Wings of Steel

Wings of Steel

My Great Uncle, George Clarke Robertson

A Left Winger in the Steel Towns

First published by Pitch Publishing, 2014

Pitch Publishing
A2 Yeoman Gate
Yeoman Way
Durrington
BN13 3QZ
www.pitchpublishing.co.uk

A CIP catalogue record is available for this book from the British Library.

ISBN 978 1-90962-634-8

Typesetting and origination by Pitch Publishing
Printed in Great Britain

CONTENTS

For my late parents, Robert Campbell Paterson and Edith Ellen Nicholls, who gave me an enquiring mind; and my wife, Barbara, and sons, Andrew and David, for putting up with my obsession.

Iain Paterson – 2014

‘Chasing the wings of steel
Chasing the ghost of time’

Collide

INTRODUCTION

IN late May 2011 an official-looking white envelope, ominously bearing the stamp Room 101, popped through my letterbox. It contained the death certificate of a long-lost relative and ended a search for what became of him which had occupied much of my time for the best part of 20 years.

I didn't know of the existence of my great uncle George until I inherited my grandmother's collection of postcards and photographs on her death in 1974. Among her treasured memories were a number of photographs and postcards of a young man in vintage football kit and proudly sporting a Scottish cap bearing the date 1910. My father identified the mystery man as George Robertson, my grandmother's older brother, and revealed that he had played professional football for Motherwell and Scotland before the First World War.

My grandmother's collection of postcards and photographs formed the core of an exhibition on the history of the village of Menstrie which was mounted by the local Community Council and managed to stir a few memories. It was very well received by those who visited it. Many people asked about the football player and I was embarrassed to say that, although we were distantly related, I knew nothing of his life and background. After the exhibition was dismantled my father surprised me by telling the story of his uncle causing a riot at an international football match in Dublin in 1913.

It was to find out more about this family legend that finally spurred me on to begin researching my own family's history and specifically to learn more about George and his distinguished football career. Further digging revealed that my great uncle George Robertson had indeed played for Motherwell and Scotland over 100 years ago. He first made a name for himself as a part-time player with Motherwell in the first decade of the 20th century and it is a tribute to his skills that he became the first Motherwell player to be capped for Scotland while still holding down a full-time job outside football.

George eventually swapped life in one major steel centre for full-time football in another, moving to Sheffield to join The Wednesday (later to become Sheffield Wednesday) in 1910. Here he probably reached the pinnacle of his career, being once described as the best outside-left in Britain and winning the hearts of one half of the football fans in his new home city, where he won three more caps for his country.

A serious knee injury and the little matter of the First World War deprived George of a few playing years when he could have been expected to be at the peak of his powers. He was ultimately let go by Wednesday and returned to Scotland and joined East Fife who were then playing in the Central League.

George packed a lot into his years in the professional football ranks. He won two Lanarkshire Cups while with Motherwell. He was the first Motherwell player to be selected for the Scottish League team in 1910 although he was unable to play because Motherwell were involved in an important Scottish Cup quarter-final tie. He became Motherwell's first full Scottish international player that same year.

He took part in The Wednesday's first continental tour to Scandinavia where he played against Danish and Swedish international sides. He took part in Wednesday's first Sunday match during that tour. He was responsible for Wednesday becoming nicknamed The Owls. He was at the heart of the riot which followed the Ireland v Scotland international in Dublin in 1913. He was part of the East Fife squad which won the Qualifying Cup in 1920 and he took part in East Fife's first ever Scottish League match in 1921.

When I was a child my father was often away for long periods so it was my grandfather, Andrew Paterson, who took me to my first football match. My grandfather was a good all-round sportsman in his day and had, I think, some vague connection with Falkirk Football Club so it was at their Brockville ground that I saw my first football match. Together we saw Falkirk's great Scottish Cup-winning side of 1957 although I wasn't allowed to go to the semi-final or final.

It wasn't long after that season that we switched our allegiance to Motherwell and my grandfather would take me along to Fir Park for every home game. It wasn't until I started the research for this book that I began to question why we made the lengthy bus and train journey from Clackmannanshire to Motherwell every second week rather than follow the fortunes of one of our local teams, Alloa or Stirling Albion.

It soon became obvious that there was some old family connection in addition to the fact that my grandfather appreciated the brand of football played by the Motherwell team under the stewardship of the legendary Bobby Ancell.

This little book is the product of many years of pleasurable research and tells the story of the football career of my great uncle, George Robertson – a distinguished player of his day with Yoker Athletic, Motherwell, Sheffield Wednesday, East Fife and Scotland. George is mentioned in numerous football histories but over the years so many inaccuracies have attached themselves to his biographical notes that it seems only right to correct these errors based on the documentation I have managed to gather together.

George's football career spanned some momentous events in world history from the Boer War, the death of Queen Victoria, the first powered flight, the establishment of the Suffragette movement, Bleriot's cross-Channel flight, the race to the South Pole, the sinking of the *Titanic*, political tension throughout Europe culminating in the carnage of the First World War, the sinking of the *Lusitania*, the Easter Uprising in Ireland, the Russian Revolution, the scuttling of the German fleet in Scapa Flow, women getting the vote and the discovery of Tutankhamun's tomb.

In the football world it takes us back to the days of only two points for a win; when goalkeepers wore the same jerseys as outfield players and were usually distinguished only by a cap; when jerseys didn't bear a number or player's name and sponsorship was unheard of. When attacking players had to have three defenders between them and the goal to be onside and when playing two or three games in a matter of days was not unusual. They were hardy souls then.

George's story had a beginning, a middle, but, until recently, no ending. After the death of my grandmother, George's youngest sibling, the two branches of the family lost touch. It has taken the best part of 20 years, pursuing a whole host of false leads in the New World from as far apart as Canada and Florida, to find out where and when he died or how his family prospered in the home that he established for them in the USA.

Interesting scraps of information keep cropping up though. Recently I discovered that George's son, also George, had been elected to the New England Soccer Hall of Fame and that his oldest son, Robert, had also played professional soccer.

Somewhere across the Atlantic Ocean there may be some families who are, perhaps, unaware of the exploits of their illustrious Scottish forebear.

This book is to help them understand the high regard in which George was held in the steel centres of the UK.

My principal sources for all the football material were the local papers – in Motherwell, the *Motherwell Times* and in Sheffield the *Football & Sports Special* (known as the *Green 'Un*). I have trusted their match reports as their reporters were more familiar with the players in their areas rather than the national daily papers whom I have found to be, on occasion, wildly inaccurate. For example, one Scottish daily listed George in a Motherwell team line-up on a day that he was on international duty with Scotland.

1

HEARTH AND HOME – THE MENSTRIE YEARS

GEORGE Clark Robertson (the spelling used on his birth certificate) was born on 7 March 1885 at his parents' home in the village of Menstrie, Clackmannanshire. George's father, Robert, was one of a long line of joiners and wrights who had originated in Perthshire then moved south into Kinross-shire before turning westward into Clackmannanshire.

The family business had been established on the banks of the Menstrie Burn by Robert's father, David, and Robert inherited the business when his father retired. Robert Robertson married Isabella Campbell, the daughter of Samuel Campbell who kept sheep at Jerah, up Menstrie Glen, high in the Ochil Hills. On settling in Menstrie, Isabella become the village midwife, and was popularly known as 'Easy', a play on her name but also recording her skill at easing the mothers of Menstrie through childbirth.

Robert and Isabella had seven children, of whom five survived beyond childhood. Their first-born, David Clark Robertson, was born in Menstrie in 1874 but died aged only 18 months from bronchitis and emphysema. Samuel Campbell Robertson was born only four months after his brother died but sadly only lived for eight years before succumbing to scarlet fever.

Mary Clark Robertson was the first girl of the family. She was born in 1878 and like many young girls of the time, went into service, later working in some grand town-houses in Cheltenham and Leamington Spa. Mary never married but returned to Scotland to live in the family home at Croft House, Middletown, Menstrie. She died in a nursing home in Alloa in 1967.

Robert and Isabella's next two children, Robert Robertson Jr. and Hugh Campbell Robertson, were born in 1879 and 1881 respectively. Both followed their father into the joinery trade and eventually moved to Glasgow where they raised their families. Robert returned to Menstrie where he died in 1966 but Hugh remained in the city where he passed away in 1978.

George was the sixth child, the fifth and final boy of the family. His primary education was at the village school in Menstrie and he probably received his secondary education in nearby Alva. His birth certificate records his full name as George Clark Robertson, the Clark (sometimes spelt with an 'e') coming from his grandmother, Mary Clark(e), who hailed from Madderty in Perthshire.

My grandmother, Helen Kirk Robertson, the youngest of the family, was born in 1892. She worked as a French polisher in a furniture factory in the village where she met her future husband, wood-turner Andrew Paterson. The couple married in 1919 after Andrew returned from service with the Argyll and Sutherland Highlanders in France. Mary and Helen (Nellie) inherited the family home after the death of their mother and remained there until the house was demolished in 1967.

George's early years are still largely undocumented but we know that he received his primary school education at the village school in Menstrie where he appears in a group photograph in 1894. His secondary school education would likely have been completed at Alva Academy two miles to the east of Menstrie. Sadly Clackmannan County Archives do not have the school rolls for the period between 1892 and 1904 when George would have been a pupil.

The 1901 Census reveals that the 16-year-old George was an apprentice baker, living then with the family at Croft House – later allocated the address 21 Ochil Road – with mother Isabella, brothers Robert and Hugh and sister Nellie (Helen) along with boarder William Cumming. We do not know where George worked but it is possible that he was employed by one of the local Co-operative Society Bakers or by one of the four family bakery firms working in nearby Alva. As George married a girl from Alva I strongly suspect that he began his working life in that town.

George's older brothers Robert and Hugh were both joiners to trade and moved to Glasgow in the early years of the 20th century where there were plenty of opportunities for good tradesmen in the rapidly expanding city. The boys' uncle James had a successful joinery business in the Gorbals area and it is possible that they worked with him for a while.

George, too, clearly moved to the west of Scotland to advance his career. When we next come across him it is in the pages of the *Motherwell Times* newspaper of 27 July 1906 which listed the players

Motherwell Football Club had signed for the coming season, describing George as the former Yoker Athletic forward. On 3 August 1906 the *Clydebank and Renfrew Press* confirmed that Yoker's left-winger Robertson was one of two players to turn senior and had joined Motherwell. It is unlikely that junior club Yoker had scouts operating as far afield as Clackmannanshire so it is safe to assume that he had moved to the Glasgow area some time between the Census in 1901 and joining the Fir Park club in 1906.

Yoker Athletic, nicknamed the Whe Ho, were formed in 1886 and still operate from their Holm Park ground in Clydebank, near the city of Glasgow boundary. As of 2013 they operated in the Super League First Division of the Scottish Junior Football League. Sadly, Yoker Athletic have no records surviving from that period so it is impossible to check how long George played for them.

I have long wondered why every published biographical note on George gives his birthplace as Stonefield, Lanarkshire. His birth certificate does not give a precise address but does confirm that he was born in Menstrie, Clackmannanshire, and his birth was registered in the parish of Logie. It is clear that George moved to the west of Scotland to pursue his career as a baker sometime between 1901 and 1906 and it is possible that he may have lived in Stonefield (which is now part of the town of Blantyre, close to Motherwell) at some time in his early working life.

This is not the only occurrence of the name Stonefield in the west of Scotland. Much of the Gorbals area of Glasgow was built on the site of the historic estate and mansion of the Waddell family, which also bore the name Stonefield, and the name was commemorated in an elegant terrace overlooking the River Clyde. Just a stone's throw away from Stonefield Terrace was the United Co-operative Baking Society whose massive complex of buildings was located in nearby McNeil Street.

Since George's uncle James lived in Abbotsford Place and both of his brothers lived locally in Oatlands and Hutcheson town, it is quite possible that George also moved to the vicinity of Gorbals and found employment with the UCBS who were one of the area's major employers. This may possibly explain his connection with the name Stonefield.

2

1906/07 – MAKING HIS MARK AT FIR PARK

GEORGE Robertson signed for Motherwell Football Club on 30 June 1906. Motherwell Football Club was a relatively young organisation having been formed when two local clubs, Glencairn and Alpha, merged in 1886. In the early days of the club they had no regular league to play in and had to content themselves with challenge matches and the Lanarkshire Cup. Motherwell's colours were initially blue and white reflecting those of each of the teams who combined to make up the new club. The club finally achieved league status in 1893/94 when the Scottish League was expanded to two divisions and Motherwell were elected to take their place with nine other aspiring clubs in the Second Division. Motherwell were quickly nicknamed The Steelmen, reflecting the town's association with the heavy industries prevalent in the Lanarkshire coalfield. For the start of this new adventure the club changed their kit for this season to maroon shirts with exotic satin knickerbockers.

They made a creditable showing in their first season, finishing in fourth place, six points behind the eventual winners Hibernian. Their second season saw them even better placed, this time finishing runners-up behind champions Hibernian (promotion was not automatic – third placed Clyde were invited to join the First Division after 1893/94). The next three seasons found the club continually slipping down the league table finishing third bottom, second bottom and then, finally, bottom of the Second Division in 1897/98.

Their form continued to fluctuate over the next few years until 1902/03 when they finished runners-up to local rivals Airdrieonians and were promoted to the First Division. Motherwell struggled in the top flight and actually finished bottom of the table in 1904/05 and had to apply for re-election. They were ultimately saved from relegation when the First Division was expanded from 14 to 16 teams.

The season before George joined the club they had reached their high at the time in Scottish football, finishing in ninth spot in the First Division. Unlike the top English sides, most provincial clubs in Scotland employed part-time professionals who would come along to training in the evenings after their shifts in the steel works, mines and workshops of Lanarkshire, or, in George's case, the bakery.

George was pitched straight into the Motherwell first team (squads were small then), making his debut in a pre-season Western League evening match with Kilmarnock on Wednesday 15 August 1906 at Fir Park. He obviously did not shape up well and Motherwell went down easily 4-0. George was not mentioned in the match report which stated that the forwards performed reasonably but needed to improve their pace and shooting.

George was not in the team which kicked off the season at home to Celtic on 18 August and suffered a 6-0 drubbing which left them languishing at the bottom of the league after the first fixture.

Motherwell stuck with their regular first-team left-winger Bob Findlay, a former internationalist with Kilmarnock, for the second match of the season, away to Queen's Park when the Steelmen were again defeated, this time by the more respectable margin of 2-1. Armour's two goals put Queen's in front with David Richmond scoring their first goal of the season just before the break. Motherwell could have snatched a deserved equaliser late in the match but Queen's goalkeeper Adams saved Findlay's penalty kick.

George made his Scottish League debut in the home game against local rivals Airdrieonians on 1 September in front of a 7,000 crowd on one of the hottest days for many a year. Happily his debut was a scoring one as the teams drew 1-1. The *Motherwell Times* reporter remarked, 'From the kick-off the Motherwell forwards made headway, and put remarkable life into their play, notwithstanding the heat. Their energy was fully rewarded, however, for in less than four minutes Robertson had Duncan [the Airdrie goalkeeper] beaten with a clever shot.'

The players began to wilt in the heat and Graham grabbed a late equaliser for the Diamonds. Motherwell's forwards came in for some criticism from the *Motherwell Times* man at the match who suggested they had a lot to learn in the art of goal-getting.

The *Motherwell Times* thought that Motherwell's play deserved at least a share of the points against Falkirk at Brockville on 8 September. Logan put the Bairns in front and Simpson controversially added a second goal which the referee allowed despite Motherwell protests for a blatant handball. Reid deservedly pulled a goal back for the Steelmen before half-time, slamming home a rebound off the post. The referee lost control of the game until the break and both sides were guilty of a series of niggling fouls.

Motherwell were effectively reduced to ten men in the second half with Donaldson limping badly. Despite concerted pressure the Fir Parkers could not penetrate the home defence and the game ended in a 2-1 win for Falkirk. The defeat saw Motherwell slip to the bottom of the table with only one point from four games.

Motherwell were confident of their first win of the season when they made the trip to Meadowside to take on Partick Thistle on 15 September. Thistle started briskly and took the lead through McGregor who emerged from a ruck of players to beat 'Well keeper Montgomery.

George was having a good game but his shooting was lamentable and he missed a clear-cut chance to level the match. Gibson then scored a second for Thistle with a glorious 20-yarder and this prompted a Motherwell revival. After a tussle in the penalty area Motherwell were awarded a penalty and Willie Reid made no mistake from the spot.

Almost straight from the restart Reid picked up the ball and ended a great solo run with a fine equalising goal. The half-time break came at the wrong time for a clearly dominant Motherwell side and the teams took to the pavilion tied at 2-2.

A hastily reshuffled Thistle side started the second half better and McGregor gave them the lead again with a neatly taken goal. Motherwell pushed hard for the remainder of the game but couldn't overcome Thistle's strong rearguard action.

The *Motherwell Times* reporter felt that the home supporters needed the patience of Job in waiting for that elusive first win. That patience was to be tried again when St Mirren visited Fir Park on 22 September. Tom McDonald of Blantyre Victoria took over from Montgomery in goal but he couldn't prevent Hamilton giving the visitors an early lead. George was having another good game on the wing but, once again, his shooting was poor and he scorned a number of chances.

James Sneddon, in his first Motherwell game of the season, surprised Saints keeper Rae and himself with a long-range equaliser but Wilson put Saints back in front before the break. The second half was a fiercely contested affair with the home side having slightly the better of the exchanges but neither side could add to their tally, leaving Motherwell propping up the table with only one point from a possible 12.

Motherwell's first win of the season finally came at Fir Park on 29 September when Aberdeen were defeated 3-2. The Steelmen took the game to the visitors from the start and Reid gave them the lead with a low shot which the Dons' goalkeeper McFarlane could not save. Aberdeen had a chance from a free kick but the Fir Park outfit broke and quickly resumed their attacks on the visitors' goal. From one of these, according to reports, 'Robertson put on a second goal for Motherwell'. It was 2-0 to the home side at the interval and they seemed to have things well under control when Reid drove home a Richmond cross shortly after the resumption.

George and his opposite wing George Nicol were performing really well and Motherwell were cruising to a 3-0 win with 15 minutes remaining but two goals in quick succession put Aberdeen well and truly back in the match. 'Well were hanging on desperately in the last few minutes but managed to secure the victory and the precious two points which lifted them off the bottom rung of the ladder.

There was a bumper crowd at Douglas Park for Motherwell's much-awaited clash with local rivals Hamilton Academical on 6 October. Motherwell continued their good form from the early part of the Aberdeen match with both Nicol and George again showing up well and it was no surprise when Andy Donaldson put them ahead.

Hamilton held out bravely until Nicol fired in a second goal through the legs of an Accies full-back to put the Fir Parkers comfortably ahead at half-time. 'Well threw everything at the beleaguered Accies defence in the second period but were only able to add another goal when Reid scored from Richmond's excellent pass. The *Motherwell Times* reporter was delighted with the whole team's effort but singled out Nicol, Richmond and George for special praise.

Joint-leaders Dundee brought Motherwell back down to earth the following week, winning 3-0 at Fir Park. The defeat was no great surprise but home fans were disappointed that the Fir Parkers only managed one shot on target in the first period. The team played well in midfield but carried little attacking threat against the much larger and more physical Dens Park outfit. The *Motherwell Times* remarked that, 'the brilliant runs of both the home wings which so delighted the home forwards at Douglas Park the previous Saturday were absent on this occasion'. Goals from Webb and Fraser, in the first half, and Russell, after the break, secured the points for the Dark Blues.

Stewart returned for his first outing of the season after a lengthy injury and Montgomery returned in goal for the match against Hibernian at Easter Road on 20 October. The match was fairly evenly-contested with both sides having periods of dominance. Findlay gave Hibs the lead in the first half but Motherwell fought back after the break and only a last-ditch tackle by Main prevented George from equalising at the expense of a corner.

The Steelmen drew level when Nicol picked up Stewart's pass and shot against the legs of goalkeeper Rennie, the ball rebounding to Andy Donaldson who slid it into the empty net. The match finished all square at 1-1.

Motherwell disappointed at home to Clyde on 27 October, slumping to a 1-0 defeat by the Bully Wee. The home side were very much in charge in the first half but their failings in front of goal were to cost them dear. Clyde turned things around in the second period and Walker gave them the lead that their attacking play deserved and they also missed an opportunity from the penalty spot when the ball came back off the post.

The *Motherwell Times* reporter expressed his concern over the Steelmen's future in the top flight, writing, 'The season is now far enough advanced to give the followers of the game an opportunity of gauging the team's chances in the League, and everything seems to point in the direction of the Fir Parkers having a life and death struggle to escape the ballot next year.'

These remarks provoked the perfect response from the players and Motherwell enjoyed a purple patch in November 1906, winning all four of their games that month.

George was in first-class form as Motherwell took both points from their trip to Port Glasgow Athletic's Clune Park on 3 November. The *Motherwell Times* reported, 'Several excellent cross-passes came from Robertson, which frequently placed the Port goal in jeopardy. Shaw however saved well.'

Port did have a couple of chances in a first half that the visitors dominated but, 'Just before half-time Motherwell scored through [stand-in centre-forward] Miller, who accepted one of Robertson's accurate centres.'

Port came back strongly in the second half and the 'Well defence was severely tested. Ritchie should have equalised for the home side from the penalty spot but his shot cannoned off the post to safety. Goalkeeper Montgomery was the hero for the visitors in the closing stages, pulling off several vital saves to keep his goal intact.

Motherwell climbed three places up to 13th in the table with a comfortable 3-0 win over Kilmarnock at Fir Park the following week although good football was not much in evidence. McDonald and Colman stood in for Montgomery and Rattray, absent through illness. In front of the poorest home crowd of the season, play swung initially from end to end. Miller raised the hopes of the home fans with the opening goal for the Steelmen and appeared to have clinched the match with a second goal just before the break.

Kilmarnock were down to ten men after half-time, losing Shaw through injury and Motherwell took advantage to secure the points when George netted his third goal of the season to complete the scoring. It was a far from impressive performance by the hosts and the *Motherwell Times* thought that George's efforts just about deserved pass marks, adding, 'Robertson put in a few good runs, and was by no means the worst of the [forward] quintette.'

Motherwell fielded the same eleven players who defeated Kilmarnock the previous week for the home match with Morton on 17 November. The Fir Park surface was soft and slippery and the home side were first to adapt to the difficult conditions. 'The first serious effort at goal came from Robertson, who sent in a shot which struck the cross bar,' wrote the *Motherwell Times*.

Andy Donaldson eventually put Motherwell ahead and Alex McCallum soon made it 2-0 for the Lanarkshire men with a long-range effort which deceived the keeper. The home forwards were in scintillating form and it was no surprise when John Miller continued his scoring streak by adding a third from close range. Nicol (though some authorities say McAlpine) grabbed a fourth goal before the interval to put the home side firmly in control.

Morton made some positional changes in the second half and were much more effective defensively but rarely troubled the 'Well defence. Dart scored a late consolation goal for the Greenock side but the match was over as a contest by half-time. The *Motherwell Times* man at the match sang the praises of the home forwards who showed great dash, saying, 'the wings being particularly clever'.

The Motherwell team turned in their most impressive performance of the season in defeating Third Lanark at Fir Park to continue their fine sequence of wins in November. Motherwell faced a strong wind in the first half but soon put visiting goalkeeper Brownlie under constant pressure. Miller in particular was proving to be a real handful for the Thirds defence and Brownlie had to be at his best to keep the score-sheet blank.

The relentless threat finally told and Nicol deservedly put the Steelmen ahead. Just before the interval Thirds broke down the right and Gilchrist drove home McGrain's perfect cross to level the scores. Motherwell began the second half in determined fashion and Miller eluded full-back McGhie two minutes after the restart to give the home side the lead again.

Good fortune and good goalkeeping kept the Steelmen at bay for another ten minutes when Miller fired a powerful shot past Brownlie to give his side a two-goal lead. Donaldson finished off an excellent, flowing Motherwell move which appeared to put the home side three ahead but, according to the press, 'The referee, to the surprise of everybody, gave off-side, and robbed the Fir Parkers of quite a legitimate goal.' Very late on Thirds pulled a goal back from the penalty spot much to the annoyance of the home fans who felt that the whistle should have gone minutes earlier.

St Mirren ended Motherwell's four-game winning streak on 1 December at Paisley, winning by the only goal of the match. It was a fiercely competitive game and the referee had to warn some of the players to calm down. Motherwell were unlucky to lose the match. They conceded an own goal just before half-time and were reduced to ten men, when full-back Rattray had to retire injured and missed the entire second half. Despite these reverses the team gave a good account of themselves and were considered unlucky not to come away with a share of the points.

George was well to the fore as Motherwell continued their good form with a fine win over Hearts at Fir Park on 8 December. The ground was soft and the showery weather clearly affected the day's attendance. 'The game opened briskly, and quite early Robertson had a fine try for goal, but he missed the mark by a few inches,' wrote the *Motherwell Times*.

'Well centre-half Hugh McNeil was injured shortly into the match and left for treatment. He was able to return later but was a limping passenger for the remainder of the contest. Despite this setback, according to the newspaper, 'The first goal of the game came from Miller, who took up a nice centre from Robertson, and beat Allan.'

The home side had a chance to double their advantage when they were awarded a penalty just before the interval. Miller was entrusted with the kick and the *Motherwell Times* reporter claimed that his effort was nearer to the corner flag than the goal. The Fir Parkers' fine form continued after the break and it was no surprise when McAlpine added a second goal with a clever shot. Hearts fought to get back into the game but could not break down the well-marshalled defence of the home side. This win against the odds helped Motherwell into 11th in the table.

With Rattray, McNeil and Miller all absent through injury Motherwell were expected to struggle against fourth-placed Rangers at Ibrox on 15 December. Willie Reid was restored to the centre-forward berth and scored the single goal which defeated the side that he was destined to sign for two seasons later.

The weather was foggy and the recent snow and ice had created a treacherous surface. The early pace of the game was frenetic and both sides made light of the conditions. The home side started well but the Steelmen came more into the match, a report read, 'principally owing to the clever play of Robertson and Donaldson'.

'Well went in front when Rangers goalkeeper Newbigging cleared a Donaldson effort and Reid picked up the ball and shot home. The Ibrox side pushed hard for the equaliser before half-time but found 'Well keeper Tom McDonald in sparkling form. His defiance continued throughout the second period and included a miraculous stop late in the game when he was spread-eagled on the ground.

The *Motherwell Times* writer concluded his report with the news that Motherwell had been drawn against non-league Galston in the Scottish Cup. He expressed his disappointment that the match would not be a great financial draw but felt there was a strong chance of Motherwell advancing to the next round.

Such was the delight in Steelopolis at the win over Rangers, a few locals penned poems in praise of their heroes. One by J. McC. was printed in the columns of the *Motherwell Times*:

THE FIR PARK LADS

Shout harrah for the Fir Park lads,
We're proud of them today,
With victory triumphant
They've returned from the fray,
'Gainst a team that has few equals
They've brought away points two,
An' shown football admirers
What our Fir Park lads can do

CHORUS

Success attend our football lads –
If they're only kept together –
They'll rank among the foremost
Of the lads that kick the leather.
The Thirds, the Hearts, an' Rangers
Are trophies to their fame.
They've shown our two big cities
That our lads can play the game

Play up, ye football heroes,
The football season's young;
There's glorious possibilities

Before the season's done.
There's honours for the winner
There's trophies for to 'cop'
When the League table is totted up
They'll find you near the top

Play up lads, be cheerful,
Old Motherwell's proud of you;
To make her famed for football
That task, she knows, you'll do,
An' see people in their thousands
Thronging along her pads
To watch her football heroes –
The gallant Fir Park lads

'Such are the ups and downs of football,' mused the *Motherwell Times* reporter in the 28 December issue. Following the euphoria over the team's win over Rangers, Motherwell were humbled 2-0 by local rivals Hamilton Academical at Fir Park on 22 December. Motherwell were badly hit by illness and injuries and George missed his first match since becoming an automatic choice on the left wing.

Accies were the better side on the day and two first-half goals by their centre-forward Forrest gave them both points to lift the team off the bottom of the table at the expense of Kilmarnock. It was a passionate derby game and Accies' McGettigan and Motherwell's McCallum were both sent off in the final minute. George was clearly missed and the *Motherwell Times* man remarked that Richmond, his replacement in the side, was 'not a patch on Robertson'.

The severe winter freeze looked to have put paid to Motherwell's home match with Hibernian on the last Saturday of 1906 but, surprisingly, the referee declared the Fir Park pitch playable although the surface was hard and icy. The weather badly affected the attendance as few fans believed that the match would go ahead. Good football was impossible as the players struggled to keep their footing and numerous chances were squandered by both teams in a goalless first half. Motherwell had the better of the exchanges in the second period but neither side could put the ball in the net and, in the end, both were happy with a share of the points.

Motherwell closed off 1906 with a good 3-2 away win against Third Lanark on Monday 31 December. Cathkin Park had a loose covering of snow and the adverse weather conditions once again meant a poor turnout of spectators. Despite the conditions the players contrived to put on a good show although some of their falls greatly amused the sparse crowd.

The match was fairly evenly-contested in the first half and it was the visitors who took the lead when Nicol stabbed home a cross from the left wing. Thirds then took over and Munro gave them the equaliser after Montgomery had blocked Johnstone's shot. Despite their superiority Thirds couldn't add to their tally and Reid put the Steelmen back in front when Thirds goalkeeper Needham missed his kick.

The visitors went in 2-1 ahead at the interval. After the break Reid added a third goal for the Fir Park outfit and the Volunteers scored a second goal although the *Motherwell Times* reporter neglected to fill in the scoring details. Motherwell held out for the win as Thirds pressed hard in the closing stages.

George missed the first match of the New Year, a goalless draw away to Port Glasgow Athletic in the first round of the West of Scotland Shield on 2 January 1907. Bob Findlay, who took George's place on the left wing, put in a good cross which Miller just failed to reach. McCallum then had a fine shot but it just skimmed past the post. Apart from these incidents Port were the principal aggressors but their shooting was extremely poor. The home side were on top for much of the match but couldn't convert their territorial advantage into goals.

Motherwell first-footed local rivals Airdrieonians at Broomfield Park on 5 January in the first league game of 1907. Both sides made injury-enforced changes and play got under way on a soft slippery surface not conducive to good football.

Although the visitors had the advantage of a stiff breeze in the first half they could make little headway against a stout Airdrie defence and chances were evenly shared between the sides with the game reaching the halfway mark without any scoring. Motherwell performed better against the wind in the second period and McAlpine missed a simple chance which would have given his side the lead. Airdrie had chances too and once again Tom McDonald in the 'Well goal performed heroics to keep them at bay.

The match finished goalless which was probably the right result on balance of play. George had another good game on the left wing where he and his partner Andy Donaldson were forming a formidable partnership.

The *Motherwell Times* carried news of a specially convened Scottish Football Association meeting to deal with a large number of disciplinary issues. It meted out a one-month suspension for Motherwell's Alex McCallum for the incident with McGettigan in the match against Hamilton Academical.

Partick Thistle were the first visitors of 1907 to Fir Park. In an entertaining opening spell, play swung from end to end with both sides scorning a few chances; Reid being the chief offender for the Steelmen. Donaldson looked set to give 'Well the lead when he was brought down in the box and a penalty was awarded. Thistle keeper Howden got fingertips to the ball but couldn't keep out Reid's spot-kick.

Motherwell were reduced to ten men when a Thistle defender fell on the grounded figure of Donaldson who had to retire with an injured back. Thistle were then awarded a penalty after a foul by McLean but Tom McDonald came to his side's rescue with a magnificent save to keep Motherwell in front.

Partick's numerical advantage eventually paid off and Kennedy levelled the scores after a bout of pressure from the visitors. Motherwell were not done though and Hugh McNeil put them back in front just before the interval although Thistle players claimed that Howden had cleared the ball off the line (clearly goal line controversies go back a long way).

It was a second half punctuated by a series of offside decisions as Motherwell went into a single back formation. This was to prove their undoing as McLean stopped, appealing for offside but the referee allowed Thistle's Gray to run through and score what proved to be the final goal of the game. The *Motherwell Times* reporter was pleased with the 2-2 draw which he considered creditable after playing so long without Donaldson and felt that George 'put in some good work' on the wing. Motherwell's hard-earned point took them up to the heady heights of eighth in the table.

The reporter expressed his concern about Motherwell's trip to second-placed Dundee minus Donaldson and McCallum but revealed that the directors had signed John McConnell of Ashfield who, he hoped, would be able to play at Dens Park.

Despite their injury problems the Fir Parkers gave a really good account of themselves away to Dundee on 19 January 1907. George made an early dash down the left and sent in a quick cross which was just missed by Reid. Dundee gradually began to take control of the game and the Motherwell defence had to be on their toes to keep out their eager forwards. It was not all one-way traffic though and Nicol brought out a fine save from Dundee keeper Muir before half-time arrived without a goal being scored.

The second half was similar to the first with the home team in charge but not able to convert any of their chances. They may have been made to pay for their profligacy when, with ten minutes remaining, Nicol put Reid through but he slipped at the final moment. The supporters were leaving the ground when former Motherwell favourite Fraser swung over a corner which was knocked into the net by Dundee's inside-left, McFarlane. The referee almost immediately blew the final whistle leaving the visitors shattered after coming so close to earning a crucial point against the high-flying Dundee side. George had another fine game; his runs down the left helping to relieve the pressure on the Motherwell defence.

The weather intervened to postpone Motherwell's Scottish Cup first-round tie against Scottish Football Combination side Galston on 26 January. The draw for the second round had already been made and awarded the winner of this match a highly lucrative home game against Rangers. There was a thaw on the Friday before the match but the ground was considered to be still unplayable on the appointed Saturday. Motherwell offered to host the tie at Fir Park but Galston were unwilling to yield up home advantage.

The match was rescheduled for the following Saturday 2 February 1907 and the weather was the winner once again although Motherwell, having made the trip to Galston, agreed to play out a 'friendly' on the snow-covered, frosty pitch. The match finished with the scores level at 2-2 with Reid scoring both goals for the Steelmen. George was absent for this match with Bob Findlay making a rare appearance on the left wing for the visitors.

George's first Scottish Cup tie was in the replayed match on 9 February 1907 when the Steelmen were surprisingly beaten 2-1 on Galston's tight, muddy, little Riverside Park pitch. The Ayrshire men were obviously in the mood for this match and 'put in some hard and plucky work' according to the report, while their opponents, on the other hand, were struggling to come to terms with the small, non-regulation pitch and the cloying glaur.

Both sides had chances in the first half but the score remained goalless at the break. Motherwell continued to try to play football in the second half but could not adapt to the deplorable ground conditions. The First Division side were stunned when Galston's inside-left Young beat 'Well full-back Rattray and opened the scoring for the Ayrshire men. When Morrison added a second minutes later, it was reported that 'the hearts of the Motherwell fans sank into their boots'.

Some desperate play from the Lanarkshire side saw McAlpine reduce the deficit but, try as they might, they could not produce an equaliser. The *Motherwell Times* felt that the Steelmen lost because, 'They tried to play nice football under impossible conditions.'

The defeat was a financial disaster for the club who would have made a tidy sum from the visit of the mighty Rangers in the next round and Motherwell might have fancied their chances against an Ibrox side that they had already beaten away from home.

The *Motherwell Times* bard-in-residence penned a lengthy poem which expressed the sense of disbelief felt by the townsfolk at the defeat of their heroes. It is too long and depressing to repeat in full but these two verses convey the sense of anguish felt by Motherwell supporters.

GALSTON'S WON

The shades of night were falling fast,
As out from Riverside was cast,
A youth who seemed to be in pain,
As he cried out time and again,
... Galston's won.

A prying 'Bobby' then did say,
Young chap, wha's won the tie the day,
He turned on him a withering eye,
And half evasive did reply,
... Galston's won.

Back on league business the following week, Motherwell's poor form continued with a 5-0 thrashing by Queen's Park in front of their concerned home fans. The *Motherwell Times* reporter wondered whether the rot had set in at Fir Park after their recent good form. The early play was fairly even but there was a hint of desperation in the Motherwell forwards' shooting; almost as if they were anxious to atone for their Scottish Cup defeat.

Queen's shooting proved to be somewhat superior and goals from Paul and Armour put them two ahead at the half-time whistle although they 'were by no means value for this'. A third goal, from a corner, early in the second half effectively killed the game and home players' heads began to droop. It was no surprise when the visitors rattled in a further two goals, one of which came in the final minute.

After two humiliating defeats Motherwell steadied the ship with a creditable 2-2 draw against Aberdeen at Pittodrie on 23 February. From the start the visitors streamed towards the Dons goal and Nicol quickly had the ball in the home net but the strike was disallowed for offside. Aberdeen gradually came more into the contest and McDonald had to concede a couple of corners from difficult shots by the home forwards.

Motherwell's attacks were more dangerous though and, according to the *Motherwell Times*, 'McFarlane failed to clear a slow shot from Reid, and Robertson ran in and easily scored.'

Aberdeen later equalised when Low converted from McDonald's cross but Motherwell stormed back on the offensive and won a penalty when Miller was tripped in the area. Reid strode forward and made no mistake from the penalty spot to give the visitors the lead at the break. Wilson equalised for Aberdeen early in the second half and the home side increased their efforts in search of a winning goal. Both goalkeepers were kept busy in the latter stages and a draw was probably a fair result in the end. George was increasingly growing in confidence and his pace and crossing ability was becoming a feature of Motherwell's forward play.

Motherwell fans were left wondering what might have been in the Scottish Cup when they succeeded in completing the league double over Rangers on 2 March. Rangers were missing four players on international duty but despite their loss they came closest to opening the scoring in the first half when Hendry's shot rattled the bar and went over. Motherwell were having more of the game though and their constant pressure finally wore down the strong Rangers defence when, with five minutes remaining, Andy Donaldson got the goal which secured the points for the hosts.

The game was perhaps one of the best and most enjoyable seen on Fir Park that season. The home players all performed splendidly according to the *Motherwell Times* scribe and George was the first to be mentioned in his report. 'Robertson played a strong game, but he was well watched by the defence.'

Clearly opposition managers were beginning to sit up and take notice of the dangers posed by the left-winger in his rookie season. The reporter concluded with a complaint from patrons of the Fir Park grandstand regarding the 'filthy' conditions encountered on match day, particularly regarding bird droppings on the seats they had paid their hard-earned cash for.

The Steelmen built on their good form from the Rangers match when seven days later Falkirk came calling at Fir Park. The cold and showery weather had kept the crowd down but those in attendance witnessed a sensational start. Almost from the kick-off Motherwell raced towards the visitors' end 'where Robertson centred beautifully, and Reid headed through'.

Falkirk came back strongly and came close with a couple of shots, one of which rebounded back into play off the crossbar. Motherwell gradually got back on top and added a second goal when keeper Allan could only parry Miller's shot and Reid ran in to slip the ball into the net. Nicol fired home a third goal to give the home side a well-deserved 3-0 lead after 45 minutes.

Motherwell were well on top in the second half when some of the Falkirk players became a little physical and the referee was called in on several occasions to speak to the offenders. The referee finally 'awarded a penalty against Falkirk for Craig fouling Robertson within the line, and from this Reid scored the fourth and last goal of the game'. The *Motherwell Times* man at the match was impressed with the entire team and felt that George and his opposite wing George Nicol put in some good work.

As in the past few games George was in excellent form against Morton at Cappielow on 16 March. George and Donaldson carried the main threat to the Greenock defence in the early part of the game but Morton, prompted by ex-Motherwell favourite Galbraith, came back into the fray and the first half finished goalless and pretty even territorially.

Morton started the second half briskly and Gillies gave them the lead after outstripping McLean and sending a powerful shot past McDonald. Motherwell were stung into retaliation and laid siege to the Morton goal. Their efforts were rewarded when McConnell found Nicol who cleverly beat 'Ton keeper Oliver.

This hard-fought match ended at 1-1 and the vital point gained saw Motherwell climb to seventh place in the First Division, the highest position they had occupied since joining the Scottish League. George and Donaldson combined well again but came in for some criticism for not delivering the ball earlier to the waiting Reid and Miller.

The *Motherwell Times* correspondent frequently remarked on the quality of George's crosses and noted that he turned in a number of really strong performances later in the season. In the 3-2 defeat to bottom club Kilmarnock at Rugby Park on 23 March, played in the teeth of a gale-force wind, Motherwell found themselves 3-0 down at half-time. The wind reduced considerably in the second half but Motherwell used it to their advantage and fought back bravely.

Donaldson almost reduced the deficit in the first few minutes but the travelling Motherwell fans did not have long to wait for a goal. The left-wing pairing of Donaldson and Robertson combined well to find Miller in the clear and he easily beat the Killie keeper. The same player notched a second goal as Motherwell swarmed all over the overworked Killie defence.

The visitors piled on the pressure but no more goals were forthcoming and the final whistle came as a great relief to the home team and their supporters. The *Motherwell Times* applauded the fightback and thought the Steelmen unlucky to lose. The newspaper wrote, 'Motherwell were strongest on the left wing, Donaldson and

Robertson playing a fine game, especially Robertson who improves every Saturday.' Despite this defeat Motherwell retained their seventh place in the league.

For the second time in the season Motherwell went down to a single goal to Clyde, this time in the away fixture at Shawfield on 30 March. In a poor game Motherwell performed well below their recent form with Nicol spurning several opportunities in the first half. Miller should have given them the lead but, with only the goalkeeper to beat, smashed the ball against the bar. Motherwell were made to pay for their slack play when Clyde centre-forward McLean mishit his shot which, luckily for the home side, finished in the net for the only goal of the game.

Motherwell were unfortunate not to pick up both points from their visit to Tynecastle on 6 April. They were vastly superior to Hearts on the day and their passing game gave the home defence considerable trouble. Despite controlling the first 45 minutes the visitors could not find an opening and the match remained goalless at the break. Hearts improved considerably in the second period but neither side could capitalise on the many chances created.

The match appeared to be heading for a goalless draw when Yates snatched a goal for Hearts in the last few minutes. 'This success seemed to put beyond doubt the issue of the game, but Motherwell came away grandly, the left wing sending a fine pass to Nicol, who converted it into a brilliant and well-deserved goal,' wrote the *Motherwell Times*. The final whistle immediately sounded giving the teams a share of the spoils.

Motherwell's final home league game of the 1906/07 season was against struggling Port Glasgow Athletic on 13 April. With nothing really at stake for both sides and a chilly wind blowing around Fir Park the poor turnout of spectators was not surprising.

Motherwell had the advantage of the strong wind in the first half and the locals were confident that their team would put a few goals past the visitors' keeper. Nothing could have been further from the truth as the home forwards struggled to crack the visitors' tight defence and even contrived to miss a penalty.

They fared better against the wind in the second half, having the bulk of the play, and it came as no surprise when Reid put them ahead. That proved to be the only goal of a disappointing match. Despite the acquisition of both points, the poor performance of the team ended the season on an anti-climactic note for their home fans. At the end of the match report the *Motherwell Times* correspondent revealed that the Motherwell directors had already signed up players, Rattray,

McCallum, McConnell, Sneddon and Robertson for the forthcoming 1907/08 season.

With only one league game remaining Motherwell turned their attention to the Lanarkshire Cup. In the first round they faced Hamilton Garrison at Fir Park on 17 April in front of only a small attendance. It was a one-sided affair and the Steelmen thrashed the Garrison 7-0 having gone in 5-0 up at half-time. The scorers for Motherwell were Miller with three, Nicol, Donaldson, Robertson and James Stewart. No team lines were listed in the *Motherwell Times* for this match.

The semi-final of the Lanarkshire Cup was played on Saturday 20 April at Wishaw and was an acrimonious affair. The appointed referee, Mr Nisbet, who hailed from Cowdenbeath, was late in arriving so the teams had agreed to play a friendly match which was under way for about 20 minutes when the official appeared. The teams were then instructed to commence the cup tie; Wishaw refused and left the field. Thistle were then persuaded to play but under protest. The match was hopelessly one-sided and at 7-0 the Wishaw backs left the field. The match finished 8-0 to the away side but Wishaw immediately lodged an official protest. The Lanarkshire Association dismissed Wishaw's protest and the tie was awarded to Motherwell. The goals came from Reid (four), Donaldson (two), Stewart and Nicol.

Motherwell took the opportunity to try out a few new players in a friendly match with Hamilton Academical on Saturday 27 April at Fir Park. The Steelmen fielded some players that they hoped to sign for the following season including Peggie of Hibs and Temple of Maryhill. The home side won a close and entertaining match 1-0 but the *Motherwell Times* did not list the teams or the scorer.

On Monday 29 April Motherwell narrowly beat Port Glasgow Athletic 1-0 in the delayed replay of the first round of the West of Scotland Shield. Nicol was the scorer for the home side but, once again, the *Motherwell Times* did not provide any match details.

Despite this fixture pile-up Motherwell attempted to complete their league fixtures with the final match against Celtic at Celtic Park on Wednesday 1 May in appalling weather conditions.

Motherwell fielded their regular first team and they made a brilliant start when Nicol, already in a rich vein of form, opened the scoring in the first minute. Orr equalised for the Celts from the penalty spot after McNeil had handled in the area. Reid's magnificent jinking run from the halfway line was capped by a fine shot to put Motherwell back in the driving seat. Celtic stormed back and Bauchop and Hamilton combined to get the home side back on level terms. At the end of a breathless first half the teams were locked together at 2-2.

The second half continued in the same frantic manner and Somers gave Celtic the lead early on. Motherwell retaliated immediately and Reid put them back on level terms again. Bauchop put Celtic back in front as the match continued at a furious pace but 20 minutes from the end the referee blew his whistle to abandon the match with Celtic leading 4-3. The abandonment meant that the result would not count and the match would have to be replayed.

It was reported in the *Motherwell Times* that the game had been played in 'distressing conditions' with all the spectators present huddling under a covered enclosure, most likely to avoid a typical west of Scotland rainstorm.

The *Motherwell Times* carried the news that East Stirlingshire had been beaten 3-0 in another friendly match at Fir Park on 4 May. This was another match arranged to try out some new players for the coming season but the paper did not give any details of the match. The *Motherwell Times* reported two significant pieces of player news: Andy Donaldson had accepted terms for the following season and Bob Findlay, whom George replaced in the left-wing berth, had been transferred to Hamilton Accies.

Motherwell's involvement in the West of Scotland Shield ended at the semi-final stage away to Clyde on Wednesday 8 May. The match was a tight affair with the Shawfield men winning by the odd goal in three. Clyde had the advantage of the high wind in the first half and pressed continuously. After 20 minutes they got their reward when a long-range shot from Walker surprised McDonald in the Motherwell goal. When Turner headed home Cowie's corner the home side were very much in command.

Motherwell fought back and Reid burst past the two Clyde full-backs to latch on to McConnell's through-ball to put the Steelmen back in the hunt. Reid came close again before the interval when his shot clipped the bar and bounced over. With the wind at their backs Motherwell pounded the Clyde defence in the second period but they could not get the vital breakthrough and the Bully Wee advanced to the final.

In a warm-up for the Lanarkshire Cup Final Motherwell travelled to Peebles to take on the local Rovers in another friendly match on Saturday 11 May. The Steelmen came out on top 1-0 and again the *Motherwell Times* gave no details of the game.

The Lanarkshire Challenge Cup was won for the fourth time in the club's history when Motherwell defeated Airdrieonians 1-0 at neutral

Douglas Park, Hamilton on Monday 13 May 1907 in front of a crowd of 3,500. Motherwell lined up with: Montgomery, Colman, McLean, McConnell, McNeil, McCallum, Nicol, Stewart, Reid, Donaldson, Robertson. According to the *Motherwell Times* the first half was a tense, closely-fought affair with few chances falling to either side, and half-time arrived without any scoring.

The newspaper wrote, 'Motherwell resumed in promising fashion and were soon swarming round Duncan [the Airdrie keeper] like bees, his charge having a miraculous escape, as nearly all the forwards had a shot at goal.

'Airdrie were kept defending for some time, the crosses of Nicol and Robertson causing them no end of trouble, and had Motherwell got a goal at this time it would have been no more than they deserved. Stewart did try on several occasions to give his side the lead, but his shooting was a bit off.

'The Broomfield lads were now working desperately, but Motherwell's half-backs were playing a strong game and seldom allowed them over mid-field.

'After 20 minutes' play Robertson fastened on to the ball and despite the close attention of Davidson he crossed right in front of goal, and Reid lying handy banged it against Duncan and from the rebound Stewart slipped the ball to Nicol, who had no difficulty in finding the net.

'A strong appeal by Rombach for offside was useless, the referee having no hesitation in awarding the goal.

'From this to the end Motherwell easily held the upper hand, on several occasions coming within an ace of scoring, McConnell and Robertson having several good tries at goal, which were luckily stopped before reaching the net. For the winners the best men were McLean, McNeil, Nicol, and Reid. Airdrie – Duncan, Davidson, McGran, Hunter, and Thomson.'

This single-goal victory was Motherwell's first appearance in the final since their 3-1 win over Hamilton Academical in 1901. The handsome trophy was presented to the team in the Royal Hotel (Mr Dodd's) where each team toasted the other and the proceedings were closed by the singing of 'Auld Lang Syne'.

I am now the proud owner of George's medal from that Lanarkshire Cup Final which he presented to his mother and was passed down to me via my grandmother and then my father. It is nice to have a tangible link with George and an event which took place over one hundred years ago. The medal bears the legend 'Lanarkshire Football Association' on the front and is inscribed on the reverse:

WON BY MOTHERWELL F.C.
1906/07
G. ROBERTSON

Motherwell were finally able to conclude their 1906/07 First Division programme on Wednesday 15 May when they visited Celtic Park to replay the match abandoned two weeks earlier. The strong wind favoured the Bhoys in the first half and they took full advantage to put the visiting defence under extreme pressure. Motherwell resisted well but after 30 minutes Bauchop beat McDonald with a good shot to put the league champions ahead.

Motherwell dug in and were able to get to half-time only one goal behind. With the wind in their favour, Motherwell were a vastly improved side in the second half and Reid came up with an equalising goal with 25 minutes to go. The visitors almost snatched a winner in the closing minutes but the match finished level at 1-1, probably a fair reflection of the play.

The point gained from the last match raised Motherwell's points total to 33, their highest since joining the top flight of Scottish football. At one point in mid-March they stood seventh, the highest place they had occupied in the First Division. The team finally finished tenth, one place lower than the previous season when they registered only 26 points. Willie Reid was the club's top scorer in league and cup matches with 16 goals, the only player to reach double figures.

Although George's form faded in the closing matches of the season he could be rightly proud of his contribution to the team in his first season in senior football. He had displaced the regular incumbent in the team (a former international player) and become an automatic choice in the left-wing position. His performances in the early stages of his career were mostly workmanlike as the young man learned his trade against more seasoned campaigners but his reputation grew as the season progressed and defences became aware of the threat he posed with his pace and crossing ability. Towards the end of the campaign he was being more tightly marked than he was in his early matches.

Apart from one week out through injury in December 1906 and missing the first, abandoned, Scottish Cup tie at Galston in February 1907 and the first round of the West of Scotland Shield, George was an ever-present for the rest of the season. In his first season with Motherwell he scored a total of four goals in his 31 league appearances.

SCOTTISH LEAGUE FIRST DIVISION 1906/07

	Pl	*W*	*D*	*L*	*F*	*A*	*Pts*
1 Celtic	34	23	9	2	80	30	55
2 Dundee	34	18	12	4	53	26	48
3 Rangers	34	19	7	8	69	33	45
4 Airdrieonians	34	18	6	10	59	44	42
5 Falkirk	34	17	7	10	73	58	41
6 Third Lanark	34	15	9	10	57	48	39
7 St Mirren	34	12	13	9	50	44	37
8 Clyde	34	15	6	13	47	52	36
9 Heart of Midlothian	34	11	13	10	47	43	35
10 Motherwell	34	12	9	13	45	49	33
11 Aberdeen	34	10	10	14	48	55	30
12 Hibernian	34	10	10	14	40	49	30
13 Greenock Morton	34	11	6	17	41	50	28
14 Partick Thistle	34	9	8	17	40	60	26
15 Queen's Park	34	9	6	19	51	66	24
16 Hamilton Academical	34	8	5	21	40	64	21
17 Kilmarnock	34	8	5	21	40	72	21
18 Port Glasgow Athletic	34	7	7	20	30	67	21

MOTHERWELL APPEARANCES AND GOALS 1906/07

	League		*Scottish Cup*	
	Apps	*Goals*	*Apps*	*Goals*
Colman, Donald	12	0	0	0
Donaldson, Andrew	33	4	1	0
Findlay, Robert	2	0	0	0
Laughlan, John	1	0	0	0
McAlpine, William	13	1	1	1
McCallum, Alexander	30	1	1	0
McConnell, John	6	0	0	0
McDonald, Thomas	23	0	1	0
McLean, John	30	0	1	0
McMillan, David	3	0	0	0
McNeil, Hugh	31	1	1	0
Millar, John	21	9	0	0
Montgomery, John	11	0	0	0
Nicol, George	33	7	1	0
Rattray, James	27	0	1	0
Reid, William	27	16	1	0
Richmond, David	6	1	0	0
Robertson, George Clarke	31	4	1	0
Sneddon, James	26	1	1	0
Stewart, James	8	0	0	0

3

1907/08 – ALWAYS DANGEROUS

RESEARCH for George's second season in Motherwell colours was made more difficult by the acquisition by the club, in July 1907, of another player bearing the name George Robertson. He had spent the previous six seasons with Port Glasgow Athletic and signed on a free transfer to fill the right-back slot vacated by Donald Colman who had refused terms and would eventually sign for Aberdeen.

The *Motherwell Times* reporter sang the praises of the Motherwell directors for resisting many tempting offers from a number of English and Scottish clubs for several of their key players despite not being the most affluent club in the league.

It was hoped that keeping the nucleus of the previous season's side together would permit the club to improve on their tenth place in 1906/07. The reporter noted that Fir Park was in splendid condition and that the playing surface had been lengthened by around six feet.

George Clarke Robertson, by this time, was a regular first-team player and an automatic choice on the left wing where he had established a fine partnership with inside-forward Andy Donaldson. George had developed into a player noted for his pace and dribbling skills and his ability to deliver telling crosses into the danger area, although the *Motherwell Times* reporter was critical of his tendency to shoot from difficult positions. The team made a slightly poorer start to this season, recording seven wins, four draws and ten defeats before the New Year holiday.

Motherwell kicked off the 1907/08 season against St Mirren in front of 2,000 spectators at Fir Park. McAvoy gave Saints the lead from the penalty spot on the half-hour mark after Rattray had handled in the area. Reid pulled Motherwell level, also from the spot, in a downpour just before the interval but the Buddies regained the lead just before the break.

Motherwell pressed hard in the second period but found Saints keeper Grant in great form. Eventually McCallum levelled the scores but the Paisley outfit broke from the restart and Cunningham put them back in front. 'Well dominated the remainder of the game but were unable to get the equaliser.

Despite their defeat in the opening league match Motherwell fans were so pleased with their side's form that they took two special trains through to Glasgow for the clash with Celtic. Motherwell were without their stalwart centre-half Hugh McNeil, whose father had died the day before, so the new George Robertson stood in for the popular pivot.

In front of a crowd of 12,000 spectators Jimmy Quinn gave the Bhoys an early lead. The visitors were further disadvantaged after ten minutes when Donaldson got in the way of a powerful clearance, taking the ball full on the head at close range, and had to leave the field with concussion.

Quinn doubled his side's advantage early in the second period and Bennett completed the scoring for the home team. Despite Motherwell playing for 80 minutes with ten men, George Clarke Robertson gave a good account of himself even though his wing partner was absent.

'He played a good game, time and time again tricking Young [the Celtic right-half], who resorted to tactics which a more capable referee would have had something to say about,' wrote the *Motherwell Times*.

Despite two defeats in the opening matches the *Motherwell Times* reporter was happy with the performance of the local team and felt that the directors had assembled a good squad and could look forward to the rest of the season with confidence.

Motherwell arranged a midweek friendly match with Wishaw Athletic at Fir Park to give some of their fringe players and recent signings some much-needed game time. The Steelmen won comfortably 3-0 and were in fine fettle for their next league match against Port Glasgow Athletic. At Fir Park 3,000 fans witnessed a 6-0 thrashing of Athletic despite the home side not being on their best form. Reid gave 'Well the lead after 15 minutes and added another three minutes later. Nicol scored the next goal just before the interval to send the home side in 3-0 ahead at the break.

It was one-way traffic again in the second half with Stewart making the score 4-0 before Donaldson completed the scoring with a well-taken double. Reid could have had a hat-trick but for a bad miss from the penalty spot. The *Motherwell Times* man at the match felt that the home side played well within themselves and had a little in reserve had Port put up more of a fight. George had a disappointing day 'and did not get away with his usual dash on the left'.

The Steelmen continued their good scoring form the following week with a 3-1 victory over Third Lanark at Cathkin Park in front of a large attendance. Thirds had the best of the early exchanges but it was Motherwell who took the lead, Donaldson giving future Scottish international keeper Jimmy Brownlie no chance with a magnificent shot. Motherwell were buoyed by this success and the home side were still reeling from this blow when Sneddon added a second goal for the visitors a minute later. Motherwell fans couldn't believe their good fortune and were almost incredulous when Donaldson and George combined well down the left to set up Reid for a third goal before half-time.

Thirds pressed hard in the second half but couldn't find their way past Motherwell goalkeeper Tom McDonald who defied the home forwards with a series of fine saves. He was eventually beaten late on from the penalty spot but Motherwell held on for their second successive win.

Motherwell made it 15 goals in three games with a 6-1 thumping of Queen's Park at home on 7 September with Nicol notching a hat-trick. George was quickly in action and, in only the second minute, won his side a penalty when he was fouled by Queen's right-back Young. The other George Robertson, the 'Well full-back, gave Queen's goalkeeper Purdie no chance from the resulting spot-kick. The home side were rampant and George Nicol doubled their lead after four minutes. The visitors pulled one back through Fitchie but Nicol restored his side's two-goal advantage as the Steelmen continued to dominate the match. Stewart looked to have increased Motherwell's lead but his strike was disallowed for offside so the home side had to content themselves with a 3-1 lead at the interval.

Queen's Park came out in determined fashion after the break but, after an initial flurry of activity around McDonald's goal, Motherwell re-asserted their dominance and it was no surprise when Donaldson made it 4-1 five minutes after the break. The resistance was broken and Nicol and Stewart completed the scoring for the Fir Park men.

Motherwell were brought back down to earth in front of 8,000 fans in the next fixture when Falkirk inflicted a humiliating 5-1 defeat on a below-par 'Well on 14 September at Fir Park. The Steelmen conceded two early goals and struggled to get back into the match despite sterling efforts from Nicol and Stewart. The Bairns were 3-0 up at half-time although play was pretty even after the loss of the early goals.

Centre-forward Reid gave 'Well fans hope of a revival but the difference between the sides was in the quality of their shooting. In this department Falkirk were vastly superior and it was no surprise when they were able to add two further goals to their tally despite being reduced to ten men when inside-forward Mitchell was carried off with a broken leg.

Motherwell travelled to Easter Road the following week and fought out a 1-1 draw with Hibs. Harkness gave the home side the lead which they held at half-time although Reid missed a gilt-edged chance to level following a defensive error. With ten minutes remaining Reid made up for his earlier miss, scoring with a powerful shot from a difficult angle.

George was going through a real slump in form during the early part of the season and the *Motherwell Times* reporter was scathing in his criticism, 'Robertson was completely off colour: this player had many chances given him to distinguish himself in the first half, but waits too long before parting with the ball, a very bad fault in an outside-forward, and one he should get out of at once if he is to be the effective player he once was.'

The fixture list gave Motherwell a chance to improve on their poor showing at Easter Road when Hibs were the visitors to Fir Park in the reverse fixture on 28 September. Sadly the match produced a dull goalless draw with defences very much on top and neither keeper greatly troubled during the proceedings. Motherwell should have secured both points when they were awarded a penalty in the second half but Nicol's weak effort from the spot went wide.

Reid was the principal sinner in front of goal and letters from fans to the editor of the *Motherwell Times* the following Friday made a number of suggestions to improve their flagging side. A common theme was the suggestion that Reid be rested in favour of the reserve centre-forward Walker or moving full-back George Robertson into the striking role.

Dundee were the next visitors to Fir Park on a dull and showery Saturday in early October 1907 and succeeded in carrying off both points with a narrow 1-0 victory. Motherwell gave Walker his first-team debut in place of Reid in an effort to get back among the goals. They could and should have won the match but spurned a number of good chances in front of goal. They should have taken the lead after 20 minutes when Stewart was fouled in the area and a penalty was awarded. McLean took the kick but Dundee keeper Crumley pulled off a magnificent diving save. The Dundee custodian was having an inspired day and made a series of saves from all of the Motherwell forwards, including a couple of good efforts from George, to keep his side in the match.

As is often the case the side pressing hard is hit with a sucker punch, and 12 minutes after the break Fraser beat Tom McDonald with a shot from distance to give the Taysiders the points. Once again the *Motherwell Times* reporter was highly critical of the team and George's performance in particular, 'Robertson, also, is needing to improve his form. On Saturday he was not effective in the least, and a change in his tactics of fumbling with the ball will be welcome.'

A special train carrying between five and six hundred Motherwell fans made the trip to Paisley for the return fixture with the unbeaten league leaders St Mirren on 12 October 1907. In a desperate attempt to solve their goalscoring problem the Motherwell board followed one of the suggestions mooted in the local press and tried out burly full-back George Robertson in the centre-forward role.

Motherwell almost made a sensational start to the match when outside-left George Clarke Robertson missed by inches from the kick-off. From the resultant goal kick Saints' forwards combined well to set up Milne for the opening goal of the match. The league leaders then dominated for a short period but could not increase their lead and gradually the visitors began to bring concerted pressure on the home defence, besieging Grant's goal for the remainder of the first half. Tempers were more than a little frayed as the first half drew to a close but, fortunately, the interval allowed passions to cool.

'Well began the second period in lively fashion and, following good pressure, Stewart beat Grant with a good shot to level the scores. Play then swung from end to end as both sides went all out for the winner. The decisive goal was headed home by Milne for Saints after Rattray had conceded a free kick on the edge of the penalty area.

The experiment of playing full-back Robertson at centre-forward was considered to be an abject failure but, despite the lack of a cutting edge up front, Motherwell gave the league leaders a real run for their money. This defeat, however, saw Motherwell slip down the league table to tenth place.

Only 200 Motherwell fans made the trip by rail on the supporters' special to 'the town of sugar and rain' but by the time they arrived at Cappielow so had the sun although the visitors kicked off against Morton into a stiff breeze. Reid was restored to the centre-forward slot and just failed to give the Steelmen an early lead following George's great run and cross. Good work by the Greenock side's right-wing pairing of Urquhart and Dart set up Spiers whose lucky shot managed to beat the impressive Tom McDonald in the Motherwell goal for the opening score of the day. The home side went in at the break with a slender 1-0 lead.

Early in the second half clever pay by Stewart allowed Nicol to firmly plant the ball in the Morton net only to be whistled up for offside. Motherwell's good play deserved at least an equaliser and that duly arrived in somewhat bizarre circumstances. Morton's goalkeeper Oliver was adjudged to have carried the ball too far (presumably outside his penalty area) and from the resultant free kick centre-half Hugh McNeil levelled the scores.

Then 5,000 fans watched both teams go all out for a winning goal but they had to settle for a hard-fought 1-1 draw and a share of the points. After some disappointing results the *Motherwell Times* reporter was happy with the team's performance on the day and sang the praises of those who had been less than convincing in recent weeks, 'The men who have been considered the weaklings this season, all gave a capital display on Saturday, Rattray and Robertson putting in some good work which was quite a treat to look at: Rattray being the best back of the four, and Robertson into his old form again.'

Motherwell's third away match in a row saw them make the short trip to Broomfield to enjoy the hospitality afforded by local rivals Airdrieonians in their bright new pavilion. In bright sunshine, before a large Lanarkshire crowd, Motherwell made an electric start and George had the ball in the Airdrie net within three minutes. The *Motherwell Times* reporter and his colleagues were astonished that the referee chalked off the goal for offside as the Airdrie keeper Duncan had handled the ball and, therefore, put all the players onside.

Motherwell were not disheartened and pressed hard for the opener with Andy Donaldson in particular showing outstanding touches. The visitors finally got their reward when Reid put them ahead before the interval. The home side came out for the second half in spirited fashion and piled pressure on the Motherwell defence using kick and rush tactics. Their deserved equaliser came 15 minutes from the end when Boyd beat Tom McDonald with a good shot. Although the home side pushed hard for the winner McDonald denied them with a string of fines saves to keep the scores at one goal apiece. The point from this game kept the Steelmen in tenth.

Motherwell were expected to pick up both points at home to Kilmarnock on 2 November but the visitors were able to return to Ayrshire with the spoils following a late winner against the injury-hit ten-man home side. McDonald's saves kept the Steelmen in the contest early on and the visitors were unlucky not to take the lead when Howie's shot rattled the crossbar. The hosts could also have gone in front when George made a great run down the left wing and sent in a powerful shot which Strachan only managed to parry and Stewart headed over the rebound.

The match was goalless at half-time but just before the interval Motherwell's McConnell was injured and had to retire to the pavilion. He began the second half but retired permanently soon afterwards, reducing the home side to ten men. Killie took advantage of their superior numbers and Barton eventually gave them the lead despite a spirited rearguard action by the Fir Parkers. Stewart gave the home side hope of sharing the points with a well-worked goal created by the forward line. 'Well hearts were broken in the 89th minute when McLean slipped allowing Howie to nick in to secure the points for the visitors.

George's form was returning gradually and Motherwell were finally able to end an eight-game winless spell with a 3-2 away victory over local rivals Hamilton Academical on 9 November when Reid was the hero with a fine hat-trick. Initially things did not look promising for the Fir Park outfit when left-winger Finlay, whom George had displaced in the Motherwell team in 1906, gave Accies the lead after five minutes. Their lead was short-lived and ended when hard-pressed Accies keeper Slavin attempted a clearance which struck Reid and rebounded into the empty net. Accies were stunned and went behind almost from the restart when Reid fired past Slavin from 20 yards.

Motherwell were now firmly in charge and just before the interval Reid notched his hat-trick when he stroked home Stewart's clever pass. Accies upped their game and dominated the second half, pulling a goal back through Arnott with 15 minutes remaining.

Try as they might the home side could only rarely get past the resolute Motherwell defence and found McDonald in sparkling form between the sticks. Motherwell held out for a hard-earned derby win. George had a fine game and linked well with Stewart and Reid in the Motherwell front ranks. This win lifted Motherwell to ninth in the table, ten points behind leaders Dundee.

Defeat by the odd goal in five at home to Aberdeen the following week typified Motherwell's inconsistent league form. The match was fought out in atrocious weather with high winds and driving rain which lashed the faces of the home side in the first period. Aberdeen took advantage of the conditions and were two goals to the good after only ten minutes through McDonald and Murray. The home side managed to stem the flow of Aberdeen attacks and at the interval the scoreline remained unchanged.

With the strong wind advantage in the second half Motherwell were expected to make a fight of it but Aberdeen managed to threaten again despite the elements being against them. The weather prevented any outstanding football being played and with 20 minutes remaining Motherwell still hadn't made the expected comeback. Andy Donaldson then found an opening in the Dons rearguard and brought the home side back into the match with a well-taken goal. A few minutes later Aberdeen's left-back Hume fired the ball into his own net in attempting to lift the ball over the bar to relieve strong pressure from the Motherwell forwards.

The momentum was now clearly with the Lanarkshire side who might have been expected to push forward and secure both points but, instead, their efforts waned and left-winger Lennie gave his side what proved to be the winning goal late on in the contest. The *Motherwell Times* reporter was not happy with the performance of the local side, conceding that Aberdeen were much smarter in all departments, especially in front of goal.

The continuing dismal weather and the previous week's poor performance against Aberdeen were reflected in the poor attendance at Fir Park for the match against Morton on 23 November. Rumours were rife in the town prior to the match about some new players being brought in to strengthen the side but the Motherwell board simply made a few changes to the line-up for this match, introducing Walker in the outside-right position and switching Nicol to left-half in place of McCallum.

Happily Motherwell made an altogether better showing against their Renfrewshire opponents than against Aberdeen and led 2-0 at half-time thanks to goals from Reid from 20 yards and Donaldson just before the break. Despite some good second-half form from the Greenock men Stewart and Reid brought the Motherwell tally up to four without reply and the Steelmen ran out comfortable 4-0 winners. The *Motherwell Times* man at the match reckoned George, 'Showed improved form, and got away with some dashes, but a better understanding between him and his partner might still further improve things.'

The win over Morton brought the crowds back and 6,000 were present at Fir Park on St Andrew's Day for the visit of fifth-placed Hearts. Motherwell made an enforced change with Robertson returning at right-back for the injured Rattray and David Richmond replacing the ineffectual Walker on the right wing.

The early play was evenly shared but gradually Motherwell began to get on top and only some erratic shooting prevented them going ahead.

At half-time the deadlock had not been broken despite the home side's better finish to the first period. After the interval Motherwell picked up where they had left off and laid siege to Allan's goal. After concerted pressure they had the chance to go ahead from the penalty spot when Donaldson was brought down in the penalty area. Right-back Robertson took the kick but Hearts goalkeeper Allan pulled off a sensational save to keep the scores level.

'Well were not to be denied, however, and Donaldson gave them the lead with a soft shot following good lead-up play by Richmond and Reid. An excellent pass from Richmond allowed Reid to add a second goal shortly after and Hearts were in disarray. Richmond capped a fine display by adding a third goal ten minutes from time.

That old inconsistency returned in December when fourth-placed Falkirk completed the double over Motherwell with a 2-1 win at Brockville. Five thousand spectators witnessed some fairly even early exchanges but Falkirk began to assert themselves and soon won a penalty when Rattray fouled Simpson. Tom McDonald kept Motherwell on level terms, saving Falkirk right-half Reid's poor spot-kick.

The Bairns did take the lead shortly afterwards in controversial circumstances when their centre-forward Skene shot home from a blatantly offside position. Both sides were surprised when referee Murray from nearby Stenhousemuir awarded a goal to the home side. Falkirk keeper Allan made two fine saves from Richmond and Donaldson as an aggrieved Motherwell side fought to gain the equaliser but the Bairns responded to the challenge and doubled their lead when McDonald could only block a shot from Davidson and Mitchell pounced on the loose ball and drove it home. The half-time break arrived with the visitors trailing 2-0.

Motherwell made a rousing start to the second half and the home goal had a few lucky escapes. The Steelmen forced two corners in quick succession and from the second of these Nicol forced the ball over the line to reduce the deficit. Falkirk were awarded another penalty shortly afterwards when Simpson was once again brought down. Reid was again entrusted with the spot-kick but was unable to find the Motherwell net.

The visitors redoubled their efforts to get back on level terms but the Falkirk defence were in excellent form and kept them at bay to run out 2-1 winners. The *Motherwell Times* reporter was delighted by the team's application and felt that their play at least merited a draw.

Motherwell fans packed another special train bound for Glasgow on 14 December for the visit to Ibrox. Motherwell's recent form gave cause for optimism and the play in the early stages swung from end to end. Motherwell were briefly down to ten men when McConnell had to seek treatment on the sidelines and during his absence Rangers took the lead when Smith crossed for May to beat McDonald with a fierce rising shot.

The home side were now rampant and Speirs added a second goal for the Ibrox men from a corner. It was no surprise when the same player repeated the performance, putting Rangers 3-0 ahead at the break. Motherwell looked to be in for a real thrashing when Kyle added a fourth goal for the Gers immediately after the resumption.

The *Motherwell Times* reporter was delighted at his team's reaction to going four goals down. Instead of throwing in the towel, 'They stuck to their task in a manner that showed they were yet to be reckoned with, and [George Clarke] Robertson with a nice pass from Reid cleverly tricked [Rangers right-back] Campbell and with a splendid shot beat Newbigging, thus scoring his first goal of the season.'

A minute or two afterwards a well-taken corner by Richmond was slipped into the net by Donaldson. Motherwell were on top for most of the remainder of the match but Rangers came back strongly at the end though neither side could add to their tally. The reporter felt that Motherwell could have had a share of the points if they had started the match as they finished it. He closed his report with news of a new signing; full-back Ballantyne from Bellshill Athletic and of the injury to regular left-half Alex McCallum who it was feared might lose the sight of one eye through an accident at work. Fortunately his eye was saved but he never played for Motherwell again and was released by the club.

Motherwell introduced their new signing Ballantyne at left-back for the visit of Third Lanark to Fir Park on 21 December. George was into the action straight away and should have had a penalty when he was fouled as he tried to find his left-wing partner in the area but the referee waved play on. Play was pretty even in the first period with both sides failing to create many chances. Just before the interval Motherwell took the lead from the penalty spot through centre-forward Reid after Thirds goalkeeper Jimmy Brownlie fouled Stewart in the box.

Thirds restarted in determined fashion and quickly equalised through their left-winger, ironically called Motherwell. The home side then upped the tempo but couldn't find the net with Brownlie in the Thirds goal showing why he was soon to be an automatic first choice for Scotland. Seven minutes from the end 'Well got the vital second goal that their pressure deserved when Stewart nipped in to shoot past Brownlie for what proved to be the winning score.

After displaying some good form in their last two matches, local hopes were high of collecting both points from the visit to Kilmarnock's Rugby Park on 28 December. On a windy day in Ayrshire Motherwell started well with George and his wing partner Donaldson prominent in their attacks. Come the interval, however, the match was still without a goal.

Kilmarnock went on the offensive in the second period and looked the more likely outfit to score. With the second half only a few minutes old, Armour headed Killie in front from a suspiciously offside position. Although Motherwell created a few goalscoring opportunities it was the Ayrshire men who made sure of both points when Templeton tried a long drooping shot which Tom McDonald turned into his own net as he tried to clear.

The *Motherwell Times* reporter felt that the match was a poor one but that the visitors were unlucky to lose. He thought George was the pick of the Motherwell forwards and could have brought them level after the first Killie goal with a fine solo run. The reporter wrote, 'After the first reverse, Robertson got off on his own, and with a little steadiness might have equalised, but his parting shot went over the bar.'

The result against Kilmarnock brought 1907 to a disappointing close, but Motherwell fans were hopeful of a return to good form in 1908 as Fir Park was scheduled to host two games in 24 hours over the Ne'er Day holiday period. Clyde were Motherwell's first-foot but the hosts were less than hospitable and saw them off with a comfortable 3-0 win. Clyde had the better of the first half but could not convert any of their chances. Their right-back Gilligan was having a fine match, keeping George and his new wing partner Walker in check so, 'seldom was it that Robertson got in one of his clever crosses' according to the press.

It was goalless at half-time but Reid broke the deadlock three minutes after the restart. The same player doubled Motherwell's advantage minutes later with a soft goal that Clyde keeper Mason clearly thought was going wide. Stewart capitalised on some hesitancy between the Clyde full-backs and nipped in to score his side's third goal of the afternoon.

The sun was shining but the Fir Park pitch was somewhat hard for the visit of Airdrieonians on 2 January. Motherwell were in charge from the kick-off. Hugh McNeil had the ball in the Airdrie net following a corner but the goal was disallowed for offside. Stewart then sent in a stinging shot which the Airdrie custodian Duncan tipped over the bar. From the resulting corner Stewart's powerful 20-yard rocket rattled the visitors' crossbar.

Motherwell continued the second half on the offensive and Duncan performed heroics in the Airdrie goal. 'In the subsequent raids that took place, Motherwell's left wing was prominent but Duncan seemed able to save anything. Robertson sent in two beauties from the touchline in succession. The first one Duncan dealt with successfully. The second was just a trifle too high,' wrote the *Motherwell Times*.

Airdrieonians fans were relieved to hear the half-time whistle and amazed that their favourites went in on level terms but Motherwell finally took the lead seven minutes after the break. Rombach conceded a corner and from the resulting kick a melee ensued in the Airdrie goalmouth and Duncan, with the ball in his hands, was charged into the net by either McNeil or Reid (the *Motherwell Times* reporter was not sure which) much to the chagrin of the visitors.

George headed what looked like another goal for Motherwell but it was disallowed for an infringement. Motherwell continued to press and a few minutes from the end Donaldson got the second goal that their attacking play deserved. The reporter was enthusiastic about the whole team's performance and singled out George for some praise, 'Robertson, the forward, was up to his old form, his "slickness" and beautiful placing being quite a treat.'

Motherwell were scheduled to play Partick Thistle at Partick on 6 January but the game did not take place, presumably because of adverse weather conditions, so they were able to play their third match in a row of 1908 at Fir Park on 11 January when the opposition was another local rival, Hamilton Academical.

Motherwell gave a debut to their new signing, right-winger James Johnstone from Irvine Meadow. With a tricky crosswind and treacherous under-foot conditions Motherwell attacked from the start and had the better of the early exchanges, although Accies were always dangerous on the break. Hamilton forwards claimed a goal when McDonald, under severe pressure, threw the ball from his goalmouth but the referee adjudged that he had not crossed the goal line. They had another chance to take the lead when they were awarded a penalty for Sneddon's foul on McGraw. Wardrop took the kick but McDonald pulled off a spectacular save to keep the scoresheet blank at the interval.

Accies pushed hard for the opener in the second half but gradually Motherwell's superior play began to tell and McConnell opened the scoring for the home side when his powerful low shot beat Slavin in the visitors' goal. Atkinson headed Accies level from a corner while McDonald was still groggy from an earlier knock but almost straight from the restart the Steelmen surged forward and Reid slipped the ball to George who easily netted what proved to be the winning goal. George turned in another good performance, 'showing good pace and putting in some good work' according to the newspaper.

Three wins from three games in 1908 had lifted Motherwell to ninth place and it looked that they might continue that winning form when they surged into a two-goal lead over Celtic before 10,000 fans on 18 January at Fir Park. In bright sunshine and on a soft pitch Motherwell took the field wearing a smart new kit of blue shirts and white knickers. The visitors' play was as smart as their new strips and new-boy Johnstone set up Stewart for the opening goal after only ten minutes. Celtic were further stunned two minutes later when clever play by Reid created space for George to net his second goal in two games.

Motherwell were good value for their lead which they held comfortably until half-time. Celtic, after the half-time team-talk, came out intending to take the game to the visitors but Motherwell held out until an injury to Nicol, who had been in brilliant form, turned the tide in favour of the home side.

With 13 minutes remaining a dipping shot from McNair rebounded from the crossbar, hit the back of the hand of diving goalkeeper McDonald and, luckily for Celtic, finished in the back of the Motherwell net. A few minutes later Somers grabbed a second goal for Celtic and the game finished with some thrilling end-to-end action but without any further scoring.

Motherwell were the better side and probably would have won but for the injury to Nicol in midfield. George turned in another good display, putting in a power of work speeding down the left wing. According to the *Motherwell Times* reporter a feature of this game was the number of times he was erroneously pulled up for offside, denying his side several goalscoring opportunities.

The first round of the Scottish Cup pitted Motherwell against non-league side Dumfries on 25 January. The memory of defeat at the same stage a year previously to Galston, another non-league side, was still fresh in the memory of the 500 Motherwell fans who boarded their special train for Dumfries with an air of trepidation. It proved to be an unhappy Burns night for the Dumfries club who went down 4-0.

A severe hailstorm battered the players in the first half and the pitch began to cut up badly. George was having a fine game and came close with a shot following a mazy run down the wing. His next attack was more productive. Although his cross was missed by Reid, Johnstone was on hand to drive home an 'unsavable shot' to give the visitors a 1-0 lead which they held at half-time.

The Steelopolins imposed themselves on the locals from the start of the second half and were soon two goals in front. George 'again broke away, beating half-back and back, and centreing accurately, Reid had no trouble in tipping the ball into the net'. Motherwell's superior stamina began to tell and their pressure soon yielded another goal. 'The third goal was a very fine effort of Robertson's, who from well out, completely beat Breckenridge with a long drive.'

The *Motherwell Times* man at the match does not make it clear which Robertson scored; George or his full-back namesake but, given the way he was playing, and his eye for a goal, I suspect that it was my great uncle.

Reid added a fourth goal just before the end to reflect the league side's superiority. The *Motherwell Times* enthused about the team and George's performance in particular and the way he, 'Repeatedly tricked the opposing defence. The forwards all did well, especially Robertson, who was always dangerous.'

February proved a less fruitful month for Motherwell as they failed to record a single win. They picked up a solid away point against the new league leaders Dundee at Dens Park on 1 February in a hard-fought goalless league match before their second round Scottish Cup game which was scheduled for 8 February.

The draw had thrown up a home tie with St Mirren who were in good form at that time, sitting in seventh place in the league and just two points ahead of Motherwell so a close match was on the cards. A good cup run was vital for Motherwell in financial terms and 12,000 spectators, including a large contingent from Paisley, turned up to see this keenly-anticipated contest.

Injury had taken its toll on the home side's ranks and a forward reshuffle saw regular right-back George Robertson take flu victim Johnstone's berth on the right wing. The makeshift winger made an impressive start, slamming the ball past Grant in the Saints' goal from Reid's pass. Home supporters were disappointed when the goal was disallowed for offside.

Both sides had chances to take the lead in a fairly even contest before Wylie put Saints in front just before the interval. The Steelmen turned up the heat early in the second half and McConnell and Donaldson both came close before Clements scored what looked like a decisive second goal for the Buddies. With ten minutes remaining McConnell found Reid from a throw-in and he beat the previously invincible Grant to give home fans hope of a revival.

St Mirren were clearly rattled and it was no surprise when Stewart equalised within a minute of Reid's goal. Reid came close to snatching a late winner but Saints held out desperately for a replay. Apart from some good early play Motherwell were disappointing until their very late rally and George himself was 'completely off'.

The replay was scheduled for the following weekend and 3,000 Motherwell fans on three special trains made the journey to Paisley for the match. Motherwell made a bright start but Saints took advantage of a mistake by right-back Robertson and Milne burst through to give Saints the lead. Near the end of the first half Motherwell began to exert a little pressure but could not convert any of their chances and went in at half-time trailing 1-0.

Saints started the second half well but Motherwell were able to contain them until goalkeeper McDonald's attempted clearance rebounded off Saints centre-forward Wylie and into the net to totally deflate his team's morale. Thereafter St Mirren proved too strong for a lacklustre 'Well side and won comfortably 2-0. The *Motherwell Times* reporter reckoned the better side won and cryptically said of George, 'Robertson got nothing to do and did it.'

George scored Motherwell's second goal against Rangers on 22 February in a match at Fir Park re-arranged from October when Rangers were involved in a Glasgow Cup tie. This farcical game was played out in a blizzard of wind and rain, hail and snow with the pitch covered in pools of water so good football was not likely to be on display.

Rangers had the advantage of the elements and Cunningham opened the scoring for them after seven minutes. Speirs added a second wind-assisted goal shortly afterwards to put the home side firmly in the driving seat. They even survived a Motherwell penalty which keeper Newbigging turned around the post. Just before the break Motherwell hit back and Johnstone netted their opener from a corner.

The second half began in a severe hailstorm and within two minutes George took advantage of the strong wind to lash home a surprise equalising goal. George Robertson, the Motherwell full-back, soon had to retire with a knee injury, reducing the visitors to ten men. This was to be the last match he played for the club so the injury must have been severe. As he does not appear on any other players' lists thereafter it may well have ended his senior football career.

Despite this disadvantage Motherwell were shaping up well but with 15 minutes remaining the storm got worse and the referee had no choice but to abandon a match which should never really have started.

The Motherwell ground staff were only able to partially clear the pitch of snow for the visit of Partick Thistle on 29 February and it was extremely heavy in places. The adverse conditions did not seem to affect the visitors who dominated the early play and deservedly took the lead through their inside-right Robertson. Stewart, in a breakaway, managed to pull the Steelmen level but the visitors continued to have the better of the exchanges. It was no surprise, therefore, when McGregor put Thistle back in front and just before the break a clever shot from Ballantyne beat McDonald in the 'Well goal to increase their advantage to 3-1.

Motherwell came out determined to pull themselves back into the match and while they were pressing, Thistle broke down the right wing and, although McDonald saved Robertson's initial shot, the Thistle forward netted the rebound to put his side 4-1 ahead.

The home team fought hard to get back into the match and controlled the remainder of the game. Donaldson's goal gave Motherwell some hope and tempers became a little frayed as they fought hard to get on level terms. With Motherwell now totally on top, George slotted home a third goal and it looked as if they could go on to get at least a draw from what seemed a hopeless position. Motherwell's reserve half-back John Dick thought that he was the hero of the hour when he scored what 'seemed a legitimate goal, but for some unexplainable reason the point was disallowed' and Motherwell fans were so outraged by the referee's decision that they pelted the official with snowballs.

The *Motherwell Times* reporter was highly critical of the team's performance and mystified by some of the refereeing decisions. George, despite scoring his team's third goal, had a miserable day on the wing and was well below par.

Motherwell made the long journey to Pittodrie on 7 March to face an Aberdeen side level with them on points in the league table. There was very little between the teams in this match but the home outfit ran out 2-1 winners largely because of their better finishing.

Motherwell took advantage of a strong wind in the first half and Nicol gave them the lead with a close-range shot from Johnstone's cross from the right. Aberdeen raised their game and levelled soon afterwards and at the half-time break the teams went to the pavilion on level terms.

With the wind behind them in the second half the Dons set about the Motherwell goal with gusto. The Lanarkshire side defended well but finally succumbed to a late goal from O'Hagan who shook off his marker to beat McDonald for the winning counter. George was one of his side's better performers of the day.

Motherwell were on their travels again the following week, making the trip to the capital to face Hearts at Tynecastle. On a beautiful spring day in Edinburgh both sides were under-strength; Motherwell being without the injured McNeil and Stewart while Hearts players Walker and Thomson were on international duty for Scotland.

George was involved in the early action around the Hearts goal and 'got a nasty kick through coming in contact with [Hearts right-back] Reid, which caused him to retire for repairs'. While George was off the field Hearts mounted attack after attack but the 'Well defence was resolute and managed to hold out.

George eventually re-appeared 'but was limping badly, and was not likely to be of much service to his side, although a cross of his was badly muddled between Johnstone and Reid, and Allan came to the rescue and cleared'.

McConnell eventually gave Motherwell the lead with a long drive and despite severe Hearts pressure the Steelmen went in at half-time leading 1-0. The Lanarkshire outfit made a great start to the second period and Nicol almost scored in the first minute. They didn't have too long to wait for a second goal. It came when Reid surged forward and picked out Johnstone. The winger saw Allan off his line and gave the keeper no chance with a carefully placed shot.

Two minutes later Nicol completed a miserable day for the Edinburgh side when he shot home for the final goal of the game. The locals thought Motherwell lucky to win the match but the *Motherwell Times* scribe reminded them, 'Robertson was practically useless after the first five minutes of the game, a fact that does not seem to be taken into consideration.'

The injury sustained at Tynecastle kept George out of the Motherwell side for two weeks, missing the away games against the two bottom clubs, Port Glasgow Athletic and Clyde. Motherwell started well at Port Glasgow's Clune Park with Stewart going close in the opening minutes. The Steelmen took the lead when Johnstone cut inside and fired in a shot which the Port keeper could only block and Reid, running in, banged the ball into the empty net. Athletic fought back and missed a couple of chances to equalise before Donaldson found Reid with a neat pass and he made no mistake so at half-time the visitors went in two goals ahead.

Port began the second period in fine style, harrying the visitors into making basic mistakes. Within a few minutes they pulled a goal back when Lynch's shot flew past the unsighted McDonald. Port had a chance of drawing level from the penalty spot when the ball struck Donaldson on the arm. Hamilton took the kick but shot feebly past. When Athletic were awarded another penalty shortly afterwards for McLean's handball, Ruddiman stepped forward and showed his team-mate how it should be done. Despite some good pressure from the home side there was no further scoring, the match finishing 2-2.

After a draw at lowly Port Glasgow, Motherwell were more hopeful of securing both points against bottom club Clyde at their Shawfield home on 28 March. The Fir Park men bore down on the Bully Wee goal from the kick-off and shots rained in with monotonous regularity on McTurk's goal but the Clyde keeper was equal to all that was thrown at him, ably assisted by his full-back colleagues.

There were strong claims for a goal from the visitors when Hugh McNeil's powerful free kick squirmed from the grasp of the Clyde keeper and trickled through his legs but the referee adjudged that the ball had not crossed the goal line (no hope of sophisticated goal line technology in Edwardian Scotland).

As is often the case the team doing all the pressing frequently falls victim to a smash and grab counter attack. As 'Well pushed men forward, Clyde broke swiftly down the right and a beautiful cross was headed past McDonald by centre-forward Graham. Clyde held out to lead 1-0 at the interval. More relentless pressure from Motherwell after the break failed to produce any goals and Clyde began to grow in confidence, ultimately taking charge of the latter stages of the match. It was no surprise when they added a second goal to dash Motherwell's hopes of a late revival. Two successive defeats to the bottom clubs in the league did not bode well for Motherwell's prospects in their remaining fixtures.

George returned to the Motherwell team for the abandoned match with Rangers which was played out at Fir Park on 4 April and had the air of a real end-of-season affair, this being the last home league match for the Steelmen. Rangers were the more aggressive side in the early stages but it took them 15 minutes before Campbell beat McDonald to give them the lead. Motherwell came more into the match later in the first half but their shooting was poor and rarely troubled Gers keeper Newbigging so the visitors were able to take to the dressing room at the break with a one-goal lead.

Motherwell made a better start to the second half and Andy Donaldson brought them back into the match with a well-taken goal. The home side were on level terms only very briefly before conceding a penalty. Campbell made no mistake with the spot-kick to put the Ibrox outfit back in front.

The remainder of the match was a real end-to-end affair and Motherwell had an opportunity to snatch a share of the points late on when Johnstone was brought down in the area. The normally reliable Reid took the resultant penalty but Newbigging saved to ensure that both points went home with the Glasgow team. The *Motherwell Times* man at the game felt that Rangers were the slightly better team and the difference between the sides was in the quality of their shooting. George made a quiet return to the side after his injury lay-off and was not even mentioned in the match report.

Motherwell's Lanarkshire Cup semi-final against Royal Albert took place in front of 2,000 fans at Fir Park on 11 April. It was a dull and depressing game which perfectly matched the weather. The visitors made a lively start but Motherwell gradually took control and could have gone in front when they were awarded a penalty following a stramash in the Larkhall team's area. After Reid's failure from the spot against Rangers, Stewart was entrusted with the kick but his well-struck shot rebounded off the crossbar and was cleared.

Although the home side were well on top, the interval was reached without any score. Motherwell finally took the lead after the break when Reid smashed home a beautiful shot from well out which gave the keeper no chance. The Royal Albert players then became a little more physical as the second half progressed and the match degenerated 'as the hooligan instincts of some players seemed to be aroused'. This violent conduct resulted in Johnstone and Royal Albert's left-back Armstrong being sent off and all of the players being lectured by the referee. A poor match ended with the Steelmen advancing to the final by that single goal.

Motherwell's penultimate First Division match on 18 April took them across Glasgow to play Partick Thistle at Meadowside in a match postponed from 6 January because of the wintry conditions. A poor crowd turned out for the match despite the sunny weather, largely because of the local spring holiday. Again Motherwell started well but Thistle's bustling centre-forward Kennedy gave them the lead against the run of play and they held that one-goal advantage at half-time.

The quality of play deteriorated in the second half but Motherwell's efforts merited at least a share of the points. They were to be denied however when Thistle added a second goal from a free kick to run out 2-0 winners. The team appeared to be jaded at this stage of the season as did the *Motherwell Times* reporter whose weekly match reports were becoming shorter every week. The *Times* man concluded his report by reminding fans of the visit of Woolwich Arsenal to Fir Park on the evening of Monday 27 April.

Motherwell concluded their league programme on 25 April with a visit to Hampden to face Queen's Park. Motherwell played with a strong wind in the first half and after some early dominance, Johnstone opened the scoring for the Steelmen. Queen's fought hard for the equaliser before the break but could not penetrate the Lanarkshire side's defence.

With the wind at their backs in the second half Queen's resumed their assault on the Motherwell goal but could not make the vital breakthrough. Motherwell appeared to have the points in the bag when they were awarded a penalty and Reid made no mistake from 12 yards. Logan did pull a goal back for the amateurs but, despite their best efforts, they could not deliver an equaliser and Motherwell were able to end the season with a 2-1 win. The two points from this match ensured that the Steelmen would finish tenth in the First Division.

Motherwell 'fought out' a 1-1 draw in a glamour friendly with the formidable Woolwich Arsenal on the Monday following the last league match. A respectable crowd turned up to watch the game, which was evenly contested with both sides scoring in the first half. The second half was a disappointment for the paying customers, with the players hardly exerting themselves, but the match was a valuable exercise for the Motherwell management who took the opportunity to try out three promising juniors who all performed well. Sadly the *Motherwell Times* did not list the line-ups and scorers for this fixture.

The Lanarkshire Cup Final, played at neutral Douglas Park on Tuesday 28 April, saw Motherwell triumph by 4-2 over Wishaw Thistle. Wishaw's kick and rush tactics deservedly gave them a 1-0 half-time lead with a goal by Laughland but Reid levelled the match ten minutes into the second half. When Reid put Motherwell ahead with a lovely drive the fight seemed to go out of Thistle. Reid soon completed his hat-trick to effectively make sure of the trophy.

Wishaw reshuffled their line-up, promoting May to centre-forward, and he pulled one back for Thistle before Stewart restored Motherwell's two-goal advantage to seal the victory. George was not mentioned in the report of the match and he was clearly not back to full fitness following the injury to his knee sustained in the match against Hearts.

Mr T. Dodd presented the cup to the winning Motherwell team after the match.

Motherwell's side for the final was: Tom McDonald, John McLean, James Rattray, John McConnell, Hugh McNeil, George Nicol, James Johnstone, James Stewart, William Reid, Andy Donaldson, George Robertson.

Motherwell, for the second season running, finished tenth in the table despite registering two points fewer than the previous season. On the positive side however, they did increase their goals-for tally from 45 to 61. Willie Reid was, once again, their leading marksman with an impressive tally of 23 goals. He was ably assisted in the scoring charts by Andy Donaldson with 11 and James Stewart with ten goals.

The 1907/08 season saw George make a total of 32 league appearances (excluding the match against Rangers in February which was abandoned after 75 minutes because of atrocious ground conditions with the score at 2-2; George having scored one of the goals) and three in the Scottish Cup. He scored five goals over the season.

The end of this season brought about a number of changes to the team. Alex McCallum played his last game for Motherwell following a serious eye injury at work and George's namesake, the full-back, retired following a serious knee injury sustained in the abandoned match with Rangers. Andy Donaldson, George's regular left-wing partner, moved on to local rivals Airdrieonians along with regular wing-half John McConnell who later joined the team of 'Macs' at Liverpool.

Centre-forward Willie Reid and goalkeeper Tom McDonald both joined ambitious Portsmouth in the Southern League in England. Reid and George would become team-mates again, but at international level after Reid later joined Rangers.

During the close season the *Motherwell Times* reported the signing of centre-forward Robert Tait from Carlisle United and indicated that the club were about to sign three players from junior clubs; Alex Jones of Rutherglen Glencairn, Robert McArthur of Shotts United and goalkeeper Chris Wakeman of Clydebank. All of these players would make their first-team debut the following season.

The important off-the-field news for local football fans reported in the *Motherwell Times* was that the Motherwell executive were considering the erection of a new stand at Fir Park.

SCOTTISH LEAGUE FIRST DIVISION 1907/08

	Pl	*W*	*D*	*L*	*F*	*A*	*Pts*
1 Celtic	34	24	7	3	86	27	55
2 Falkirk	34	22	7	5	102	40	51
3 Rangers	34	21	8	5	74	40	50
4 Dundee	34	20	8	6	70	27	48
5 Hibernian	34	17	8	9	55	42	42
6 Airdrieonians	34	18	5	11	58	41	41
7 St Mirren	34	13	10	11	50	59	36
8 Aberdeen	34	13	9	12	45	44	35
9 Third Lanark	34	13	7	14	45	50	33
10 Motherwell	34	12	7	15	61	53	31
11 Hamilton Academical	34	10	8	16	54	65	28
12 Heart of Midlothian	34	11	6	17	50	62	28
13 Greenock Morton	34	9	9	16	43	66	27
14 Kilmarnock	34	6	13	15	38	61	25
15 Partick Thistle	34	8	9	17	43	69	25
16 Queen's Park	34	7	8	19	54	84	22
17 Clyde	34	5	8	21	36	75	18
18 Port Glasgow Athletic	34	5	7	22	39	98	17

MOTHERWELL APPEARANCES AND GOALS 1907/08

	League		*Scottish Cup*	
	Apps	*Goals*	*Apps*	*Goals*
Ballantyne, John	1	0	0	0
Dick, John	3	0	0	0
Donaldson, Andrew	31	11	1	0
Johnstone, James	11	2	2	1
McCallum, Alexander	15	1	0	0
McConnell, John	28	2	3	0
McDonald, Thomas	34	0	3	0
McLean, John	27	0	1	0
McNeil, Hugh	29	1	3	0
Nicol, George	32	7	3	0
Rattray, James	28	0	3	0
Reid, William	32	20	3	3
Richmond, David	7	1	0	0
Robertson, George	15	1	3	0*
Robertson, George Clarke	32	4	3	1*
Sneddon, James	12	1	0	0
Stewart, James	31	9	3	1
Walker, John	6	0	2	0
Hume (Aberdeen) OG	-	1	-	-

* Degree of uncertainty which George Robertson scored this goal.

4

1908/09 – DEADLY AND DECEPTIVE

BY the end of July 1908 Motherwell had signed 15 players for the upcoming season including new goalkeeper Robert Young from Kilmarnock. The *Motherwell Times* praised the directors of the club for their ambition and was pleased to report that work was nearing completion on the new grandstand at Fir Park. However the *Times* sports reporter castigated the directors for allowing Andy Donaldson to be transferred to rivals Airdrieonians.

The left-wing partnership he had forged with George was one of the strongest elements of the team and Tait and McArthur, who were tried in his place, did not measure up to their illustrious predecessor.

Motherwell prepared for the start of the First Division season with a practice match against Dalziel Rovers at Fir Park on Wednesday 5 August. According to the *Motherwell Times* the team gave 'general satisfaction' and easily won 4-0. Motherwell were still hopeful of recruiting a few new players and an amateur figured at right-back on trial and gave a good account of himself. 'The left wing [presumably George and McArthur] also put in some good work, and altogether the team shaped up well,' according to the newspaper.

A second warm-up match took place against Wishaw Thistle at Fir Park on Saturday 8 August. There was a good turnout of fans anxious to see their new players in action. It was reported, 'The new grand stand came in for some attention, and it was voted on all hands to be quite a substantial-looking structure, but the general opinion also seemed to be that the management might have made it a little longer when they were at it. The management, however, say that they will be satisfied if they get the stand filled every Saturday, as it is.'

On the whole the team put up a fairly good show and the *Motherwell Times* was particularly impressed by both wings. Motherwell won comfortably 5-1.

A crowd of 4,000 enjoyed the summer sunshine when Third Lanark were the visitors for the opening match of the 1908/09 season at Fir Park on 15 August. George was quickly in action with a strong early shot. Motherwell were in command from the start and Thirds keeper Brownlie was under great pressure as the home side sought an early breakthrough. It took Thirds fully 20 minutes to bring out a save from Motherwell's new goalkeeper Robert Young, and thanks largely to Brownlie's efforts the teams turned around with the match still goalless.

The visitors made a bright start to the second period but Motherwell soon regained the upper hand and Brownlie had to be on the top of his game again. The match looked to be heading for stalemate when Robert Tait, Motherwell's new centre-forward, beat Brownlie with a splendid shot with only a few minutes remaining. George was 'in grand form, and got away with some fine rushes, some of which deserved a better finish. He also crossed and shot well, and but for the cleverness of Brownlie, he would have had several goals to his credit'.

Motherwell staged a benefit match on 17 August for half-back George Nicol who had been on their books for five years. The opposition was provided by local rivals Airdrieonians who included former 'Well heroes McConnell and Donaldson in their line-up. Motherwell took the opportunity to give some game time to some of their new signings. The Broomfield men dominated proceedings and led 1-0 through McMeekin at the break. The same player added another goal in the second half and Motherwell could only muster a single counter from Stewart and went down 2-1. The game was played in great spirit and much enjoyed by the crowd.

Four hundred Motherwell fans on a special train made the trip to Brockville to see their favourites take on Falkirk on 22 August. The Steelmen continued their good form from the opening match and took the lead after only five minutes when Stewart headed home McArthur's pass. An injury to winger James Johnstone then changed the course of the match as while he was receiving treatment McTavish equalised for Falkirk.

Johnstone did return to the field but was limping badly and Motherwell were effectively down to ten men. Tait hit the bar for the visitors but thereafter Falkirk dominated proceedings and it came as no surprise when Clark put them ahead and a Skene header gave them a two-goal lead at half-time.

Second-half injuries to Young, Sneddon, Rattray and McArthur did little to help Motherwell's faint hopes of a fightback. Simpson added a fourth goal for Falkirk who looked set to run riot. The Bairns were awarded a penalty when Rattray brought down Skene but Young made an excellent save from Simpson's low spot-kick. At the end of this match report the *Motherwell Times* reporter advised that the club had signed left-half Archibald Buttery of Cleland Rangers.

After the bruising encounter with Falkirk the previous week a few Motherwell players were carrying injuries for the visit of Port Glasgow Athletic to Fir Park on 29 August. New full-back Breslin was due to make his debut in this match but his train was delayed and a hasty reshuffle of the team was necessary.

The home side took control early on and pinned the visitors back in their own penalty area with Tait, Nicol and Sharp all having good chances to open the scoring. George 'was conspicuous' at this stage, his runs causing confusion in the Port ranks and he was unlucky not to score.

The *Motherwell Times* wrote, 'Robertson again nipping the ball up sent in a rocket shot which Thomson could not hold. The ball, however, went from the keeper's hands against the crossbar, and rebounded into play.'

The home side's continuous pressure was to no avail and the sides retired at half-time without a goal being scored. Motherwell resumed in the second half where they left off and their relentless pressure simply had to tell. They had the chance to go ahead from the spot when Port's Jackson handled in the penalty area. Sharp, who had a reputation as a penalty taker, sent his shot wide. Motherwell suffered another blow when Nicol had to go off for treatment. He was able to return but his effectiveness was considerably reduced.

It was reported in the newspaper, 'At last the ill luck seemed to forsake the Fir Parkers, and about fifteen minutes from time they scored the only goal of the game. Sharp sent in a magnificent shot, and Thomson was making a good attempt to save, when Robertson rushed the ball through.'

George's performance caught the eye of the *Motherwell Times* sports reporter, 'Robertson was in excellent form, and his deadly finishes were a delight to behold. None of his efforts were very far astray.'

The win took Motherwell up to eighth place with four points from their opening three fixtures.

George took part in a benefit game for Dalziel Rovers against Kilmarnock on Monday, 31 August. The Steelmen used the match to try out some of their newcomers and the match was halted as darkness descended with the score at 1-1.

Old rivals Airdrieonians, including former Fir Park favourites McConnell and Donaldson, were Motherwell's next First Division opponents at a windy and rain-soaked Broomfield Park. Motherwell faced the elements in the first half and, after a good spell of play, there were loud appeals for a penalty when Rombach brought down George in the penalty area but the referee dismissed the claims. Stewart then brought out a great save from Duncan as Motherwell began to get on top. As the rain continued to pour down the referee blew for half-time.

Airdrie began the second half and immediately began to put pressure on the 'Well full-backs. Goal line controversies are nothing new. Airdrie's opening goal came from a McLay free kick which slipped through the hands of goalkeeper Young and bounced on the line. The keeper recovered and cleared the ball but referee Hamilton had already awarded a goal. The official was surrounded by a crowd of Motherwell players led by keeper Young who vociferously contested the decision.

A few bad-tempered moments followed which the *Motherwell Times* described as 'more bootball than football'. The incident clearly disturbed the Motherwell keeper who was still seething when Airdrie added a second goal. It was all over for the Fir Parkers when Hunter scored a fine third for the home side. George had a disappointing day in the appalling conditions and was well marked by his former colleague John McConnell.

More misery was to follow when Hearts inflicted a 6-1 thrashing on a dismal Motherwell side at Fir Park. Former Clydebank Juniors goalkeeper Chris Wakeman made his debut in place of Young but he could not be held solely responsible for his side's crushing defeat. 'Well were sorely pressed from the kick-off and Walker, Scott, Hynds and Scott again had the game won for the Edinburgh men by half-time although Stewart had reduced the deficit just before the break when Hearts were temporarily down to ten men.

Motherwell's anxiety to get back into the game in the second half meant that their efforts were hurried and Hearts' more composed approach brought them two more goals from Devine and Sinclair. The defeat by Hearts saw Motherwell slip three places down the league table to 11th, leaving the *Motherwell Times* reporter wondering if the outstanding display against Third Lanark in the opening game was a flash in the pan. This shameful performance brought forth another poem in the pages of the newspaper by Knowetap Lad. Its chorus expressed the town's disillusionment with all departments of the current team:

'I care not for the forward line,
Our half-backs never seem to shine,
Our backs, how can we love you
When you're losing every time'

Kilmarnock rubbed even more salt into a gaping Motherwell wound at Rugby Park on 19 September when the Lanarkshire side found themselves on the wrong end of a 4-1 scoreline. Young returned in goal for Motherwell against his old colleagues but he couldn't do anything to prevent them securing both points. The game began in sensational fashion with the referee awarding the home side a penalty after only two minutes when McLean handled and Mitchell made no mistake from the spot.

The *Motherwell Times* reporter was mystified at the award of a second penalty to Kilmarnock, when the hand that touched the ball clearly belonged to a Killie player. Mitchell once again clinically dispatched the kick. Despite these setbacks Motherwell played well and had the best of the first half but couldn't convert any of their chances and went into the pavilion at half-time 2-0 down.

Killie added a further two goals in the second period and Motherwell scored a consolation goal through their new centre-forward, as reported, 'Tait scored the goal from a cross by Robertson, who never had half enough of the ball, McArthur being out of it completely.' Killie thus leapfrogged the Steelmen in the table, the Fir Park men slipping down to 13th and provoking more critical odes in the columns of the local press.

To their credit the critics were prepared to eat humble pie and penned a couple of poems of praise when Motherwell recorded their third win of the season, at home to Hibernian the following week. Rain was falling and the Fir Park pitch was heavy as the home side, and George in particular, made a spirited start. 'Robertson on the left wing early tested the Hibs defence, that player sending in a rocket shot which Allan had to negotiate on all fours. Another good shot from the foot of Robertson, just missed the net by inches,' wrote the newspaper.

'Well opened the scoring minutes before half-time when Tait slammed the ball home after the Hibs left-back failed to clear and the home side led by that counter at the break. Hibs came into the match a little more in the second half but their shooting posed no problems for 'Well keeper Young. Fifteen minutes from time Stewart scored from Tait's cross and added another just before the finish. The *Motherwell Times* man at the match was pleased with the team's overall performance and praised the left-wing pairing, 'McArthur and Robertson made light of the Hibs defence, the latter's shooting was deadly and deceptive as usual.'

James Johnstone's first goal of the season was the difference between the two sides when Queen's Park were beaten 1-0 in beautiful weather at Hampden on 3 October as Motherwell recorded their first back-to-back wins of the season. Queen's monopolised the early possession but their shooting was poor with only a Bowie effort which hit the bar causing Young any concern. Motherwell gradually asserted themselves and play was finely balanced as the first half ended without a goal.

Johnstone's rather soft goal put Motherwell ahead shortly after the interval with the Queen's keeper unable to hold the winger's shot. Queen's pushed hard for the equaliser and Young pulled off a remarkable save from Queen's Park's legendary centre-forward R.S. McColl. Motherwell managed to repel all the homesters' attacks and won by the only goal of the match. George had another fine game and it was reported, 'Robertson played well, his shots as usual being dangerous.' This win propelled Motherwell up to ninth in the table.

Remarkably, it was three wins in a row the following week when Morton were beaten 2-1 at Fir Park. At the last minute a nervous-looking Wakeman replaced Young, who felt unwell in the dressing room, in goal for Motherwell. Motherwell won the toss and took advantage of the strong wind. Play was fairly even in the opening period and the deadlock was not broken until ten minutes from the interval when Tait, Stewart and Johnstone combined well down the right with the winger finishing off the move. Just as the referee was about to blow for half-time Morton snatched an equaliser when Hamilton was on the mark.

With the advantage of the wind Morton should have piled on the pressure but the home side seemed to fare better against the elements. Their persistence paid off when Stewart put Motherwell back in front with a well-taken goal. Play thereafter was pretty even and the Steelmen held out for the win which they just about deserved on the balance of play. George had a quiet game by his recent standards and was criticised for not bringing the opposite wing into play more often.

Motherwell fans packed another special train for the trip to Ibrox on 17 October to meet a Rangers side who had just suffered their first league defeat of the season the week before. Despite going down 3-1 Motherwell turned in another good performance but their shooting was a major let-down. George was one of the chief offenders, spurning a number of good chances. 'Indeed, twice Robertson with good work, put himself in a position to score, and failed miserably,' reported the *Motherwell Times*.

The visitors were having the better of the exchanges but, against the run of play, Livingstone gave Rangers the lead from a Bennett corner. Smith added a second goal for the Gers when Young failed to hold his swerving shot. After the break Rangers took charge and Smith added another goal. This sparked a Motherwell revival and Tait ran on to

Stewart's pass and beat keeper Rennie. Tait should have closed the gap further when the Steelmen were awarded a penalty but Rennie held the centre's spot-kick. Motherwell were now in command and were still pressing hard when the final whistle blew with the home side leading 3-1. Apart from his shooting George played well. 'When once Robertson is able to finish more deadly, he will rank high as an outside-left,' bemoaned the *Motherwell Times* reporter.

Motherwell fell to unbeaten Clyde at Fir Park on 24 October although they had more of the play than the Shawfield men. Clyde bossed the early part of the first half but never looked like scoring against a resolute home defence. Gradually Motherwell came more into the match and put the visitors under some pressure, 'Robertson having a fine shot for goal and 'Nicol testing [Clyde keeper] McTurk'.

Just before half-time Spiers luckily latched on to a cross from Kirwan to put the Bully Wee 1-0 ahead at the break. Motherwell totally dominated the second half and created numerous chances but their shooting left much to be desired. They were hampered by a knock to Tait whose pace was seriously limited by the injury. George had another reasonable game but his reputation was now such that he was being closely marked, according to the press: 'Robertson was well watched by Gilligan, but he had many good runs.'

Remarkably results elsewhere over the past two weeks meant that Motherwell were able to retain ninth spot in the table.

That was to change when their third successive defeat, by high-flying Dundee at Dens Park on 31 October, saw Motherwell slip back down to 13th. The home side were quick off the mark, opening the scoring after four minutes when Bellamy's shot was deflected by a defender's foot into the corner of the net. Young was under considerable pressure and it was no surprise when the rampant Dundee side added a second goal, Hunter tricking McLean and shooting home. The Motherwell goal had some miraculous escapes and the Steelmen were lucky to go in at half-time only 2-0 down.

In the second half the Dark Blues resumed their assault on the visitors' goal but the Motherwell defenders were beginning to get to grips with their opponents and kept them at bay while starting to prompt attacks of their own. From one of these Stewart headed past Crumley to give the visiting fans some hope of a revival. The game could have been level minutes later when Stewart 'missed a splendid pass from Robertson when he had no one to beat'. Dundee had other ideas and 'Sailor' Hunter (later to become a Motherwell legend – as manager, secretary and director of the Lanarkshire club from 1911 to 1959) added a third goal for them after Young had blocked his first effort. Motherwell forced the pace again and Crumley made an excellent save from Tait and the home side ran out 3-1 winners.

The *Motherwell Times* reporter berated George for trying to do too much, 'Any goals that are scored are generally from Robertson's crosses, yet he persists in trying to shoot from impossible positions, when a cross in front of goal might mean victory for his side.'

The Steelmen picked up another vital point with a hard-earned 2-2 draw in the derby game at home to Hamilton on 7 November. The Accies were still without a win, all of their seven points coming from drawn matches. A crowd of 5,000 witnessed a fast-paced start to the game with the home side going in front after only four minutes through Stewart who beat Mason with a grand shot. The Douglas Park side stormed back and Miller equalised after a great run down the right wing.

After this sensational start the game settled down and both teams played some attractive, crisp, passing football. Play was fairly even but Motherwell luckily took the lead just before the interval when Accies right-back Brownlie, under severe pressure, headed into his own net.

The game resumed in the same frenetic manner as the first half with a nervy-looking Young having to look lively to deny the Accies forward line. The visitors eventually beat the Motherwell keeper for a second time and both teams then went flat out for the winning goal. In a pulsating end to the match neither side could make their chances count and the *Motherwell Times* reporter felt that a draw was a fair reflection of the play. George had another good match, 'Robertson was the best of the Motherwell forwards. He put in some good work, and was well supported by his partner.'

The Motherwell management clearly felt that the team's deficiency in front of goal was a problem. The *Times* indicated that the club were on the point of agreeing terms with Sam Hill, the centre-forward of the Belfast club Mountpottinger, and one of the directors had already made a trip to Ireland to secure his signature although Hearts had also expressed an interest in signing the young player.

Motherwell played a friendly match with local club Dykehead on Wednesday 11 November in aid of that club's pavilion fund. The Fir Parkers won the match 3-0 with all the goals coming in the first half from Nicol, Stewart and Kennedy.

Owing to family illness at home in Belfast, new signing Sam Hill was unable to take his place in the Motherwell side on 14 November for the trip to Love Street to meet St Mirren. Motherwell could have done with the services of their new man as the team's poor shooting probably cost them the points.

Saints took the lead through Brown after two minutes but Motherwell soon settled and started to exert some pressure on the home defence with the left-wing pairing prominent in their attacks. A rash tackle by McLean after 15 minutes gifted Saints a penalty and Brown scored his second goal of the match from the spot. Just on the half-time whistle Motherwell appeared to have pulled a goal back when Tait netted but the referee disallowed what seemed to be a legitimate counter.

The second half was a ding-dong affair and Saints had the match sewn up when Milne and Cunningham combined to beat Young for a third time. Motherwell retaliated and mounted several attacks and from one of these George finally beat keeper Grant. The Steelmen continued to attack furiously but their shooting let them down badly. The *Motherwell Times* felt that the team played well enough in parts and deserved better than a 3-1 defeat, suggesting that the referee was wrong in disallowing Tait's 'goal'.

The reporter also castigated the forwards for their deplorable shooting and remarked that George's left-wing partner McArthur 'has not yet come up to expectations and Robertson did not get enough work to do in consequence'.

The *Motherwell Times* report of the home match against Queen's Park on 21 November cocks a snook at city sportswriters and Queen's supporters for their Glasgow bias and getting so many details of the Motherwell team wrong in their accounts of the match. Fir Park was once again lashed by high winds and heavy rain for the visit of the amateurs and all the spectators took cover in the new stand.

The home side took the lead when Johnstone and Stewart worked their way down the right and Johnstone's cross picked out George who had no difficulty in beating Queen's goalkeeper Adam. There is evidence that George's performances were attracting the notice of the Scottish national press. The city papers must have stated that George played at outside-right and was a native of Montrose or Dumbartonshire for the *Motherwell Times* reporter questions their knowledge of the geography of Scotland, explaining, 'Robertson, by the way, comes from Montrose. What part of Dumbartonshire is that in? And I might also add he plays outside-left, not outside-right.'

The Spiders were keeping Young busy and he did well to save good efforts from Dixon and Leckie as the play swung from end to end. Debutant Sam Hill's impeccable pass sent Johnstone free and the right-winger calmly put Motherwell two goals ahead and there was no further scoring at the break. According to the *Motherwell Times* man, the first half was a cracker and he felt Queen's were desperately unlucky to be two goals behind.

Queen's began the second half in positive fashion and a good run and cross from Paul set up Leckie whose goal deservedly brought the Hampdenites back into the match. The Glasgow side's cheers had barely died down when Motherwell scored a third goal through Stewart. The young amateurs were undaunted and forced corner after corner as the Fir Parkers began to wilt. From one of these Rattray got his head to the ball and diverted it into the path of Dixon who steered it past Young. However, another poor clearance fell to Paul whose drive beat Young to draw the sides level.

Yet Motherwell could have won the match late on, as it was reported, 'Johnstone gave Robertson a beautiful opportunity of pulling the points back, but Geordie struck the bar with his shot. A touch would have done it, of course. That was not bad luck, bad play better describes it.'

The *Times* man rated this match the best and most exciting of the season and the 3-3 draw a fitting result. With Tait now moved to the inside-left position the *Times* reporter thought that he might prove a good partner for George, 'A little study and he and Robertson would make quite as effective a pair as the other. Robertson was in spanking form, and has started to get goals, yet he might get more with a little steadiness.'

Motherwell adapted better to the treacherous conditions at Pittodrie on 28 November to record a fine 3-1 win over Aberdeen. Motherwell moved the ball about quickly and took the lead after five minutes when Stewart beat Mutch in the Aberdeen goal with a long-range daisy-cutter. Aberdeen fought back and pushed 'Well back on the defensive and their efforts finally brought about an equaliser. The home side were now on top and Young did well to keep them from adding to their tally.

Motherwell's confidence began to grow as they took inspiration from their goalkeeper's performance and the pendulum began to swing in their favour again. After harassing the home side's goal the prolific Stewart fired home a second goal to put the Steelmen in front after 45 minutes. Both sides had chances in the second half but near the end young Irishman Sam Hill scored his first Motherwell goal to make the score 3-1 and secure the points for the visitors.

After a deluge, the game against Celtic kicked off amid the rain and mud at Fir Park on 5 December. Celtic won the toss and chose the advantage of the wind and rain at their backs in the first half. The pitch cut up badly and the players soon had difficulty in moving the ball about. Celtic's kick and rush tactics were ideally suited for the conditions and Quinn gave the Motherwell defence a torrid time with some powerful shooting although George managed to test Adams when he sent a stinging shot straight at the Celtic goalkeeper.

Celtic took the lead in controversial circumstances when referee Jackson of Glasgow awarded a goal after a shot from Loney was touched by Young on to the post and, as reported in the newspaper, 'rolled into the centre of the goal almost under the bar, but not over the line. The ball was allowed to remain untouched in its position, and the Motherwell players tried to induce the referee to come down and examine the position of the ball, but he would not, and ordered the game to proceed.'

The Motherwell players continued to hold out manfully against the elements and the Celtic forwards but were powerless to prevent McMenemy scoring with a rasping shot. Motherwell did better in the second half and after ten minutes' play Stewart headed home George's cross to set up the home side for a grandstand finish. Despite having the bulk of the play the home side could not add to their tally and the Bhoys took the points with a 2-1 win.

The *Motherwell Times* announced that Messrs A. & W. Smith, the hatters, would present a new felt hat to the first Motherwell player to score two goals in a match. The *Times* reporter indicated that there would be a change in the Motherwell line-up for the next match when McArthur would come in for George.

The reason for George's absence was that he had a match of another kind on his mind that day when he married Jessie Greig in McArthur's Hall in Alva, Clackmannanshire, on Friday 11 December 1908. Jessie was born on 29 July 1886, the daughter of Robert Greig, a weaver, and his wife Catherine Greenlee, and lived at 185 Stirling Street, Alva. The couple may have met at secondary school at Alva Academy or during the early years of George's apprenticeship as a baker.

George's address at the time of his marriage was 6 Findlay Street, Motherwell. The marriage certificate gives George's occupation as baker (journeyman), clearly indicating that he was not a full-time professional with Motherwell. Jessie was described as a power loom weaver, presumably in one of the many woollen mills in Alva.

George missed his only game of the season, the 2-0 win over homeless Partick Thistle at Ibrox, the day after his wedding when Tait played a starring role in his place on the left wing. Stewart continued his great scoring streak, giving his side the lead after six minutes and late on in the second half the limping Johnstone sent over a cross which Hill slammed past Eadie in the Thistle goal. The *Motherwell Times*, at the end of the match report, noted that Motherwell had been drawn away from home to Highland League side Elgin City although the paper hoped that Elgin might be induced to switch the tie for financial reasons.

George was back in the Motherwell ranks and enjoyed a few good runs the following Saturday when the Steelmen were away to Hibernian at Easter Road. In a match played out in failing light the Steelmen went down 3-0 to a Hibs side three places and three points above them in the league. Paterson gave the Edinburgh team the lead and Peggie added a second before the interval. Peggie's great solo run and finish completed the scoring in the late afternoon gloom – a goal probably missed by many of the spectators present.

It was a disappointing display from the Motherwell men who might have been expected to come away with both points given their easy win when the sides met earlier at Fir Park. Chances went begging throughout the match and George was one of the main culprits, 'Robertson was let away by Tait, and had no one to beat but the goalkeeper, but carelessly he banged the ball against the keeper.'

Fir Park was hard and frost-bound and somewhat dangerous but the referee gave the go-ahead for Motherwell's match against Falkirk on Boxing Day 1908. Four thousand fans saw Falkirk make a bright start but Sam Hill gave the homesters the perfect response when he netted after only a few minutes and it wasn't long before George added a second to put the Steelmen two up. According to the newspaper, 'Following shortly upon this success, Robertson had a splendid run, and McKenna was once more beaten by a beautiful shot from that smart forward.'

Just before the interval Devine got through the Motherwell defence and pulled a goal back for the Bairns and at the turnaround Motherwell led 2-1. James Johnstone restored Motherwell's two-goal advantage early in the second period and the home side seemed comfortably in command of the match. With ten minutes left Falkirk mounted a frantic all-out attack on the Motherwell goal but Young and his defence held them at bay to run out 3-1 winners. The *Motherwell Times* reporter was enthusiastic about George's performance, 'Robertson was magnificent in his tackling, travelling; and shooting.'

If the team had displayed inconsistency in the early part of the season, 1909 began even more alarmingly with five straight league defeats and a first round exit from the Lanarkshire Cup.

Motherwell hosted the 1909 Ne'er Day derby encounter with near neighbours Airdrieonians. Airdrie were the vastly superior outfit throughout the match but surprisingly found themselves two goals down to the Steelmen at the half-time break. Goals from Tait and Johnstone did the damage, the Motherwell forwards taking advantage of two of the rare opportunities presented to them in the first half. Justice was done in the second period when Airdrieonians got the goals that their good play and possession deserved. They managed to put four goals past Young in the Motherwell goal without reply and were good value for their 4-2 win.

The 'Well defenders suffered a New Year hangover when they shipped another four goals at home to Dundee the following day. Injury-hit Motherwell were without regulars Rattray, Jones and Tait and were overwhelmed by the high-flying Dundee side who coasted home 4-1. Johnstone provided the one crumb of comfort for the home fans with his side's only goal in the second half.

In between league matches Motherwell relinquished their hold on the Lanarkshire Cup on Monday 4 January 1909, going down 2-1 to Hamilton Accies at Douglas Park. Having lost eight goals in his last two matches Young was dropped and Wakeman took over goalkeeping duties, but otherwise the team was almost back to full strength. Honours were fairly even in the first half. Accies took the lead through Robertson but Sam Hill levelled for 'Well just before the change of ends. In the second half, former Motherwell favourite John Miller scored what proved to be the winner for a much more dangerous Accies side.

As if the crowded fixture list wasn't busy enough at this time of year, Motherwell staged a benefit match for popular veteran full-back John McLean against Hibs on Wednesday 6 January 1909. The Motherwell side contained a few first-team players and some guests from other sides. The Motherwell XI led 1-0 at the break but eventually succumbed 3-2 to the Edinburgh side.

For their fourth competitive match in nine days, Motherwell made the trip to the south side of Glasgow to face Third Lanark at their Cathkin Park home on 9 January. Thirds were totally in command in the first half but only had one goal to show for all their superiority. It came just before the interval when their appropriately named left-winger, Cross, centred for Thirds' Johnstone to head past Young. Motherwell performed better in the second half against the stiff breeze but couldn't take advantage of the few chances they created.

Thirds looked to have the points secured when Young got his fingers to a shot from Cross but couldn't keep the ball from crossing the line. Motherwell eventually came back into the game after Stewart beat Thirds' formidable keeper Brownlie with a long-range goal late on.

'Well pushed hard for an equaliser but Richardson broke away and scored a third goal for the Volunteers to effectively end the contest with the score 3-1 in favour of the home side.

George was good in spells, according to the *Motherwell Times*, 'Johnstone was the only forward who could be classed as good, the others played hard but made little progress, with the exception of Robertson in the second half.' This defeat saw Motherwell slide down to 12th in the table with 18 points from their 23 matches played.

The Lanarkshire side's dismal run continued the following week when they travelled to the capital to face Hearts on 16 January. Motherwell set the early pace and McArthur had them in front after only ten minutes. The lead was relatively short-lived as Hearts deservedly drew level five minutes later. Motherwell were not downhearted and went back on the offensive and George was directly involved in Motherwell's second goal. 'Success again came to Motherwell, however, as Collins, in trying to clear a shot from Robertson, put the ball through his own goal,' according to the report.

That proved to be the final score of the first half. Hearts took advantage of a good spell of pressure to equalise within the first ten minutes but afterwards the second half was fairly even with play swinging from end to end. With both sides missing a host of chances, the match appeared to be heading for a draw. Then, in the last few minutes, Courts popped up in the Motherwell area to fire the ball past Young to give the Tynecastle side both points.

The only bright spot for Motherwell in a thoroughly miserable January came in a break from league business when the luckless Elgin City were crushed 6-1 at Fir Park in the first round of the Scottish Cup on 23 January. Elgin had been persuaded to relinquish home advantage in the tie in the hope of a big crowd but, sadly, there was a disappointing turnout on a fine but chilly day, with few fans making the trip from Morayshire.

There was a clear gulf in class between the two sides and the visitors were scarcely able to get out of their own half as the First Division side piled on the pressure. A wonderful display in goal by Elgin's goalkeeper Davidson kept the score respectable as Motherwell fired in shots from all angles. Davidson's heroics kept 'Well at bay for some time but eventually Hill made the breakthrough and a second goal from Stewart quickly followed. Before half-time Motherwell made it 3-0, when Hill got his second of the match.

Motherwell picked up where they had left off in the first period and Stewart, Nicol and Hill added second-half goals to complete the rout of the Highland League outfit. Elgin towards the end threw caution to the wind and managed to force a few dangerous attacks and from one of these Guthrie got them a consolation goal. Sam Hill's three goals proved to be the young Irishman's only hat-trick in Motherwell colours.

Motherwell welcomed Rangers as their guests to Fir Park for the return league encounter on 30 January. The visitors initially appeared to be having an off-day, having much of the play but missing countless easy chances. Their supporters were dismayed when, 'just on the call of half-time, however, Hill beat Rennie from a pass by Robertson' to give the hosts a shock 1-0 lead at the interval.

After the refreshments Rangers came out with all guns blazing and McPherson quickly restored parity with a simple goal. The home side were not a spent force though and, 'Robertson soon put his side in the lead again with the best goal of the game.' This audacity only spurred on the Ibrox side who soon equalised and then added a further three goals to run out comfortable 5-2 winners.

The Motherwell board were clearly worried at the way the defence had been leaking goals and the *Motherwell Times* concluded the match report with the news that the club had signed a new goalkeeper, McFarlane of Aberdeen, and hoped to acquire additional players to strengthen the half-back line. With all the other teams around them in the league faltering, Motherwell, despite this loss, held on to 12th place.

McFarlane made his debut as Motherwell were bundled out of the Scottish Cup in the second round by Falkirk on 6 February when the Bairns exacted a little revenge for their Boxing Day league defeat. The Brockville pitch was in relatively good condition but a trifle frosty in places. Both sides began tentatively as they probed for an early opening and the first goal arrived on ten minutes when Stewart headed home a good cross to put the visitors ahead. The honours were pretty even for the remainder of the half, with both sides going all out for goals, but at the changeover, Motherwell still led 1-0.

Fifteen minutes from time it looked as if Motherwell would be advancing to the third round despite strong pressure from the Bairns attack. At this point Falkirk switched Simpson to the centre-forward position and their fortunes changed dramatically. With ten minutes left Simpson got the equaliser, despite protests from the visitors that he was offside. The same player, within minutes, put the Bairns in front and Motherwell looked down and out.

Bravely they threw almost everyone forward but Falkirk broke quickly and McLean conceded a penalty in the last minute which Simpson converted to make the final score 3-1 to the home side.

Simpson's penalty completed a remarkable quick-fire hat-trick and advanced his side to the next round when all seemed lost.

Motherwell managed to halt the run of five league defeats with a 1-1 draw against Clyde at Shawfield on 13 February. 'Well started briskly and a great piece of dribbling by Tait ended with Stewart firing in an unsaveable shot for the opening goal, his 17th of the season. The visitors led by that solitary goal as the teams crossed over at the break. Clyde came out strongly in the second half and were swarming dangerously around McFarlane's goal for long periods.

The equalising goal, when it came, arrived in bizarre fashion. In a desperate scramble in the Motherwell goalmouth Sneddon tried to thump the ball clear but it struck Clyde's Stirling and sailed past the helpless McFarlane into the net. Stewart missed a chance in the closing minutes to steal both points but a draw was a fair result in what was an evenly contested match.

George had a poor game against the Bully Wee, and it was reported, 'The game could hardly be described as exciting, but it was on the whole interesting, with some very pretty footwork, especially on the part of the Motherwell forwards, who, with the exception of Robertson, all played well – with Hill and Tait outstanding.'

Despite earning a valuable point, results elsewhere ensured that Motherwell slipped down to 13th in the league.

George returned to something like his old form in the 3-3 draw with Partick Thistle at Fir Park on 20 February. Motherwell's left wing was prominent in the early stages and Hill scored from a pass from George within two minutes. Partick began to improve and McGregor put them back on level terms after five minutes. Things looked bleak for 'Well when McFarlane couldn't stop Lyle's shot and the ball trickled over the line to give the visitors the lead but Hill finished a clever run with a fine shot to draw the Steelmen level. At half-time the score was 2-2 although Motherwell should have gone in ahead, having spurned several good chances after equalising.

Motherwell started the second half vigorously and George was unlucky when 'a beautiful shot by Robertson, worthy of a goal, glanced off the crossbar'. Motherwell were now buzzing around the Thistle goal and seemed to do everything but find the net. The Jags seemed a spent force but, on a rare visit to McFarlane's goal, they surprised the hosts by going in front against the run of play. From the kick-off Motherwell promptly raced downfield and Johnstone made it 3-3 with a snap shot which beat Massey.

After this goal there were some ill-tempered displays from the Thistle players as Motherwell went in search of the winner but all their efforts proved fruitless. Motherwell were the better team and probably deserved both points but their shooting let them down badly. However the point gained manage to elevate them to 11th place with 20 points from their 27 games.

Motherwell finally achieved their first league win of 1909 when Aberdeen were beaten 3-2 at Fir Park on 27 February and George was first on the mark, as reported, 'Motherwell forwards again got on the run, and Robertson scored the first goal in less than ten minutes of the start.'

Once again Motherwell's failings in front of goal were very much in evidence and, despite calling the shots for much of the first half, they went in at the break on level terms when Blackburn's shot swerved past McFarlane and into the corner of the net for Aberdeen's equalising goal.

Motherwell reshuffled their line-up after the interval including switching Rattray to George's position on the left wing. The new formation proved largely ineffectual but leading scorer Stewart soon bagged another goal to put the home side in front again. When Niblo levelled things for the Dons in the closing stages it seemed that the homesters would have to go another week without a win. Salvation came in the shape of a penalty in the dying seconds of the match when Hill was brought down in the Aberdeen box. Stewart calmly tucked away the spot-kick to the huge relief of the Fir Park faithful.

George was beginning to turn on the style again and had a good game against his former Motherwell team-mate, Aberdeen's right-back Donald Colman. Motherwell remained 11th, now with 23 points.

Only a handful of spectators were present at the start of Motherwell's Lanarkshire derby match against Hamilton Academical on 6 March. The weather was appalling for players and public alike and as the teams took the field the snow began to come down so heavily there was the possibility that the match might have to be abandoned. Fortunately the snow ceased fairly quickly and additional fans began to drift into Douglas Park. Both teams began cautiously as players regularly found themselves floundering on the icy surface.

The Accies seemed more willing to take risks and eventually got in a shot which beat Rab McFarlane. In endeavouring to stop the shot McFarlane dislocated a finger and had to leave the field to have it strapped up. Right-back John McLean had to take over in goal and gave a good account of himself in the keeper's absence.

Accies led by the only goal at the break and Motherwell already looked a beaten and disjointed unit. Little Robert Tait was the best of the Motherwell players but even he was unlikely to pose any real threat to the Accies defence and 'even Robertson was at sea against Davie'. Accies added another goal in the second half after some clever work by Glasgow and Finlay McLean and closed out the match to claim both points.

The following week Motherwell were held to a 1-1 draw by Morton at Cappielow. Morton started with the wind and sun in their favour and took the game to the visitors from the off. Motherwell fought back and George had 'an ineffectual try' at the Greenock side's goal. After 25 minutes of fairly even play Hamilton and Speirs combined to cut their way through the Motherwell defence and Hamilton beat Young to put Morton ahead. It looked as if the visitors had equalised almost immediately when, 'The Fir Parkers, with great dash, made for the home goal, and Robertson netted the ball but he was ruled off-side and the goal disallowed.'

At half-time the home side still led by the only goal of the game. Motherwell, with the advantage of the wind, made a strong start to the second half and, 13 minutes in, drew level when Stewart continued his fine scoring form for the Lanarkshire side with his 20th goal of the season, his final one in Motherwell colours. Despite raining in many shots on the Morton goal there was no further scoring and the Motherwell team had to settle for a share of the points. Motherwell were now sitting on 23 points from their 30 games and lay 12th in the table.

Motherwell won their next match, beating St Mirren 1-0 at Fir Park on 20 March. The margin of victory should have been much, much greater in a game in which the home side were superior in every department. Sam Hill gave Motherwell the lead in the first half but, try as they might, the Fir Parkers just could not add to their tally. That was in no small part due to Saints goalkeeper Grant who defied the Motherwell forwards time after time with a series of impressive saves.

George was one of the better performers on the day, and it was written in the *Motherwell Times*, 'Robertson and Hill were prominent with their dash and vigorous shooting, which would have taken effect more frequently had it not been for Grant in the St Mirren goal.'

In the final home game of the season, Motherwell entertained Kilmarnock on 27 March and ran out 2-1 winners. Motherwell were quickly out of the traps and Aitken did well to clear a shot off the Kilmarnock goal line in the early stages. Thereafter play was fairly even and at the interval neither side had managed to score. Motherwell were a little livelier in the second half, and Hill put them in front a few minutes after the resumption. The Fir Parkers did not hold the lead for long, for within five minutes Bulloch brought the Ayrshire men back into the game with an equalising goal. The home side threw everything at Killie in the last 15 minutes and Sam Hill got his reward for his great efforts by grabbing a deserved winning goal for Motherwell. According to the *Motherwell Times* scribe, he and George 'showed great dash'.

The season ended in disappointing manner, however, without another goal being scored. Motherwell fought out a dull goalless draw against struggling Port Glasgow Athletic at Clune Park on 3 April. Things looked promising for the visitors in the early stages when Stewart fired narrowly past former Motherwell keeper Montgomery's post. Some wild shooting then followed from both sides, notably from Gourlay who should have put the home side in front but missed the target with the goal gaping.

With the scoresheet blank at the interval there was still all to play for. Motherwell looked the hungrier side in the second half and should have won the game on the number of chances they created. Montgomery kept the sides level with a spectacular and brave diving save at the feet of Johnstone. Motherwell slipped one place down the table to 13th with 28 points and only one fixture remaining.

With the final match of the season against Celtic not scheduled until 26 April, Motherwell took the opportunity to arrange a friendly match, if local derbies can be called friendly, against Hamilton Academical at Fir Park to maintain the players' fitness. Gracie gave Accies the lead before the break and the Motherwell defence looked none too steady against the Douglas Park outfit. After the changeover Hill finished a beautiful run with a shot which crashed back off the upright and, at the other end, Gracie beat Young for a second time to double Accies' advantage. Two late penalties allowed Motherwell to draw level and, at the death, they managed to snatch a late winner.

Sadly the *Motherwell Times* provided no details of the Motherwell scorers or how the players performed generally. The *Times* considered this one of the worst matches ever seen at Fir Park but it is significant in that it is the first in which George did not appear in the left-wing berth. He was tried out in the inside-left spot, perhaps in an effort to provide a little more of a goal threat. It was evident from the report that there was also real concern over the quality of Motherwell's goalkeeping staff.

After a period of absolutely horrendous weather Motherwell completed their league programme against Celtic at Celtic Park on Monday 26 April. It was not a meaningless end-of-season match for Celtic who were still chasing Dundee in the race for the title. The *Motherwell Times* did not report at all on the game but the *Evening*

Times covered the match which took place in 'fearful weather'. Motherwell persisted with the experiment of playing George at inside-left and introducing John Tennant on the left wing but it had no effect as the Parkhead side thrashed the Fir Parkers 4-0.

Jimmy Quinn had Celtic 2-0 in front after six minutes with two headed goals, one from a free kick and another from a corner. Despite relentless Celtic pressure Motherwell managed to keep the deficit to two goals at the break. Quinn completed his hat-trick in the first minute of the second half and promptly switched to the right wing with David McLean (George's future team-mate in Sheffield) taking over at centre-forward. McLean scored the final goal ten minutes from the end when Young failed to hold his powerful drive. 'Well keeper Young was his side's hero with a string of fine saves 'while McLean, Stevenson, Hill and Robertson did well in depressing circumstances'. The Glasgow side were in simply irresistible form and went on to overhaul Dundee to take the league championship.

With so many changes among the forward positions at the start of the season it is perhaps no surprise that the Motherwell team took some time to gel. Just as they appeared to string some results together they were badly hit by injuries and difficulties with the goalkeeping position.

George's third season with Motherwell began with the team performing inconsistently, recording eight wins, ten defeats and two draws before the New Year holiday. Their record after the festive season makes disappointing reading with only three wins, four draws, and seven losses from the final 14 matches. James Stewart admirably filled the breach caused by the departure of Willie Reid and contributed 20 league and cup goals over the season. Sam Hill chipped in with 12 goals after joining the club in November 1908.

George managed to avoid injury again for most of 1908/09, playing in 33 of the 34 league fixtures. Once again he improved his goal tally, notching six goals over the season to be Motherwell's third highest scorer. Motherwell finished in a disappointing 14th place in the 18-team First Division table with a total of 28 points, three less than in the previous season.

SCOTTISH LEAGUE FIRST DIVISION 1908/09

	Pl	*W*	*D*	*L*	*F*	*A*	*Pts*
1 Celtic	34	23	5	6	71	24	51
2 Dundee	34	22	6	6	70	32	50
3 Clyde	34	21	6	7	61	37	48
4 Rangers	34	19	7	8	91	38	45
5 Airdrieonians	34	16	9	9	67	46	41
6 Hibernian	34	16	7	11	40	32	39
7 St Mirren	34	15	6	13	53	45	36
8 Aberdeen	34	15	6	13	61	53	36
9 Falkirk	34	13	7	14	58	56	33
10 Kilmarnock	34	13	7	14	47	61	33
11 Third Lanark	34	11	10	13	56	49	32
12 Heart of Midlothian	34	12	8	14	54	49	32
13 Port Glasgow Athletic	34	10	8	16	39	52	28
14 Motherwell	34	11	6	17	47	73	28
15 Queen's Park	34	6	13	15	42	65	25
16 Hamilton Academical	34	6	12	16	42	72	24
17 Greenock Morton	34	8	7	19	39	90	23
18 Partick Thistle	34	2	4	28	38	102	8

MOTHERWELL APPEARANCES AND GOALS 1908/09

	League		*Scottish Cup*	
	Apps	*Goals*	*Apps*	*Goals*
Breslin, John	3	0	0	0
Buttery, Archibald	21	0	1	0
Hill, Samuel	20	9	2	3
Johnstone, James	31	7	2	0
Jones, Alexander	17	0	1	0
McArthur, Robert	17	1	0	0
McFarlane, Robert	4	0	1	0
McLean, John	31	0	2	0
McNeil, Hugh	16	0	1	0
Nicol, George	20	0	1	1
Rattray, James	29	0	1	0
Robertson, George Clarke	33	6	2	0
Sharp, Andrew	8	0	1	0
Sneddon, James	29	0	2	0
Stevenson, Samuel	1	0	0	0
Stewart, James	33	17	2	3
Tait, Robert	30	5	2	0
Tennant, John	1	0	0	0
Wakeman, Christopher	2	0	0	0
Young, Robert	28	0	1	0
Brownlie (Hamilton) OG	-	1	-	-
Collins (Hearts) OG	-	1	-	-

5

1909/10 – CONSISTENT AND DESERVING OF INTERNATIONAL HONOURS

THE *Motherwell Times* of 13 August 1909 listed the players signed up for the coming season which the directors hoped would help the team climb the league and challenge for major honours. Additional signings were also said to be in the pipeline and, for the first time in their history, Motherwell would have sufficient playing staff to run a reserve side.

Among the new signings was goalkeeper Tom McDonald who made a welcome return to the club after a season with Portsmouth. New full-backs were John Johnston, the former Dalziel Rovers player, who was snapped up from Sunderland, and Patrick Kelly from Dumbarton. The new half-backs were William Downie, 'a half back of repute' from local club Bellshill Athletic, Henry Duff from Queens Park Rangers and David Taylor from Rangers.

There was concern in the *Motherwell Times* that the forward line would be the weakest part of the team. Motherwell had lost their top scorer James Stewart to Liverpool at the end of the previous season and were hoping that Sam Hill was going to fill that void and perhaps even improve on the 12 goals he scored in 22 matches since signing for the club. Six new forwards were added to the books; William Lawson from Reading, John Gray of Wishaw Thistle, Edward Davidson of Dumbarton, Bannerman of Kilwinning, John Tennant of Ashgill Rovers and Jimmy Murray from Shettleston who also hoped to be able to provide extra firepower in 1909/10.

Young Irishman Murray had excellent credentials having won the Irish Cup and the City Cup in 1904/05, the Irish League championship in 1905/06 and represented the Irish League against the Football League in 1905 when starring with Distillery in his native Ulster.

Unfortunately the much-changed side started the season very badly, taking only two points from their first seven league games. The opening match of 1909/10 was a Monday night affair against Clyde at Shawfield played in front of 5,000 spectators on 16 August. Things started well for the Fir Park outfit when, after five minutes, Bully Wee full-back Blair slipped and let inside-left John Gray in to give the Steelmen the lead. The home side were rattled and Motherwell looked more than capable of adding to their lead. As the match progressed the home side came increasingly into the game and should really have got back on level terms by half-time but at the close of the first 45 minutes the visitors still held their single-goal advantage.

Fifteen minutes after the restart Chalmers got the goal that the Shawfielders deserved and thereafter they ran the show. Clyde went in front through Walker and completed the scoring ten minutes from the end when Stirling got through the Motherwell defence for the best goal of the match to make the final score 3-1. George had a fairly anonymous game and was one of the poorest performers on the day.

Motherwell were not expected to pick up any points against Dundee at Dens Park on 21 August with many pundits strongly tipping the Dark Blues for either the Scottish Cup or the league title. The Fir Park forwards could make no headway against a powerful and well-drilled defence and as a result most of the traffic was headed in the direction of McDonald's goal. The major surprise of the first half was that the visitors went in at the break only 1-0 down.

Dundee were still well on top in the second period but Motherwell showed a little more fight with Taylor and Downie urging them forward. Despite their best efforts the only goal of the second half went to the home side when Bellamy slotted home from the penalty spot to give them a 2-0 victory. George was more noticeable in this match although the Dundee defence held the Motherwell forwards in check for much of the 90 minutes, and it was reported, 'Lawson and Robertson, however, were occasionally in evidence, and Gray at times showed neat footwork.'

Once again George made a rare appearance in the inside-left slot in a benefit match for Hamilton Academical's veteran right-winger Finlay McLean. Sadly, persistent rain kept the attendance down and the match finished Hamilton Accies 1 Motherwell 0. The *Motherwell Times* reporter felt that Motherwell deserved at least a share of the spoils and could even have won if Johnstone, Murray and George had taken the chances presented to them.

Motherwell's first point of the season was achieved at Fir Park when Partick Thistle were the visitors on 28 August. Thistle had the advantage of a strong wind in the first half and put the home defence under a little pressure although keeper McDonald was seldom called into action. The Fir Parkers had chances of their own and twice came close to opening the scoring, 'Once Gray had Howden almost beaten, while Robertson had that keeper under difficulties with a trying shot.'

The half-time whistle sounded with neither side having registered a score. Ten minutes after the restart Motherwell grabbed the lead when 'a clever run by Robertson and a cross from Johnstone, gave Murray a splendid opening, and that player made no mistake'. Motherwell seemed to be in command and should have gone two up. They 'were attacking in fine style, when Robertson, with the goal at his mercy, stepped on the ball and nullified a fine effort'.

Shortly afterwards the Jags lost centre-forward Branscombe through injury and finished the match with ten men. This appeared to give the visitors heart, and McGregor soon burst through the 'Well defence to give them the equaliser. Partick redoubled their efforts and were rewarded 12 minutes from the end when McGregor once again beat McDonald with a fine shot to put the ten men in front. The Fir Parkers looked like a beaten side but, as they pushed forward in the closing stages the ball struck Thistle's McKenzie on the arm and a penalty was awarded. David Taylor stepped forward and scored from the spot to spare the home side's blushes. Jimmy Murray made his first Motherwell appearance in this match and, like George, scored on his debut.

Murray held on to the centre-forward spot for Motherwell's next match, an away fixture against Celtic on 4 September 1909. With the wind behind them Motherwell took the game to their hosts but, despite all their pressure, had only one goal to show for their efforts at the interval. George played a big part in putting 'Well ahead, and it was reported, 'Robertson was in grand form, and the goal came from a piece of fine work from him. A swinging shot from Robertson to the centre gave Murray an opportunity, and that player had Adams beaten.'

Celtic came back strongly in the second half and goals from Johnstone and McMenemy put them in front. It looked to be all over for Motherwell when Rattray fouled Kivlichan in the penalty area and the referee awarded a penalty to the home side. Tom McDonald rose to the occasion and turned Loney's spot-kick around the post. This undoubtedly raised the spirits of the Fir Park outfit and 15 minutes from time 'again Robertson crossed to centre, and Murray, with a fast low drive, beat Adams a second time to the enthusiastic delight of the Motherwell supporters in the field'.

The *Motherwell Times* congratulated the team on their determined fightback which earned them a well-deserved point. The *Times* reporter was particularly impressed with the forward line with 'Robertson, Lawson and Murray conspicuous'. It was clear, even at this early stage, that George and Jimmy Murray were rapidly developing a promising rapport.

Airdrieonians visited Fir Park on 11 September and made off with both points with a narrow 1-0 victory in the first Lanarkshire derby game of the season. Motherwell took the time to pose for a team photograph – one of only two Motherwell team pictures which include George.

It was reported, 'After the Motherwell team had smiled before the photographer the ball was set in motion' to begin what proved to be an explosive start to the match. 'Within two minutes of the kick-off the ball was netted twice, once at each end. In the first minute Lawson sent the ball home but offside robbed him of the goal. From the kick-off, Airdrie rushed up and Webb was more fortunate for he beat McDonald with a pass from Donaldson, the former Motherwell player and Airdrie were a goal up.'

There were chances for both teams but the visitors probably just deserved to hold their single-goal advantage at the break. The second half continued in a similar vein but neither side could convert any of their opportunities so the visitors collected both points thanks to their early counter. The *Motherwell Times* reckoned that Airdrie were marginally the better team but both sides could and should have scored more goals. Sadly George did not play well and the *Times* reporter felt, 'Motherwell's left wing, particularly in the second half might have shown to much better advantage.'

Worryingly, Motherwell were still without a win and had only gathered two points from their first five matches to languish third from bottom of the league table. They were hopeful of securing their first victory of the season in front of their own fans, when Third Lanark visited Fir Park on 18 September but, sadly, it was not to be, with the Fir Parkers going down 3-1 to the Volunteers. The 5,000 fans saw 'Well make an encouraging start and Johnstone put them ahead as early as the second minute, a lead they maintained until the half-time whistle.

The visitors had played well enough in the first period but could make little headway against the Motherwell defence. However they made a breakthrough early in the second half when Richardson equalised for Thirds. Motherwell should have quickly regained the lead when Barr committed a foul in the penalty area but Taylor's poor spot-kick was easily saved by Brownlie.

At this point the home side appeared to lose heart and the complexion of the game changed completely. Two minutes later Thirds were awarded a penalty and Ferguson confidently beat McDonald from the spot. The referee instructed the kick to be re-taken but the result was the same and the visitors were now in front. The match was over when Johnston added a third goal for the Cathkin side who ended up running the show. The failure to record that crucial first win appeared to be getting to the Motherwell side, particularly the forwards who played well but seemed over-anxious in front of goal.

Motherwell's dismal run continued when they lost 3-1 again, to Falkirk on 25 September at Brockville with the Bairns' veteran winger Andrew Mitchell getting all his side's goals. Mitchell put the home team ahead with a powerful shot from a tight angle and that remained the difference between the sides at the break. Motherwell came out a little more positively in the second half and exerted some pressure on the Falkirk defence but 'a lack of sting and sharpness of finishing of the Fir Parkers' proved to be their undoing. Mitchell added two further goals to give Falkirk a comfortable cushion but Motherwell kept plugging away and Willie Lawson got a late consolation goal which proved to be his only score of the season.

The *Motherwell Times* reporter saw some hope in the performance of the forwards of whom 'Davidson and Robertson were the pick of the front rank'. The spectre of having to apply for re-election to the league was now looking a distinct possibility with Motherwell still sitting in the third-bottom place having earned a meagre two points from their seven matches.

The team's first win came, at last, in the eighth game of the season when they beat Hibernian 3-1 at Fir Park with George notching his first goal of the campaign. Motherwell dominated the match from the start but just couldn't turn their pressure into goals. 'Success was bound to follow the persistence of the Fir Parkers, but nearly half an hour had gone ere Robertson found the net with a fast, low shot at close quarters,' it was reported.

Motherwell went all out to kill off the opposition but were caught out by a swift Hibs break and Peggie gave them the equaliser with a headed goal. Given Motherwell's recent form, another collapse could have been on the cards but this time Motherwell were a bit more steely and were soon back on the attack, although couldn't produce another goal and the teams went in level at the break.

Hibs were the principal aggressors in the early part of the second period and they created numerous chances but some woeful shooting kept the scores even. On this occasion it was Motherwell who broke away and Johnstone sent over an immaculate cross which Murray slammed past Hibs keeper Allan. Hibs fought on gamely but Murray settled matters by adding a third goal for the visitors in the latter stages to secure both points.

The *Motherwell Times* scribe was delighted to report on a win and a good showing by the Fir Parkers, 'The front rank and Murray played judicious football, while both wings proved very speedy on the ball, and their runs were beautiful to watch although their finishing was weak. The left wing was the strong part of the Motherwell attack, Robertson being in fine form.' Despite doubling their points total with this win the Steelmen remained third from bottom.

Although George turned in a good display, Motherwell went down 2-1 to Kilmarnock at Rugby Park on 9 October. Killie started with the advantage of a strong wind and attacked the visitors from the first whistle. Despite really strong pressure from the home side, the 'Well defence performed heroically to keep them at bay until Cunningham eventually broke through to give the Ayrshire men the lead. Motherwell retaliated and Stevenson in the Killie goal was soon the busier of the two custodians, keeping his side in front with a series of grand saves including two from George, which were reported, 'Robertson had two fine efforts, but a corner only resulted.'

Motherwell were hoping to go in at half-time on level terms or, at worst, only one goal in arrears but, just before the interval, Cunningham again beat McDonald to make the score 2-0 to Kilmarnock. Motherwell utilised the wind well early in the second half but gradually Kilmarnock began to get on top and Cunningham was denied his hat-trick when Taylor cleared off the 'Well goal line. The wind-assisted ball flew downfield and caught Stevenson out of his goal, allowing Murray to run in and help it into the unguarded net. George's wing play drew praise from the *Motherwell Times* reporter who thought him the pick of the forwards. This defeat caused Motherwell to slump to second-bottom position, edging ever closer towards having to seek re-election to maintain their First Division status.

Motherwell's hopes of retaining their top-flight position were boosted by an excellent 5-2 win over St Mirren at Fir Park on 16 October as George's good form continued. The home side started in determined fashion and took the lead in less than two minutes, 'The goal resulted from a fine breakaway by Robertson, who passed into goal, and Murray put the finishing touch on the effort.'

Motherwell attacked the Saints' defence with vigour and, after 13 minutes they were rewarded when Murray added a second goal. Motherwell's third goal came from George 'who took advantage of an injudicious pass from Key to his back, and got away with only Grant to beat, and this he successfully accomplished'.

St Mirren managed to raise their game and Cunningham scored to give the Buddies a glimmer of hope of a revival. That was dashed just before the interval when Murray completed a fine hat-trick to put the Fir Parkers 4-1 ahead. St Mirren put on a better showing after the break but found it hard to get past Motherwell's full-backs, Gillespie and McLean. Fifteen minutes from time they pulled a goal back from the penalty spot but it was to no avail as the Steelmen also won a penalty just before the end and Murray scored with the spot-kick. This win propelled Motherwell to fifth from bottom with a more respectable six points scored from their ten matches.

The following week at Pittodrie, George was on target when 'Well were lucky to come away with a point in a hard-fought 2-2 draw with Aberdeen. The Dons were on top for much of the match and went into a deserved lead through centre-forward Soye. Motherwell showed some fine touches as they sought an equaliser but their finishing proved to be pretty inept. It took a remarkable goal to put them on level terms. Johnstone sent across an in-swinging corner which Dons goalkeeper Mutch thought to be going past but the ball swerved in the air and, although the keeper got fingers to it, ended up rolling into the net. The teams went in at the break with the scores even at 1-1.

Motherwell were a better side after the oranges as play swung from one end to the other. From one of the visitors' attacks, 'Motherwell scored, Robertson giving the home custodian no chance.' With time rapidly running out it looked as if the visitors would steal the points but Simpson scored a late equaliser which was a fairer reflection of the play. The *Motherwell Times* man at the match noted that Murray was now perceived as a real goal threat and, as a result, was very tightly marked by the Aberdeen defence.

George scored his fourth goal in three games as Motherwell went down by three goals to one against local rivals Hamilton at Douglas Park. Motherwell were without the in-form Murray, presumably through injury, and suffered as a result although they started the match on the offensive. George was first to try his luck but Accies goalkeeper Slavin managed to clear his lines. Accies gradually settled and took the lead when Irvine slipped Gillespie and crossed for Freeman to nod in the opener. Accies had the best of the remainder of the first half but could not add to their tally and led 1-0 after 45 minutes when the teams turned around immediately rather than resort to the dressing room.

In the second half the visitors were back on top but, surprisingly, went two behind when a McLean miskick allowed Freeman in to place the ball past McDonald. This reverse spurred Motherwell on and 'eventually Robertson, with a fine drive beat Slavin, who had no chance to save. This was easily the best goal of the match'.

Both sides went flat out for the next goal which could turn the game. Watson rattled the bar for Accies before Main settled matters with a third goal for the home side. The *Motherwell Times* reporter felt that the 'Well forwards under-performed in this match, particularly in front of goal, but George was the best of the bunch. The *Times* man expressed his concern that, unless the Motherwell management provided a brand of football 'worth following' then Fir Park gates would fall away rapidly. The directors had reiterated that the talent was there but the *Times* felt that it should now be showing itself. This latest result saw Motherwell slide back down the table to third from bottom once more, raising the spectre of re-election again.

Against Falkirk at Fir Park 'Robertson was conspicuous with his runs' although he couldn't turn the match in Motherwell's favour and it finished level at 2-2 in a ding-dong encounter. The weather was good for football so 6,000 spectators lined Fir Park and were treated to some end-to-end attacking play. The home side were first to press and Falkirk's full-backs had to be at their best to prevent Motherwell from opening their account.

Motherwell took the lead when Falkirk's Miller failed to clear his lines and Johnstone crossed to Murray, who, standing with his back to the goal, hooked the ball over his shoulder and into the net. The home side were now in full cry and should have put the match out of reach of their visitors when Murray was brought down in the area and a penalty was awarded to the Fir Parkers. Murray took the kick himself but it was a weak effort that was easily saved.

'Well were made to pay for this miss when, in a melee around McDonald's goal, Gillespie failed to clear and Logan equalised for Falkirk with the scores remaining level at 1-1 at the break.

Motherwell were under the cosh in the opening stages of the second half as Falkirk mounted attack after attack. Eventually Devine got his foot to the ball in a crowded penalty area to put the visitors ahead. Motherwell tried hard to get back on terms and succeeded when 'Johnstone netted the ball from a fine cross by Robertson'. With 15 minutes remaining both teams gave their all in search of the winner but the match ended all square. Motherwell fans were delighted to have their talismanic goalscorer back in the side after injury. It was reported, 'It was with pleasure, too, supporters of Motherwell learned that Murray would resume his place in the team, as he now seems to be almost indispensible.'

Motherwell made the trip down the Clyde to engage Port Glasgow Athletic on 13 November at Clune Park. Play was pretty well balanced as the first half progressed and it was easy to see why the home side occupied such a lowly position in the league as most of their attempts at goal were usually well off target. Port did have the ball in the net, however, when Allan headed home from close range but the goal was disallowed for a foul on a Motherwell defender. Motherwell were stung into retaliation and Murray raced through Athletic's defence to beat the Port keeper but his strike was also chalked off, for offside.

The match was goalless at the break and it appeared that it would remain that way, with both sides scorning the few chances they created. With quarter of an hour remaining, Port's Dollar miskicked in his own penalty area and Murray poked the ball home for what proved to be the winning score. The *Motherwell Times* reporter felt that the team had performed reasonably well and probably did enough to deserve the win. 'Well now had ten points from the 14 matches played so far.

A crowd of 4,000 turned up to watch Motherwell entertain Clyde in fine weather at Fir Park on 20 November. The game was fairly evenly-contested although it lacked much in the way of excitement. Motherwell's danger-man Murray was being carefully watched by Wylie and, as a result, his goalscoring chances were very limited. He did have two good opportunities in the first half but the close attentions of the Bully Wee defence prevented him putting the Fir Parkers ahead.

The left-wing pair were clearly supplying the ammunition but the bustling centre-forward was just not able to capitalise, and it was reported, 'Robertson and Gray were working well on the left, and some of their crosses deserved better fate.'

The teams turned around without scoring and the spectators were hoping for more action in the second period. It also proved to be disappointing apart from a fine goalkeeping display from Tom McDonald who denied the Clyde forwards on several occasions to keep the scoreline blank and give the teams a share of the points.

At Ibrox on 27 November, Motherwell were beaten 4-1 by Rangers in a match played in a torrential downpour. A special train conveyed a host of Motherwell fans to the game and they were shocked when the home side took the lead after only 20 seconds through Hunter. The Steelmen fought their way back into the game and Murray beat four men but couldn't get the ball past keeper Lock. 'Motherwell's left wing then got away, and Robertson and Gray between them forced Lock to give away a corner, which, however, was unproductive,' according to the newspaper.

Rangers doubled their lead when McPherson shot and McDonald saved but Hunter rushed in and charged the keeper into the net. As a result McDonald was carried off with concussion and took no further part in the game. Taylor took over between the sticks and the team underwent a hasty reshuffle. When Hunter converted a Ramage cross to put the Gers three up, the match was effectively over as a contest. Just before the break Rattray intercepted a pass to Hunter and the Rangers man caught the Motherwell left-back on the ankle breaking a bone, an injury which effectively ended his top-flight football career.

Hunter himself was injured in the clash and the second half was played out with ten men against nine. Despite being a man down Motherwell held their own in the second period until Bennett broke away and found Gilchrist who beat Taylor for Rangers' fourth goal.

'Towards the end of the game Motherwell were pressing, and Robertson was fouled in the penalty area, and from the resultant kick Murray scored the Fir Parkers' only point of the game,' wrote the *Motherwell Times*. The newspaper thought that 'Robertson and Gray played well, though the former was inclined to hang too long on the leather'.

Motherwell's game against Queen's Park at Fir Park on 4 December was in doubt until the last minute when referee Hamilton declared the surface playable, the coating of snow preventing the pitch becoming hard and dangerous. Despite the wintry weather play was fast and full of interest with Queen's performing well but lacking punch up front.

The *Motherwell Times* reported, 'The home team played a plucky go-ahead, dashing game, Gray and Robertson making a very effective left wing, with Murray always with an eye for goal-scoring. Before the interval Murray scored, and in the second half he added a second, while Robertson made matters sure by putting on the third and last goal.'

George's speed was often too fast for the officials, 'The ball, of course, was in the net several times in addition, but "off-side" deprived the player of the credit of the goals.'

Motherwell were now 15th in the First Division with 13 points from their 17 games.

The miserable drizzly and misty conditions kept the crowd down to a disappointing 2,000 when Motherwell travelled through to Edinburgh to meet Hearts at Tynecastle on 11 December. The home side had all the early pressure but Motherwell rallied and forced a corner from which Gray opened the scoring. This only had the effect of rousing the Hearts side for which Cole equalised almost immediately. It was not long until the Edinburgh team had the lead. McLean failed to clear a Hearts attack and Sinclair stepped in and beat McDonald with a shot which went in off the post. 'Well went further behind when a tricky shot from Bobby Walker was helped into his own net by keeper Tom McDonald. When Hollingworth fired in a fourth goal before the interval the visitors looked set for a thrashing after the changeover.

Motherwell could have pulled themselves back into the game when enterprising play from Gray and George sent Nicol clear but he pulled his shot well wide of the target. This seemed to knock the stuffing out of Motherwell and Hearts dominated the remainder of the proceedings but only had a late goal from Cole to show for all their efforts.

This was not one of George's better outings. The *Motherwell Times* reporter was critical of both wingers, 'Murray was the most successful of the Fir Park forwards, and his runs at times were deserving. Gray and Davidson, the inside men, played a good game but the outside men failed to cross to advantage.' Despite this heavy defeat Motherwell remained 15th in the table.

Motherwell entertained Celtic on 18 December in front of a record 8,000 crowd at Fir Park. Celtic won the toss and elected to play with the low sun at their backs. The visitors opened the scoring after only six minutes when Hay ran on to Hamilton's pass and beat McDonald. It was nearly 2-0 shortly after when Hamilton's shot ran right along the crossbar. Celtic were temporarily reduced to ten men when both Young and Loney went for the ball and Loney was kicked under the chin as his team-mate attempted to clear. Loney was carried off unconscious but bravely resumed later in the second half.

From a corner Quinn headed home Celtic's second goal and Motherwell looked down and out. The Fir Parkers did pull a goal back before the break when Murray was held by goalkeeper Adams and a penalty was awarded. David Taylor made no mistake with his spot-kick.

With Loney really only a passenger Celtic were effectively reduced to ten men but still managed to control the match. However with ten minutes remaining Motherwell still had the chance of snatching an equaliser from one of their breakaway attacks. From one of these, the Celtic defence sent a long ball downfield and as their forwards rushed towards McDonald, McMenemy latched on to the ball and scored.

Unlike the other Motherwell forwards George had a good day. The *Motherwell Times* reporter asked, 'How was it that while Robertson was in grand form, the other four should be having a day off as it were? Robertson on the left put in a power of work, and he had McNair repeatedly in difficulties, and his centres were not taken up.'

With all the bottom teams in the league losing, Motherwell remained 15th, with 13 points from their 19 matches.

Long-suffering Motherwell fans got some very welcome Christmas presents in the form of two points, five goals and a clean sheet when their team thrashed Morton 5-0 at Fir Park on Christmas Day 1909. The *Motherwell Times* reporter suspected that the forwards might have all received shooting boots as Christmas gifts.

Despite the wintry weather 5,000 hardy souls turned up to witness a comfortable win for the home side on a surface described as treacherous with a liberal sprinkling of sand. Motherwell made an impressive start with good efforts from newcomer John Atkinson and George well saved by Greenock keeper Stewart. The Fir Parkers forced a series of corners and from one of these Stewart nearly punched the ball into his own net when challenged in the air. It was reported, 'Through some pretty play by Atkinson, Murray and Robertson the home side netted the first ball. A pretty backheeler from Atkinson to Murray, who crossed to Robertson, ended in the latter player scoring from a difficult position, which shot found Stewart unprepared.'

Following this the Steelmen forced another corner and Harry Duff breasted the cross over the line for the second goal and Jimmy Murray made it 3-0 just before half-time. Morton rallied somewhat after the break and good tries from Hamilton, McCubbin and Stevenson kept McDonald in the Motherwell goal warm and on his toes. The Greenock side had no luck however and Nicol found the net for Motherwell's fourth to kill off any hopes of a revival. Atkinson completed the scoring late on to cap a memorable debut.

The newspaper continued, 'Motherwell's forward line moved with splendid combination, and the inclusion of Atkinson tended to liven things up a bit. The more prominent men of the five were Atkinson and Robertson.'

The valuable two points earned, leapfrogged Motherwell above Morton to 14th in the league table.

The 1910 Ne'er Day derby match at home to Hamilton was a fiercely contested 2-2 draw as one might expect between two local rivals close together in the league table. Curiously both teams included a player called John Atkinson in their line-ups and each played a significant part in the final result. In front of a packed Fir Park, Motherwell, with the breeze at their backs, applied early pressure and Brand missed an early chance for the home side. Motherwell eventually took the lead when George charged down the left and crossed for Murray to smash the ball past Slavin in the Accies goal. The home side's lead was short-lived as minutes later Gillespie fouled Accies' Atkinson, and Davie equalised from the spot.

The Steelmen regained the lead before the break. As the Motherwell forwards closed in on the Accies goal, Slavin tried to clear the ball downfield but missed the dropping ball and 'Well's Atkinson 'rushed in and breasted the ball through'. Accies were on top in the second period and eventually got a deserved equaliser when Freeman fired in a free kick which McDonald failed to hold. The match became heated towards the end and Accies were reduced to ten men when one of their players was dismissed for an infringement.

Two days later, on Monday 3 January, Kilmarnock were the visitors to Fir Park and brought with them two special trains full of fans. Motherwell were without prolific scorer Jimmy Murray, out through injury, so Sam Hill deputised for his fellow Irishman. The 6,000 crowd were treated to a passionate, well-fought encounter which resulted in a 3-1 win for the Lanarkshire outfit.

Things looked bleak for the Fir Parkers when Cunningham gave Killie the lead after only three minutes but shortly afterwards the Steelmen were awarded a penalty and Taylor drove home the equaliser from the penalty spot. Play swung wildly from end to end but it was the home team who grabbed the lead when Robert Brand finished off a good move down the right wing.

Leading 2-1 at the break, Motherwell had the advantage of a strong wind in the second half. Killie mastered the conditions better and pinned Motherwell back in their own half for long periods and it seemed that an equalising goal was only a matter of time. 'Instead, at the other end Robertson was the means of Motherwell getting their third goal. He ran down the wing, and when tackled shot for goal, bringing down Stevenson [the Killie goalkeeper] in his attempt to clear, and Atkinson finished the deed by putting the ball through,' according to the *Motherwell Times*. The result was pretty harsh on Killie who contributed enormously to a fine match.

Motherwell hosted Brechin City in a friendly match on Wednesday 5 January as part of the deal which brought Brechin's talented goalkeeper Colin Hampton to Fir Park. Motherwell won the match 4-1 although the *Times* did not provide any match details. Hampton was turning in first-class performances for Motherwell's reserve team and would eventually represent Scotland in the League International against the Irish League in 1912 at Windsor Park in Belfast which Scotland won 3-1.

On 8 January the now deadly double act of Robertson and Murray scored in Motherwell's home win over Aberdeen. The Steelmen made an impressive start and Murray crashed the ball off the visitors' post in the opening minutes. The Dons, with the strong wind at their backs, then pinned the home side deep in their own half and Tom McDonald kept his side on level terms with a handful of fine saves. Motherwell were dangerous, however, on the breakaway and from one of these, 'Murray opened the scoring from Robertson's neat slip.'

Aberdeen fought back but at the changeover went in 1-0 down. The wind was tending to play havoc with the shooting of both sides but George managed to get a powerful effort on target and Mutch pulled off an amazing save to turn the ball past the post for a corner. His next effort proved more successful, 'At length Robertson got away and after working his way through the defence scored a goal characteristic of him.'

Aberdeen again forced the pace and Simpson scored a smart goal after good play down the right. Aberdeen pushed hard for the equaliser but the Motherwell defence was in great form and kept them at bay to run out 2-1 winners. Strangely, both sides seemed to perform better against the severe wind. Motherwell were pleased at the number of chances created, most of which fell to Murray whose shooting was disappointing. George was once again one of the home side's best players with his speed and crossing causing severe headaches for Donald Colman, the former Motherwell right-back. Motherwell were now 11th in the table with 20 points from 23 matches.

Having seen their team pick up seven points from a possible eight in their last four games Motherwell fans were optimistic of a gradual climb up the table so it was a surprise when, on 15 January, the Steelmen went down, unexpectedly, 3-1 to second-bottom team Queen's Park at Hampden. Motherwell were badly hit by illness and George missed his first match of the season, being replaced on the left wing by John Tennant. The match was played in deplorable conditions with the rain falling in sheets rendering the pitch extremely heavy in places so good football was at a premium.

The Queen's Park players adapted better to the conditions and could have had several goals but their shooting was as poor as the weather. Motherwell's chances were few and far between but Murray should have given them the lead when he blasted over the bar from two yards out. Queen's Park's attacks were unrelenting and just before the break they got the goal their pressure deserved when Skene beat debutant goalkeeper Hampton with a low shot.

In the second half Hamilton doubled Queen's Park's lead, netting from Paul's corner kick. Shortly afterwards Paul beat Gillespie and gave Hampton no chance with a cracking shot. Jimmy Murray broke through the Spiders' defence and sent in a good drive which beat

Adam to give the visitors faint hopes of a comeback. The match was then fairly evenly-contested but no further goals were scored. The *Motherwell Times* remarked that the team 'as a whole gave a most miserable display, Robertson was badly missed on the left wing, while the defence was none too steady'. This defeat allowed Hamilton Accies to overtake Motherwell in the table, pushing the Fir Parkers down to 12th position.

George returned to the team when Forfar Athletic were Motherwell's first round opponents in the Scottish Cup at Fir Park on 22 January. The bone-hard pitch was covered with sand but the players were still having problems keeping their footing and a few hard knocks were received. Only 2,000 spectators turned up to brave the winter chill and witnessed the non-league side put up a strong showing against the First Division outfit.

Forfar's players were clearly up for it against a Motherwell side who seemed afraid to fully commit themselves on the slippery surface. No goals were scored in a poor first half but Motherwell seemed to go up a gear after the break. Chances were falling chiefly to Murray but his shooting was well off the mark and Forfar gradually came back into the contest. John Gray finally made the breakthrough for the home side when he scored with a low drive after Forfar keeper Paterson had saved a stinging close-range shot from Nicol. Forfar rallied and tried hard for the equaliser but couldn't get past a Motherwell defence who performed well below their recent league form.

Motherwell were back on league business against Rangers on 29 January. The Fir Park pitch had been cleared of snow and a layer of sand put down but the players were still finding it difficult to adapt to the bounce of the ball on the hard surface. Motherwell were 1-0 down after ten minutes when Taylor failed to clear and McPherson stepped in to beat a surprised McDonald. Motherwell, with a strong sun at their backs, came back at the visitors and Murray and Atkinson combined well but Murray's rushed shot went harmlessly past.

'Near the end of the first half Motherwell were pressing heavily on Rangers' defence, and about eight minutes from the interval Robertson, after negotiating both backs in fine style, beat Lock with a deceptive shot. This goal proved to be the best of the match, and was characteristic of the speedy left-winger,' wrote the *Motherwell Times*.

The teams retired to the pavilion with the scores level at 1-1. Motherwell resumed their offensive in the second period and soon had the visitors on the rack and deservedly went in front, 'Robertson and Gray on the left forced a corner, and from the kick by Robertson, the ball was headed past Lock by Murray.'

Rangers immediately took the ball into the Motherwell half and equalised in controversial circumstances. Millar sent in a high dropping shot and Hogg ran in and fouled McDonald before he could reach the ball while it rolled into the corner of the net. Despite howls of protest from Motherwell players and fans the referee awarded a goal to the visitors. Motherwell roared back and Lock did well to make vital saves from Gray, George and Nicol.

If Rangers' second goal was dubious there was no doubting the quality of their winning goal which came when Miller volleyed home an excellent Smith cross. Motherwell were not prepared to lie down and clearly should have had a penalty in the dying minutes when Campbell handled in the area but the referee missed the incident. The *Motherwell Times* felt that the home side deserved at least a share of the points and George had an outstanding game, 'Of the forwards, Robertson was the hero. For dash, tricking, speed and shooting there was nothing on the field to beat him. His crosses were well timed, and his shooting gave Lock some difficulty.' This second successive league defeat pushed Motherwell back down to 13th in the table with 20 points from 25 matches.

More than 6,000 fans turned up at Fir Park on 5 February to see Motherwell take on Greenock Morton in the second round of the Scottish Cup. The match was in doubt right up to the kick-off because of the extremely heavy pitch but the referee gave it the go-ahead despite the fact that the rain continued to pour down relentlessly. The home side pressed from the outset and George went close with a shot which skimmed the bar. Duff then came close before George had another effort which was cleared by Morton keeper Robertson.

After Murray had missed another golden chance, when through on his own, the Steelmen finally made the breakthrough. Following great pressure in the Morton area Gray passed forward to Murray whose low shot found the corner of the net. 'The home team still kept at it hammer-and-tongs, and were further rewarded when a second goal was scored by Robertson after a fine run on his own,' according to the newspaper, and at half-time the score was 2-0 in favour of the home side.

Morton began the second half strongly but Motherwell gradually took command again. Soon Murray broke through from midfield and 'the Morton keeper came out to meet him, and tackled Murray bringing him down. The centre made desperate efforts to get up, but seemed unable to do so, when Robertson came in from the left and slipped the ball into the net'. Motherwell were firmly in command and Murray again broke through and had the ball in the

Morton net but the referee awarded a penalty for an infringement in the area.

After some trouble between the players had been subdued, Taylor took the penalty and drove the ball straight at Robertson in the Morton goal so the match finished with the home team 3-0 winners. The *Motherwell Times* praised the home players, 'And none earned this distinction more than Robertson, who was a continual danger to the Morton defence.' After the match Morton lodged a protest that the pitch was unplayable and the lines had been obliterated but, after some advice, they decided to drop the matter.

The *Motherwell Times* of 11 February revealed that Dundee would be Motherwell's opponents in the third round to be played at Fir Park by 26 February. The scoring prowess and general play of the lanky Irish centre-forward Jimmy Murray and his principal provider George ultimately attracted the attention of the international selectors. The *Times* was pleased to announce, 'It will be gratifying to Fir Park supporters to note that George Robertson, the popular outside-left of Motherwell, has been selected to play in the "A" team trial match in connection with the League International. The trial game takes place on Monday the 21st, and it is hoped Robertson will secure his position. He is a speedy player, and the form he has shown this season has been most consistent and deserving of international honours.'

But it was the young Irishman Murray who was destined to become the first Motherwell player to play at full international level when he appeared for Ireland against England in a 1-1 draw in Belfast on 12 February 1910.

With Murray absent on international duty Sam Hill stood in for his fellow Irishman against Partick Thistle at a soft and heavy Firhill. Motherwell started the match well and George and Gray caused the Thistle defence a few headaches before the home side began to take charge. Despite their dominance the nearest the Jags got to opening the scoring was a Branscombe shot which grazed the outside of the post and at the cross-over the match remained goalless.

Motherwell were soon on the attack in the second period but Thistle once again asserted themselves and it was no surprise when Gardiner created an opening and gave them the lead with a good shot. Motherwell did well to force a corner and were unlucky when a shot through a ruck of players was cleared off the Partick goal line by Raisbeck. Thistle were soon back in Motherwell territory and another Gardiner effort doubled their advantage. Motherwell kept pegging away and Hill gave them a consolation goal in the final minute.

George and Gray were the pick of the Motherwell forwards on the day, according to the newspaper, 'The Motherwell front rank was rather one-sided, the left wing being exceedingly clever, while the right wing did not exactly shine and Murray's presence in the centre-forward was clearly missed.'

George's next match was for the Scotland 'A' team in the trial at Firhill to select the Scottish League team to play their Football League counterparts on 26 February at Blackburn. The *Daily Record* reported on the match the following day by stating that George was the outstanding performer afield and that he was a certainty to be selected for the representative match.

Daily Record, Tuesday 22 February 1910

SCOTTISH LEAGUE TEAM
STRONG ELEVEN TO PLAY AT BLACKBURN
TRIAL DISCOVERY
SFA TO BE ASKED TO DELAY THE CUP TIES
'A' TEAM 4 'B' TEAM 1

The conditions at Firhill Park yesterday were certainly not those best fitted to realise all that is meant by a trial match, but the game was not without its benefits after all, for in the discovery of Robertson, the Motherwell outside-left, the League Selectors not only solved the difficulty of a position which must have been causing them some little anxiety, but which may also be a guide to the Selectors of the Scottish Association in the choosing of their teams for future International matches.

The game was responsible for much clever forward play, especially on the winning side, but nothing bettered the dashing runs of Robertson, who after opening quietly, surprised the majority of the onlookers by his masterly performance. The manner in which he carried the ball up the field to score the second goal for his side was only equalled by the splendid drive, from a difficult angle, with which he found the net, and all through the match he was ever in the eye with delightful dribbling and accurate centring.

On the other side of the field Kivlichan was also a success and Richardson responded well to the deft movements of M'Menemy and M'Pherson, the inside wing men. The centre had the other three goals.

The forward line on the other side were handicapped for the want of a strong controlling centre, Branscombe, who has been playing on the wing for Partick, failing as a pivot. M'Tavish did much that was neat and clever, but Rankin, otherwise good, failed in his finishing. The other wing pair, Devine and Cole, were spasmodic in their efforts.

The half-back play all over reached a high standard, and of the backs there was none better than Miller. Allan was unfortunate in losing one of the goals, but Brownlie made no mistake.

'A' TEAM – Brownlie (Third Lanark); M'Kenzie (Partick Thistle) and Miller (Falkirk); Halley (Kilmarnock), Loney (Celtic) and Scott (Hamilton Academical); Kivlichan (Celtic), M'Menemy (Celtic), Richardson (Third Lanark), M'Pherson (Rangers) and Robertson (Motherwell).

'B' TEAM – Allan (Hibernian); Taylor (Falkirk) and Mitchell (Kilmarnock); M'Donald (Falkirk), Anderson (Falkirk) and Mainds (Third Lanark); Rankin (Third Lanark), M'Tavish (Falkirk), Branscombe (Partick Thistle), Devine (Falkirk) and Cole (Heart of Midlothian).

After the match the League selectors met in the Grosvenor Restaurant and selected the following team to play at Blackburn on Saturday:-

JAMES BROWNLIE (Third Lanark)
ALEX M'NAIR (Celtic)
TOM MILLER (Falkirk)
WM. WALKER (Clyde)
WM. LONEY (Celtic)
JAS. HAY (Celtic)
JAS. M'MENEMY (Celtic)
ROBT. WALKER
(Heart of Midlothian)
A. BENNETT (Rangers)
J. QUINN (Celtic)
G. ROBERTSON (Motherwell)

The following is the English League team which was chosen on Friday:-
Goal – Dawson (Burnley)

Backs – Crompton (Blackburn Rovers) and Hayes (Manchester United)

Half-Backs – Brittleton (Sheffield Wednesday), Harrop (Liverpool) and Makepeace (Everton)

Forwards – Rutherford (Newcastle United), Holley (Sunderland), Cantrell (Notts County), Bache (Aston Villa) and Wall (Manchester United)

Some surprise will doubtless be occasioned by the selection of Walker, of the Hearts; and Robertson, of Motherwell, all of whom, in the ordinary course of events, would be engaged in the Cup ties on Saturday. We understand, however, that representatives of the clubs to which the players are attached signed a petition, to be forwarded to the Scottish Football Association, asking that the ties be delayed meantime, and this will come before the S.F.A. Council at the meeting. Unless an extension of time for the Cup ties is granted the players mentioned are not likely to travel to Blackburn.

The team as a whole should give general satisfaction. After the display in the trial game, there was little doubt as to Robertson's inclusion. He and Miller, the Falkirk back, get their first caps, and Loney is the only other who has not previously played against the English League, although the Celtic half-back has had other honours.

A feature of the selection is the inclusion of M'Menemy and Walker in the forward rank, with the Edinburgh player on the left wing. This is an experiment which has been too long delayed, and it will be interesting to watch its effect.

Motherwell and Dundee had scheduled their Scottish Cup quarter-final for Saturday, 19 February but had to postpone the match because of flooding of the Fir Park pitch following a week of incessant rain. The match was re-arranged for the following Saturday, the same day as the Football League v the Scottish League fixture at Ewood Park, Blackburn. George's selection for the Scottish League team prompted Motherwell to petition the Scottish Football Association, requesting the postponement of the match against Dundee 'owing to certain players being chosen to represent Scotland in the League International v. England at Blackburn'.

The petition was unsuccessful and the council decided not to postpone the games, 'Those players chosen for the League International have been withdrawn, and their places otherwise filled.'

The *Motherwell Times* of 25 February reported that George would take his place in the Motherwell side against Dundee 'and, after all, it is just as well, as he has become such a valuable asset to the team'. George was therefore denied League International honours and took his place in the team to face Dundee. Falkirk's Andy Devine took George's place in the Scotland side which won the fixture 3-2 in front of a 30,000 crowd. The Scottish League's goals came from Quinn, Devine and Templeton. The *Motherwell Times* was also delighted to report that

Jimmy Murray had been selected by the Irish Football Association to play against Scotland in Belfast on 19 March.

The quarter-final eventually got under way at Fir Park on 26 February in excellent weather conditions in front of a bumper crowd including a large contingent from Dundee. There were around 12,000 in the ground for the kick-off and that number increased to 18,000 during the first half. The pitch was still a little sticky after the previous week's flooding but the teams managed to serve up a fiercely-contested affair with Motherwell spurning a number of early chances, centre-forward Murray being the principal culprit. Despite relentless pressure Motherwell found themselves a goal down at the interval after Hall headed home Bellamy's cross and this breakaway goal gave the Dens Parkers the half-time lead.

When Hall netted from another Bellamy cross early in the second half Motherwell's cup dream appeared to be over. The Motherwell defence managed to hold out against the now rampant Dark Blues forwards and started to push them back into their own half. With 15 minutes remaining 'the Fir Parkers raised the siege, and bore down on the visitors' defence, and after some stiff work Robertson broke through and scored a splendid goal'.

In pushing hard for the equaliser that their play merited, Motherwell were caught cold when Bellamy got away and set up Hall for his hat-trick to complete the scoring in a 3-1 win. George was obviously viewed as a potent threat and Dundee had made sure that he was marked closely by three men. Despite their close attention he was still the outstanding home forward but 'he could not work miracles'.

Although he did not know it at the time, this was to be George's last home match in Motherwell colours. The *Motherwell Times*, after its coverage of the Dundee match, congratulated George on his selection for the full Scotland side to play Wales in the international at Rugby Park, Kilmarnock, on 5 March.

George's talents were eventually recognised by the SFA, who awarded him his first full Scottish cap against Wales. By all accounts George gave a far from impressive performance. The *Motherwell Times* reporter summed it up thus:

> 'The international match v. Wales has now passed, and many were the disappointments expressed by those who witnessed the game. It was thought Scotland had a team on the field that would take some beating, but the display given all over was very poor indeed.
>
> 'The interest of Motherwell folks in connection with this game centred in Geo. Robertson, the Fir Parkers' outside left. Naturally,

> many travelled to Kilmarnock last Saturday with the object of seeing with their own eyes how this player would shape. All were disappointed, not with the Motherwell man, but with the team as a whole.
>
> 'For the first fifteen minutes of the game Robertson was giving a splendid account of himself, but after that he seemed to have been forgotten by his partner. Had Robertson been properly supported throughout the game, no doubt the opinion of many critics would have been altered. But the critics maintain he was a failure. How can a player be otherwise when he is, in a manner, "starved".
>
> 'Another matter to be taken into consideration is the fact that he was playing in front of a section of spectators who, naturally, thought their favourite could better fill the position, and shouts for Templeton [Robert Templeton, the Kilmarnock winger George replaced in the Scotland side] were pretty general.
>
> 'Such conduct on the part of the crowd was in no way sportsmanlike, and the Motherwell man ought to have been given a fair chance. We do not say Robertson is a better player than Templeton, but on present form he is every bit as good, and if neither of these two men tend to strengthen this position in our international team, then by all means, have the place made as perfect as possible.'

Despite the treatment George took from the Kilmarnock crowd, Scotland ran out winners by 1-0, Falkirk's Archie Devine scoring the only goal in the 86th minute.

Scotland's team was: James Brownlie (Third Lanark), George Law (Rangers), James Mitchell (Kilmarnock), Alex McNair (Celtic), William Loney (Celtic), James Hay (Celtic) captain, Alex Bennett (Rangers), James McMenemy (Celtic), James Quinn (Celtic), Archibald Devine (Falkirk), George Robertson (Motherwell).

While George was earning his first international cap against Wales, his Motherwell team-mates were entertaining Port Glasgow Athletic at Fir Park. Unlike the previous Saturday's crowd, a mere 2,000 spectators turned up to witness the home side's 6-3 victory played out in brilliant sunshine. John Tennant again deputised for George and was responsible for the opening goal when his dangerous cross was turned into his own net by Port's left-half Lynch. Motherwell were firmly in control and Gray added a second goal for the Steelmen as Port were pushed back into their own penalty area. Tennant, who was having a field day, soon made the score 3-0 and Gray, not to be outdone, added his second goal of the match. Port's only response was a Hagan shot which cannoned off the upright just before the interval.

Hagan was luckier after the break when his free kick flew past McDonald to give the home supporters something to cheer about. Motherwell immediately raced downfield and forced a corner from which Tennant headed home Johnstone's superb cross. The visiting side now upped their game and pulled another goal back when Taylor deflected Allan's shot past McDonald to make the score 5-2. Port drew even closer when former 'Well left-winger Bob Findlay rounded Gillespie and placed the ball past McDonald. Towards the end of the match 'Well bombarded the visitors' defence and scored a sixth goal when Johnstone completed a fine move by Tennant and Hill.

Despite the acquisition of two valuable points Motherwell still languished in 15th, although level on points with Third Lanark, Partick Thistle and Hamilton Accies.

Around 4,000 fans turned up at Broomfield Park when Airdrieonians hosted Motherwell on 12 March in the last of the Lanarkshire derby games of the season. The early play was mostly in midfield with few opportunities for the forwards of either side. Eventually George had 'a brilliant solo run, but he was pulled up before he could get his shot in'. Airdrie took the lead when Thomson shot home from Neilson's cross and they increased their lead shortly afterwards, from a penalty, when Hill beat McDonald from the spot. Gray had a chance to pull the Fir Parkers back into the match but failed with his shot and moments later McDonald pulled off a great save to prevent 'Well going three goals down.

Late on in the first half, with Motherwell still two behind, 'a miskick by Hill of Airdrie let the Fir Parkers in, and in a scrimmage round Ewart's charge Robertson got the ball through'. At the interval Airdrieonians led their rivals by two goals to one. Both sides had chances in the second half before George Nicol got Motherwell's second goal with a cute shot which beat Ewart. In a frantic end to the match both teams went all out for the winner but the whistle sounded with the sides level at two goals each. The single point earned helped push Motherwell one place up the league table.

George's last match in Motherwell colours was a 1-0 victory over Morton at Cappielow in front of a crowd of around 4,000 people on 19 March. Motherwell had already beaten Morton 5-0 in the league and had knocked them out of the Scottish Cup, winning 3-0, so the Greenock side were anxious to exact a little revenge in what was a fairly meaningless fixture for both sides.

Smith almost gave them an early lead when his shot hit the outside of the post and Hamilton shot past when it seemed easier to score.

George was in sparkling form, with his pace and trickery causing the Greenock defence real problems, 'Robertson got away on the Motherwell left, and sent across a dangerous pass, which, however, was cleared in time.'

Morton fought back and McDonald had to be at the top of his game to deny Hamilton and Smith. Again George threatened, 'The Fir Parkers again got away through Robertson, but off-side spoiled the effort. He immediately repeated the run, and his accurate centre, which he put right across the goalmouth, was not taken advantage of.'

The home side had no answer to Motherwell's left wing and were wilting under continuous pressure but managed to hold out until they lost centre-half Nugent with a thigh strain. Shortly afterwards, Brand, who was deputising for Murray – on international duty with Ireland – broke through and scored what proved to be the only goal of the game although Morton claimed that he had been in an offside position.

In the second half Brand missed a sitter for the visitors and also hit the upright while Smith sent the ball wide with only McDonald to beat. Motherwell finished the stronger side and won a penalty late in the match. Nicol scored from the spot but the referee ordered the kick to be re-taken and, on this occasion, Morton keeper Robertson pushed the ball wide. Motherwell's two points elevated them to 13th in the table with 25 points from 29 games.

Following the report of the Morton match the *Motherwell Times*, in a small paragraph headlined 'MURRAY AND ROBERTSON SIGN FOR SHEFFIELD WEDNESDAY', carried the following news:

'A representative of the Sheffield Wednesday club visited Motherwell early in the week and was fortunate in securing the signatures of both Murray and Robertson, the Fir Park centre and outside-left respectively. The transfer of these two players will considerably weaken Motherwell's team, but it is hoped capable substitutes will be found to fill the vacancies. This change, coming as it does near the end of the season, alters the outlook as regards position in the League for the Fir Parkers, who require all possible points to remain in a respectable position on the table. Murray and Robertson will figure in the Yorkshire team on Saturday first.'

Elsewhere in the paper, 'Alpha' commented in his regular column, 'Our football club funds will benefit by the two transfers this week to the extent of quite a tidy sum. Sheffield Wednesday will have no cause to regret the deal, which will well repay them.'

The circumstances surrounding the transfer and the resulting local controversy are dealt with in the next chapter but it is fitting that I conclude the story of Motherwell's 1909/10 league campaign with brief notes on the remaining five games of that season.

Motherwell's first game without their two capped players resulted in a good 2-0 win over Third Lanark at Cathkin Park on 26 March. Both sides had early chances but Thirds went into defensive mode following an injury to right-back Barr and Motherwell found it difficult to get shots in on keeper Brownlie. Despite being reduced to ten men Thirds did make life difficult at times for the visitors but Motherwell always seemed the more likely outfit to score. 'Well appeared to have taken the lead when Atkinson cut through the Thirds defence and squared to Brand who beat Brownlie but the goal was disallowed for offside. Half-time arrived without any scoring.

Both teams had good efforts in the second period but Motherwell's shooting proved to be a major disappointment. Late on in the match the visitors eventually broke the deadlock when Tennant scampered down the left and sent in a perfect cross for Brand to drive past Brownlie. A second goal followed minutes later when Gray sent in a hot shot which completely deceived Brownlie to secure both points for the Fir Parkers. The team put up a reasonable show but their shooting was a little lacklustre as if they were in awe of Scotland's formidable goalkeeper.

The points from this game, along with results elsewhere, rocketed Motherwell up to ninth, well away from the danger of having to seek re-election.

Motherwell's next opposition came in the shape of Royal Albert in the Lanarkshire Cup on 2 April at Fir Park. Motherwell fielded a team largely comprised of reserve team players and experimented with right-back John Johnston in the centre-forward role. The team played well below their recent league form and could consider themselves lucky to escape with a 1-1 draw to take the match to a replay at Larkhall.

Motherwell went behind after half an hour when McDonald attempted to punch clear a corner kick but only succeeded in putting the ball in his own net. Against the run of play, Downie intercepted a back-pass and beat the keeper with a low fast drive to make the scores level at the interval. Motherwell made a better showing in the second half and Atkinson had the ball in the net but it was chalked off for offside. Motherwell dominated for the rest of the game but could not get the winner.

Back on league business the following week, Motherwell continued their winning ways with a 1-0 over Hearts at Fir Park. In a very mediocre first half Hearts had more chances but their shooting was really inept and the 45 minutes passed without any scoring.

Motherwell were the better outfit in the second period but neither custodian was troubled greatly as the match became bogged down in midfield. The only goal of the game came when Tennant forced his way into the Hearts penalty area and was sent crashing down by Mercer. Taylor stepped forward and beat keeper Robertson from the spot. Despite another poor performance, two more valuable points were secured although the team remained ninth in the table.

Two days later Motherwell were sent crashing out of the Lanarkshire Cup by non-league Royal Albert in the replay at Larkhall. Again Motherwell took the opportunity to field some reserve players and although they looked a little more businesslike than in the first match they fell behind after 20 minutes when Dargue shot past Hampton. Motherwell forced the issue a little but couldn't beat Smith in the Royal Albert goal. Just before the half-time whistle Horn shocked the league side when he put Albert further ahead.

Motherwell fought back after the break and after a series of corners James Johnstone fired a splendid shot past Smith. Try as they might the visitors could not force their way past the Larkies' defenders who held out for a memorable 2-1 win. The *Motherwell Times* reporter heavily criticised the management for taking Royal Albert far too lightly and not fielding their strongest 11 on the day.

On Wednesday 13 April Motherwell played a friendly game against an Argyll and Sutherland Highlanders XI. Robert Brand was attached to the Highlanders and the game was to thank the regiment for his release for several Motherwell matches over the season. The Steelmen won 5-1.

The *Motherwell Times* of 15 April also intimated that Jimmy Murray had played for Ireland against Wales at Wrexham when the Welshmen scored a resounding 4-1 victory.

Motherwell's winning streak in the league extended to four games when they were 2-1 victors against St Mirren at Love Street on 16 April. The weather was once again miserable and the heavy pitch cut up very badly. Motherwell started really well and Saints had keeper Grant to thank for keeping them in the game with excellent stops from Gray, Davidson, Brand and Gray again. Saints began to grow in confidence but found it very difficult to penetrate the resolute Motherwell rearguard. Just before the interval Gray gave the Steelmen the lead with a powerful shot which Grant got fingers to but couldn't keep out. Both sides had chances before the whistle blew for half-time with the visitors leading 1-0.

Saints were a more dangerous team after the break and apart from a good run and shot from Tennant, Motherwell were finding it difficult to get out of their own half. After a lengthy spell of Saints pressure Tennant broke down the left and sent in a shot on goal which glanced off the foot of left-back Featherstone past the helpless Grant to give Motherwell a two-goal advantage. Towards the end of the match Cunningham pulled back a goal for the home side but the revival proved to be too little too late. Motherwell's win still left them ninth in the league, the lowest-ranked of four teams on 31 points.

The winning run was brought to an abrupt halt by Hibernian at Easter Road on 23 April in a howling gale and relentless rain. Good football was little in evidence as both sides found it difficult to cope with the adverse weather conditions. Motherwell started well and Hibs keeper Allan did well to hold a stinging shot from Tennant. Tennant and McNeil then had good tries as the visitors pushed hard for the opening score. When it did come, it was at the other end when Dixon, after 30 minutes, forced the ball in after a melee in Hampton's goalmouth. This gave Hibs heart and Callaghan had a couple of good efforts which failed to trouble Hampton in the Motherwell goal. Just before the interval Tennant unleashed a rocket shot which just skimmed the Hibs crossbar, leaving the visitors trailing 1-0 at the break.

After the changeover Hibs were the better side but both keepers were idle for long periods in a dull 45 minutes apart from late on in the contest when Hampton pulled off two smart saves from O'Hara and Callaghan.

Dundee, by now the Scottish Cup holders, were the visitors to Fir Park for the final league match of the season on Monday 25 April. Although the weather was fine the pitch was still heavy from recent rain and cut up as the game progressed. Dundee were quickly on the attack and Hampton was called upon to make three vital saves in the opening minutes. The visitors were very much in the ascendancy but the Motherwell defence was doing a good job in keeping them at bay so at the changing of ends the match remained goalless.

After the half-time refreshment Motherwell took the game to Dundee and Gray's shot clipped the crossbar, then another effort from Johnstone rebounded off the outside of the post. With only 15 minutes remaining Dundee right-winger Bellamy tricked Taylor and slipped the ball past Hampton to give the visitors the lead. 'From the kick-off Motherwell carried the ball right down the field, and from a neat pass by Gray, Brand equalised before a Dundee player had touched the ball,' it was reported. The *Motherwell Times* felt that it was a great match and a fitting game on which to close the season.

Motherwell finished tenth in the final league standings with 32 points from their 34 matches, four points better than the previous season, and well clear of the danger of having to apply for re-election. Jimmy Murray and George were the club's top scorers with 20 and nine goals respectively.

George Robertson's final season with Motherwell saw him reach the peak of his powers in Scottish football, culminating in being selected to represent the Scottish League against the English League and then winning his first full Scottish cap in March 1910 against Wales at Rugby Park, Kilmarnock, before being transferred to The Wednesday in the English First Division.

George missed only two games for 'Well in his final season with the club, one through illness and one while he was on international duty. He appeared 27 times in the league, in three Scottish Cup matches and scored his highest tally of 12 league and cup goals.

George's career with Motherwell lasted just under four seasons. He made 123 Scottish League appearances (excluding two abandoned matches) and scored 23 goals. He also scored a further four goals in nine Scottish Cup appearances.

SCOTTISH LEAGUE FIRST DIVISION 1909/10

	Pl	*W*	*D*	*L*	*F*	*A*	*Pts*
1 Celtic	34	24	6	4	63	22	54
2 Falkirk	34	22	8	4	71	28	52
3 Rangers	34	20	6	8	70	35	46
4 Aberdeen	34	16	8	10	44	29	40
5 Clyde	34	14	9	11	47	40	37
6 Dundee	34	14	8	12	52	44	36
7 Third Lanark	34	13	8	13	62	44	34
8 Hibernian	34	14	6	14	33	40	34
9 Airdrieonians	34	12	9	13	46	57	33
10 Motherwell	34	12	8	14	59	60	32
11 Kilmarnock	34	12	8	14	53	60	32
12 Heart of Midlothian	34	12	7	15	59	50	31
13 St Mirren	34	13	5	16	49	58	31
14 Queen's Park	34	12	6	16	54	74	30
15 Hamilton Academical	34	11	6	17	50	67	28
16 Partick Thistle	34	8	10	16	47	59	26
17 Greenock Morton	34	11	3	20	38	60	25
18 Port Glasgow Athletic	34	3	5	26	25	95	11

MOTHERWELL APPEARANCES AND GOALS 1909/10

	League		*Scottish Cup*	
	Apps	*Goals*	*Apps*	*Goals*
Atkinson, Henry	9	3	2	0
Brand, Robert	9	4	0	0
Davidson, Edward	18	0	1	0
Downie, William	7	0	0	0
Duff, Harry A.	16	1	3	0
Gillespie, James	17	0	3	0
Gray, John	33	6	3	1
Hampton, Colin	4	0	0	0
Hill, Samuel	7	1	0	0
Johnston, John	13	0	0	0
Johnstone, James	28	4	3	0
Kelly, Patrick	1	0	0	0
Lawson, William	8	1	0	0
McDonald, Thomas	30	0	0	0
McLean, John	10	0	0	0
McNeil, Hugh	30	0	3	0
Murray, James	22	20	3	1
Nicol, George	28	2	3	0
Rattray, James	11	0	0	0
Robertson, George Clarke	27	9	3	3
Sharp, Andrew	2	0	0	0
Sneddon, James	3	0	0	0
Taylor, David G.	34	4	3	0
Tennant, John	7	3	0	0
Lynch (Port Glasgow) OG	-	1	-	-

6

MOVING ON

IT was inevitable that George's outstanding performances and his pace and ability to deliver pinpoint crosses into the penalty area would soon attract the attention of wealthier clubs down south. It was no surprise that he chose to move to England to sample full-time football, improve his prospects and further his career but it was a move tinged with sadness at leaving behind many close friends at the club which gave him the opportunity to play professional football and make his mark at Fir Park.

The Motherwell supporters were not happy to see Jimmy Murray and George go. Letters to the *Motherwell Times* in the days and weeks following their departure called for the resignation of the board for disposing of the club's greatest assets. According to one correspondent it appears that both players were bent on moving following some friction between them and the club regarding wages due while they were on international duty.

Another contributory factor in George's case might have been the extra mouth to feed in the Robertson family. Jessie gave birth to the couple's first son, Robert, named after George's late father, in the early hours of 9 February 1910 at 2 Findlay Street, Motherwell. Interestingly Robert's birth certificate gives George's occupation as works despatch clerk, not baker which had appeared on the couple's marriage certificate.

The *Motherwell Times* on 1 April 1910 revealed some details of the transfers, 'Football is quite an up-to-date commercial concern. The transfer of the two Motherwell players to Sheffield was responsible for £1,200 changing hands, of which sum the football club would have about £900, and the two players about £300 divided, but not in equal shares between them.'

Such was the regard for both Murray and George that the *Motherwell Times* gave reports of The Wednesday's matches over the next few weeks and commented on the performance of both players.

Sadly Murray's career with Wednesday was destined to be a short one. Following on from his three international matches for Ireland he played all the eight remaining matches for Wednesday in 1909/10, scoring two goals. He started the 1910/11 season as Wednesday's regular centre-forward but played in only five more matches, scoring two more goals, before returning to Ireland to play for Derry Celtic. He made a brief return to Motherwell in 1911/12 but could not recapture his old form.

George was transferred to the Sheffield club on 22 March 1910, shortly after winning his first Scottish cap. His team-mate Murray was the first Motherwell player to be internationally recognised when he represented Ireland against England in Belfast on 12 February 1910.

The *Daily Record & Mail* on 23 March carried, under the heading 'Important Transfers – Motherwell Players sign for Sheffield Wednesday', this account of the double transfer deal:

> 'Yesterday Mr Brown, representative of the Sheffield Wednesday club visited Motherwell and succeeded in coming to terms with the Fir Park executive for the transfer of George Robertson, outside-left, and James Murray, centre-forward of the Motherwell Club. Both men had made their mark in Scottish football during the season. Murray came to Motherwell from Shettleston and has played for Ireland against both England and Scotland within the last few weeks. Possessing height and dash, and with a capital shot the young Irishman should come to the front across the Border.
>
> 'Robertson, who came from Yoker Athletic, is an outside-left of much promise and it is generally known that he would have played for the Scottish League team at Blackburn but for the intervention of an important Cup tie in which his club was engaged. He was in the Scottish team against Wales and the departure of these players must affect the chances of the Motherwell club in dropping their league match against Third Lanark at Cathkin on Saturday and in their remaining matches in the Competition. The club possesses one or two capable reserves however.'

In Sheffield, the *Football & Sports Special* also reported on the transfers, under the heading 'Captures by Wednesday':

> 'The directors of Sheffield Wednesday have in the past favoured the policy of obtaining little-known players of talent and training them on, if possible, into the first class article. This is the best of all ways of team-building, but it has its limits, and having been disappointed by

the general performance of the side this season, the directors during the week signed on two well-known players from the North. The expense of these captures, which may be regarded as sensational, was considerable, but if the new men prove all Wednesday think them to be, there will be complete satisfaction at Owlerton with the result of the deal. Each of the new Wednesday players has played in this season's Internationals; and as they are both young, more "caps" are likely.

'James Murray led the successful Irish attack against Scotland last Saturday, and he is undoubtedly one of the most dangerous centre-forwards in Scotland. At the present time he stands third in the list of Scottish League scorers, with about 20 goals to his credit. Murray is purely a product of Scottish football, although like John Simpson, of Falkirk, he was born in "furrin parts". In this way Ireland has gained one of the best centre-forwards she ever had, and thus Wednesday's little colony of Irishmen is increased. Murray, who is a schoolmaster, stands 5ft. 10ins. and weighs between 12 and 13 stones.

'George Robertson, Wednesday's new outside-left, has been hailed as "the discovery of the season" in Scotland, and when I was at Blackburn for the League International, I found the Scots very enthusiastic over the qualities of this young winger. Robertson should have played in that Inter-League match, but Motherwell were playing in a Scottish Cup-tie that day, so Robertson had to help his club. He played for Scotland against Wales a fortnight later, however, and he is not yet out of the running for a place in the Scottish team against England.

'Many of Murray's goals for Motherwell have been the outcome of Robertson's accurate centres, and if the pair can resume their profitable partnership in Wednesday's ranks (and there is no reason why they shouldn't), they will go a long way towards reforming the Owlerton brigade. Robertson can also claim 5ft. 10in. in height, and his weight is 11st. 10lbs.'

The same paper carried a report on March 26th on the reaction of Motherwell fans to the loss of their star players, 'It may be interesting to know, writes a Motherwell correspondent, who signs himself "Sheffield", that the transfer of Murray and Robertson from Motherwell to the Sheffield Wednesday Club is creating no little excitement there. As showing how a movement was set on foot to break into the ground, and fire the grand stand and pay-boxes, a proceeding for which the Scotch football "supporters" are becoming notorious. Happily, steps have been taken to prevent anything of this nature occurring.'

7

1909/10 – A NEW START

THE Wednesday – the Sheffield part was formally added to their name after they won the Football League championship in 1928/29 – were one of the top clubs in England at the time of George's transfer. They were league champions in 1899/1900, 1902/03 and 1903/04, and FA Cup winners in 1896 and 1907.

George would have felt very much at home in Sheffield since Wednesday had for many years boasted a large Scottish colony. When George joined the club they already had goalkeeper Henry Kinghorn (ex-Leith Athletic), defender Bob McSkimming (ex-Albion Rovers), half-backs Findlay Weir and Jimmy Miller (ex-Maryhill) and Scottish international centre-forward Andrew Wilson (ex-Clyde) on their books.

This group were joined the following season by wing-half Jimmy Campbell and forward Marr Paterson from Leith Athletic and free-scoring centre-forward David McLean from Preston North End.

Wednesday had made a bad start to the 1909/10 season and were languishing at the bottom of the First Division at the end of September 1909. By the time they signed Jimmy Murray and George Robertson in March 1910 they had fought their way up to 11th place although their performances were very inconsistent.

The two ex-Motherwell players made their debuts in front of 12,000 fans in a 2-0 defeat away to Bradford City on Good Friday, 25 March 1910, and played their first three games for their new club within the space of four days over the Easter holiday. Both were ever-present in the team for the remainder of the season.

On the day following their Wednesday debut they were once again in action, making the long journey to London where Harry Chapman's goal gave Wednesday a 1-0 win over Woolwich Arsenal at the Manor Ground. Murray and George had their revenge on Bradford City by scoring the goals in the return fixture at Owlerton on Easter Monday, 28 March, when Wednesday ran out 2-1 winners.

Although George was on the scoresheet, the three games in four days had obviously taken their toll and the *Green 'Un* remarked, 'Robertson, wasn't quite up to the form on Monday that he showed in his first match, on Good Friday. But after all, who could expect that he would be?'

The Green 'Un of Saturday 2 April carried pen portraits of Wednesday's new players along with photographs of each. The feature gives a great insight into the difference between the life of a part-time player with a Scottish provincial club and the full-time professional with a leading English club of the period. This is how it described George:

> 'You can generally tell a baker, as you can tell a miner – by the whiteness of his face. Life in the pit has its compensation for this theft of natural colour – or so an old Scottish footballer told me – in its strengthening effect upon the digestion. But whether baking offers any such compensation I don't know. There was in the past time a famous footballer who used to work at his trade as a baker half through the night before playing in his club's matches.
>
> 'But, generally speaking, one would say that a trade which so greatly affects the lungs of its workers is not one for an athlete to follow, and probably it is well for all concerned that George Robertson, Wednesday's new outside-left, has given up active participation in the trade, of which he is a skilled exponent. Still you can tell him on the field by the paleness of his countenance.
>
> 'There are other things. You can pick him out by the peculiar cunning of his dribbling, by a way he has of emerging from a tackle with the ball, when the average outside-left would have given up possession and by the extra special quality of his centres.
>
> 'Robertson has cost the Wednesday Club a pot of money. If people knew how much they would open their eyes. The fact is that the Murray-Robertson transfer altogether is one of the biggest things of the kind that have taken place, but the Wednesday have a policy of silence where the amounts of transfer fees are concerned, and so the figure is not likely to become generally known. Whatever, it may have been, however, there is a consensus of opinion among good judges that Robertson at any rate will prove worth his share. Murray I can speak of later.
>
> 'Robertson is an artist with the ball. We saw this in the first few minutes of the game at Bradford, in which he made his debut. His control of the object was delightfully sure, and the way in which he could guide it past or over hooking feet, while on the run, was

> convincing as to his outstanding merit. Several times in that game he recovered the ball from seemingly hopeless positions, and as he has done the same thing in other matches since, this power of recovery is evidently a valuable feature of his play.
>
> 'He can shoot goals from oblique angles, and he middles the ball so well that he makes scoring easy for others. Robertson has played for Scotland this season, and was picked to play in the inter-League match for the Scottish League. His build is splendid for a forward – only two inches short of six feet in height, and in weight 11st. 10lbs.'

George was off form again in Wednesday's goalless draw with Bolton at Owlerton on 2 April 1910 although he did get in an 'excellent shot from a distance', the *Green 'Un*'s man at the match remarked that he 'never seemed to get going, and in the first half was almost mediocre'.

Although Wednesday were on the wrong side of a 4-1 scoreline at Stamford Bridge on 9 April, George appears to have performed well against Chelsea. The *Green 'Un* report noted, 'A gallant individual run by Robertson nearly brought an equaliser. Beating the opposition in great style, the left-winger shot at close range, but Robinson, who had to leave his goal, managed to beat the ball down. A second time the Wednesday left-winger left the opposition standing, and this time Robinson clean missed the centre, which he placed in the goal-mouth.' Andrew Wilson scored Wednesday's solitary counter.

The following week, against Blackburn Rovers in torrential rain at Owlerton, George was once again prominent, getting in a couple of really good shots and winning the ball cleverly on the touchline. Ulsterman Andy Hunter's two goals gave Wednesday a narrow 2-1 win over the championship-contending Lancashire outfit.

Away to Nottingham Forest on 23 April the team were in sparkling form and were 4-0 ahead at the interval through goals from Murray, Chapman and two from Wilson. Play was a bit scrappy in the second half but Wednesday and George finished the game in style, 'A fine centre by Lloyd was turned to full account by Robertson, who headed a fifth goal twelve minutes before the finish,' and yet another goal to the visitors, 'Robertson making a fine run and beating Hassell seven minutes from the close.'

At Owlerton on 30 April, Harry Chapman's 20-yard goal in the second half gave Wednesday a narrow 1-0 win over Sunderland in the final game of the season although the *Green 'Un* reckoned that the winning margin should have been much greater. Wednesday's Billy Lloyd hit the post and George had two fine shots saved as well as setting up a chance for Andrew Hunter who just failed to knock in the winger's cross. According to the *Green 'Un*, George had an outstanding game, 'Robertson was in great form, and kept dribbling in and driving the ball across with fine judgement.'

This was the end of a disappointing season for the club who finished 11th in the First Division with 39 points although their mid-table position was fairly respectable given their poor start to the season. George played in the last eight games, of which five were won, one drawn and two lost. He scored three goals for his new side.

Wednesday's poor position in the league was largely due to their inability to field a settled side and the introduction of so many new signings over the season. Only Tom Brittleton and the ever-present Jimmy Spoors played more than 30 games during the campaign. Goals too were in short supply with only leading scorer Wilson and Frank Rollinson getting into double figures. Embarrassingly Wednesday failed to score in the FA Cup, losing 1-0 to Northampton Town at Owlerton after being held to a goalless draw by the Cobblers at the County Ground.

George, Jessie and young son Robbie soon settled into a house at 122 Dixon Road, only a short walk from Wednesday's ground. At the time this area was originally re-surveyed for a map in 1902, some of the streets including Dixon Road were still under construction.

Dixon Road was named after James Willis Dixon of the famous pewter, Britannia metal and silverware manufacturing firm who owned Hillsborough Hall and estate and who sold the land to Wednesday to enable them to build their ground.

The area of Owlerton (locally pronounced Ollerton, although George would probably have pronounced it as it is written) takes its name from the alder trees which flourished alongside the River Don, not from the number of nocturnal birds of prey to be found there. Many of the surrounding streets bear the names of members of the Willis family.

ENGLISH FIRST DIVISION 1909/10

	Pl	*W*	*D*	*L*	*F*	*A*	*Pts*
1 Aston Villa	38	23	7	8	84	42	53
2 Liverpool	38	21	6	11	78	57	48
3 Blackburn Rovers	38	18	9	11	73	55	45
4 Newcastle United	38	19	7	12	70	56	45
5 Manchester United	38	19	7	12	69	61	45
6 Sheffield United	38	16	10	12	62	41	42
7 Bradford City	38	17	8	13	64	47	42
8 Sunderland	38	18	5	15	66	51	41
9 Notts County	38	15	10	13	67	59	40

10 Everton	38	16	8	14	51	56	40
11 The Wednesday	38	15	9	14	60	63	39
12 Preston North End	38	15	5	18	52	58	35
13 Bury	38	12	9	17	62	66	33
14 Nottingham Forest	38	11	11	16	54	72	33
15 Tottenham Hotspur	38	11	10	17	53	69	32
16 Bristol City	38	12	8	18	45	60	32
17 Middlesbrough	38	11	9	18	56	73	31
18 Woolwich Arsenal	38	11	9	18	37	67	31
19 Chelsea	38	11	7	20	47	70	29
20 Bolton Wanderers	38	9	6	23	44	71	24

THE WEDNESDAY'S APPEARANCES AND GOALS 1909/10

	League		*FA Cup*	
	Apps	*Goals*	*Apps*	*Goals*
Bartlett, W.J.	17	0	2	0
Bradshaw, F.	12	3	0	0
Brittleton, J.T.	32	6	2	0
Chapman, H.	28	6	2	0
Davison, J.E.	24	0	2	0
Foxall, F.	16	5	0	0
Hamilton, H.G.	7	0	0	0
Holbem, W.	26	0	2	0
Hunter, A.	6	2	0	0
Kinghorn, H. McG.	14	0	0	0
Kirkman, S.	29	7	2	0
Layton, W.	6	0	0	0
Lloyd, W.	20	1	0	0
McConnell, J.E.	21	0	2	0
McSkimming, R.S.	9	0	0	0
Murray, J.M.	8	2	0	0
O'Connell, P.J.	3	0	0	0
Robertson, G.C.	8	3	0	0
Rollinson, F.	20	10	2	0
Slavin, H.	2	0	0	0
Spoors, J.	38	0	2	0
Stringfellow, J.F.	6	2	0	0
Taylor, J.	13	0	0	0
Tummon, O.	12	1	2	0
Warren, P.	1	0	0	0
Weir, W.F.	11	0	0	0
Wilson, A. McC.	29	12	2	0

8

1910/11 – THE NEW IDOL

THE 1910/11 season was George's first full one in Sheffield and he was very keen to create a good early impression with his new club but Wednesday made an inauspicious start to the new campaign. They found themselves propping up the First Division after losing their opening fixture 3-1 to Tottenham at White Hart Lane on 3 September 1910, with Harry Chapman on target for the visitors.

Wednesday's first home game of the season was on 10 September against Middlesbrough.

The *Green 'Un* reporter was in raptures about George's play although he complained that the winger should have scored, 'Robertson had made a great run on the left, in the course of which he beat man after man,' 'Robertson was in wonderful form, and several times he seemed to have the goal at his mercy. On one occasion only rank bad luck stopped him, for when he had beaten McLeod very cleverly he slipped as he shot, and the ball went harmlessly past,' 'Robertson was still doing wonders, and after getting a fine pass from Murray he ran right in and shot past the far post with Williamson beaten,' and 'Robertson had been quiet for a little, but he broke out again, and was leading the visiting defence a merry dance when force of numbers proved too much for him.' The sides finished level at 1-1 with Chapman scoring again for Wednesday.

Wednesday recorded their first win of the season against Preston North End at Deepdale where Chapman put the Sheffield side in front after seven minutes. The newspaper reported, 'It was Robertson who made the goal possible. The winger worked right through, and put a low centre in front of goal, where Chapman gave McBride no chance.'

George was also involved in the second of Wednesday's goals, 'Then the Wednesday left wing worked up another goal. Wilson started it with a good pass, which Robertson picked up at full speed. The winger, already the most brilliant forward on the field, raced like a greyhound into goal, taking the ball right in front before giving Murray the simplest of chances which the centre quickly availed himself of.'

Just before half-time Chapman scored a fine individual goal to give the visitors a 3-0 interval lead. Mounteney pulled a goal back for Preston in the second half and late in the match George took an ankle knock which left him hobbling on the wing. Wednesday's 3-1 win hoisted them to 12th in the table.

On 24 September Notts County were the next visitors to Owlerton to face the skills of the in-form winger. The *Green 'Un* proclaimed 'ROBERTSON AGAIN BRILLIANT' and praised his many runs and attempts on goal. County scored against the run of play and held that lead at half-time. The *Green 'Un* reporter highlighted an incident typifying George's determination, 'Robertson made a great effort to head a goal, but he only succeeded in putting the ball past, and at the same time damaged his clothing, and he had to go off for a change.'

While George was absent County added a second goal. Despite George's best efforts Wednesday went down 3-1 with Jimmy Murray scoring for the home side. Murray was dropped from the team following this match as Wednesday experimented with a number of players in the centre-forward role in the search for a player with the goalscoring touch.

On a scorching hot Saturday, 1 October, George scored twice against Manchester United at Old Trafford but still finished on the losing side. 'When Chapman got possession, he gave to Dowling, who passed the good work on to Robertson. We had not seen much of the left-winger so far, but this was a brilliant introduction, for he went right on and put the ball past Moger,' it was reported.

Wednesday's goalkeeper Henry Kinghorn suffered a bad shoulder injury in an accidental clash when Wall equalised for United and the teams went in level at the break. Wednesday were 3-1 down through further goals from West and Wall when George scored late on in the game, 'Then Robertson, after a fine run scored for Wednesday with a high shot.'

Wednesday dominated the closing stages but couldn't grab the vital equalising goal. They now found themselves in 17th place, perilously close to the relegation positions.

The following week, at Owlerton, George scored within five minutes of the start against Liverpool, 'The next Wednesday raid was destined to prove successful, for Robertson took a pass when going at top speed, ran right into goal and beat Beeby with a fast ground shot,' wrote the *Green 'Un*.

George was maintaining his rich vein of form with his pace, in particular, creating havoc, 'Robertson's speed was giving Chorlton any amount of anxiety, and the Liverpool back found it safer to kick into touch rather than risk a tackle.' George's counter gave the home side a hard fought 1-0 victory and took them back up the table to 14th.

On 15 October Wednesday travelled to Lancashire and came away with a share of the points following a 1-1 draw with Bury at Gigg Lane. Hibbert gave the Shakers a first-half lead from the penalty spot but Wednesday hit back and Wilson got his side's equaliser.

On the following Saturday, George experienced his first Steel City derby and turned in a performance which caught the eye of 'Looker-On', the *Green Un*'s man at the match. Wednesday emerged victorious by 2-0 at Owlerton with Harry Chapman scoring twice in the first half. According to the *Green 'Un*, Robertson shone, 'Again we saw a little of the new idol, Robertson. With exquisite skill he left Benson standing still, then cut in and blazed away like a big gun.'

This win pushed Wednesday up to tenth in the First Division. Harry Chapman's great scoring run then continued away to Aston Villa but his single goal was not enough to overcome the home side who claimed both points through goals from Walters and Bache and pushed Wednesday three places down the table.

George sustained a serious knee injury on 5 November in a tough 1-1 draw against Sunderland at Owlerton when Tom Brittleton scored Wednesday's second-half equaliser. Holley had given the home side the lead in the first period. As a result of George's injury he missed the next two matches, away to Arsenal and at home to Bradford City, which were both lost 1-0. These two defeats saw Wednesday slide down the table again to 16th place.

On his return to the side on 26 November, Wednesday were humiliated 6-1 by Blackburn Rovers at Ewood Park although they did have several chances to level the match at 2-2 either side of half-time. Wilson was the sole Wednesday scorer. This defeat plunged Wednesday, worryingly, to second from bottom as their run of inconsistent results continued.

This match proved to be the last in Wednesday colours for George's former Motherwell team-mate Jimmy Murray who returned to Ireland to play for Derry Celtic before making a brief and unsuccessful return to Motherwell the following season.

Wednesday got back to winning ways on 3 December when George received some rough treatment against Nottingham Forest but was able to lay on the third goal for Wilson in a 5-2 win at Owlerton. Top scorer Chapman contributed two goals, one from the penalty spot, with Frank Rollinson and Sam Kirkman the other Wednesday marksmen.

One week later Chapman and Wilson gave Wednesday a 2-1 win over Manchester City at Hyde Road to lift them back up the table to 13th.

A 2-0 home defeat at the hands of Everton on 17 December pushed Wednesday down to 15th as the crowded Christmas fixture list loomed. Wednesday faced a busy schedule of five matches in ten days over the festive season with three of those games coming within a four-day period.

Things started badly for Wednesday with a 1-0 defeat to Oldham Athletic at Boundary Park on Christmas Eve. For the first time in English football the Wilson brothers from Ayrshire, Andrew of Wednesday and David of Athletic, found themselves on opposing sides.

A goal from the prolific Chapman and a second-half equaliser from Findlay Weir, with his one and only score for Wednesday, earned a vital Boxing Day point in a 2-2 draw against Bristol City at Ashton Gate to ease them a couple of places away from danger. Wednesday were back at home to face Newcastle United on 27 December and tamely went down 2-0, perhaps not surprisingly given the amount of travelling involved over the previous few days. The prospect of relegation was now a real possibility as Wednesday had slipped to second from bottom in the First Division.

This Wednesday side responded positively to the threat and three wins in a row within a week did much to reduce their relegation worries. Changes were afoot as veteran inside-right Chapman made way for some new blood in the forward line. Tottenham Hotspur were beaten 2-1 at Owlerton on the last day of 1910 with goals coming from newcomer Teddy Glennon and Frank Stringfellow either side of the break.

Bristol City were then defeated by the same scoreline on 2 January 1911 with Glennon bagging a brace in the first half.

In the match against Middlesbrough at Ayresome Park on 7 January, George was denied a goal by the officials in an unusual manner, 'It was Wednesday's turn now, and Robertson worked like a hero to get through. He forced a corner, and might have got a goal had not the referee got right in his line of fire.' Wednesday won the match 1-0 through Stringfellow's goal.

George's FA Cup debut came on 14 January when Wednesday made a very hasty exit from the competition, embarrassingly going down 2-1 at Owlerton to Coventry City of the Southern League. Wilson had the home side's solitary counter.

Back on league business Wednesday's 0-0 draw with Preston at Owlerton on 21 January actually pushed them up to 11th place. But Wednesday plummeted back down the table to 16th after successive away defeats, 2-0 to Notts County and 3-0 to Liverpool, which raised the spectre of relegation again.

Before the match at Anfield George shook hands with Liverpool left-half John McConnell, a former Motherwell team-mate, but it was the old Fir Park half-back who came out on top against the winger again just as he had when he joined Airdrieonians.

Wednesday moved quickly into the transfer market in an effort to reverse their fortunes by signing high-scoring centre-forward David McLean from Preston, along with wing-half Jimmy Campbell and inside-forward Marr Paterson from Leith Athletic. Coincidentally Paterson was born and raised in Alva, two miles from George's birthplace in Menstrie. Although Paterson was almost two years younger than George, the pair may have known each other from their schooldays at Alva Academy.

Paterson made his debut in the Liverpool match on 11 February but McLean and Campbell had to wait a week as both made their first Wednesday appearance in the 1-0 win over Bury at Owlerton when a Jimmy Spoors goal separated the sides. Wednesday created numerous chances and George was prominent in almost every attack but the two new forwards Paterson and McLean were not quite on the same wavelength as their Sheffield team-mates and failed to convert the opportunities into goals.

Wednesday's inconsistent form during the first part of the season had seen them slide up and down the table, although the form of the Scots contingent was still worthy of note. The *Green 'Un* reported on 18 February that, for the match with Bury, 'It was interesting to note that two members of the Scottish Selection Committee watched the game from the stand. Presumably they were looking at the form of McLean, Weir and Robertson among others.' Obviously they were not too impressed as none of the Wednesday players were selected for the international series.

Wednesday's Scots continued to turn on the style and McLean immediately endeared himself to Wednesday fans by scoring the winner over city rivals United in the 1-0 win on 25 February at Bramall Lane.

Wilson and George were at the top of their form against front-runners Aston Villa on 4 March at Owlerton. The *Green 'Un* reported, 'Wilson bustled the defence and did the donkey work, whilst Robertson slipped away with the ball at every opportunity. Once he burst away like a flash of greased lightning and slung across a centre… but unfortunately it just passed in front of the Wednesday forwards.'

The newspaper remarked on George's skill, 'One of the finest things of Robertson's play is the craft he shows in controlling a long pass without stopping. An instance of this cropped up just now when the ball went to him from a lofty kick by McSkimming, and without the slightest hesitation he shot it forward past his man in such a way that would have given him a very fine start.'

Marr Paterson repaid some of his transfer fee by scoring the only goal of the game against Villa.

It was not until 11 March that George's name appeared again on the scoresheet when he and David McLean scored the goals in the 2-1 defeat of Sunderland at Roker Park. George's goal came when Sunderland goalkeeper Worrall, according to the newspaper, 'came out of his goal and fisted away, but the ball went to Robertson, who promptly drove it into the unguarded net'.

Minutes later Wilson slipped the ball to George who sped past the full-back and sent in the perfect centre for McLean to volley into the net for the second and winning goal which hoisted Wednesday up to tenth place in the league.

Against Woolwich Arsenal on 18 March Wednesday were effectively down to nine men through injuries to McLean and Paterson but George was 'still the outstanding figure', dropping the ball dangerously into the centre for his team-mates but neither side were able to score.

Sam Kirkman scored the only goal of the game to beat Blackburn at Owlerton on 1 April and extend the team's unbeaten sequence to six matches and push Wednesday up to ninth in the table. That run was abruptly halted at Valley Parade three days later when Wilson scored twice but Wednesday conceded five against a Bradford City side, including George's former Motherwell team-mate David Taylor at left-back, who were destined to win the FA Cup later in the month. Wilson was the marksman when Wednesday bounced back with a 1-0 win over Nottingham Forest at the City Ground on 8 April to reclaim ninth spot.

Wednesday appeared, at last, to have discovered some consistency in their play and George and Wilson were the scorers in a fine 2-0 win over Newcastle United at St James' Park on Friday 14 April. The Easter fixtures were obviously to the liking of the Wednesday players for the following day they enjoyed a field day in defeating Manchester City 4-1 at Owlerton.

George was again on the top of his game. He was fouled around 20 yards from goal and from the resulting free kick Jimmy Campbell netted his first Wednesday goal. Smart work by Paterson gave reserve inside-forward Stringfellow the opportunity to beat City keeper Smith with a terrific drive. Both Paterson and Stringfellow missed another gilt-edged chance from George's cross just before the break but Wednesday went 3-0 up almost from the restart. George sent the ball across the face of the City goal to Kirkman, whose inch-perfect cross was headed home by Paterson.

'Looker-On', the *Green 'Un*'s man at the match, was concerned for George, 'The Manchester defenders were finding it difficult to stop Robertson, and to level matters up they had recourse to fouling him, and the referee was very busy in dealing out free-kicks for actions that were uncalled for.'

A defensive error allowed Lot Jones to reduce the arrears before George scored Wednesday's fourth goal, 'Then Wednesday got another goal. This was scored by Robertson from 20 yards' range after a magnificent run half the length of the field, and it was certainly one of the finest goals seen at Owlerton for many a long day. The crowd simply "rose" at that brilliant left-winger and cheered him again and again.' The win pushed Wednesday up to eighth in the table.

George was injured in the goalless draw with the eventual league champions Manchester United on Easter Monday, 17 April, and as a result missed the away trip to Everton the following Saturday which Wednesday drew 1-1. The *Green 'Un* reckoned that Wednesday's injury problems probably cost them the win, 'Wednesday were not fully represented, so they may be excused somewhat for not winning, as they undoubtedly would have done had they had Robertson and Weir in their positions.' George's stand-in Percy Wright got the Wednesday goal on his first-team debut.

George was very much to the fore in the final game of the season at home to Oldham Athletic which was used as a benefit match for Wednesday legend Harry Chapman, who had moved to Hull City. Oldham, as newcomers to the top flight, had surprised everyone by reaching fifth place going into the match so a keen contest was anticipated. Oldham had beaten Wednesday earlier in the season at Boundary Park and beaten United home and away so a visit to Sheffield held no fears for them.

For the second time, the Wilson brothers, Andrew and David, found themselves in opposition and this time it was Andrew who claimed the family bragging rights.

Chances were missed at both ends as players struggled to control the ball on the greasy surface. George was beginning to trouble the Oldham defence when he was hurt, 'A moment later Robertson was working his way up the wing, when Moffat made a back for him, and the Wednesday player came down very heavily on his head. He was attended to by the trainer, and came round after a while, but the referee earned the disfavour of the crowd by merely throwing the ball down instead of giving a free kick to Wednesday, as he ought to have done.'

These days such a head injury would have seen the player taken off but they were made of sterner stuff back then. George was quickly back in the action and soon opened Wednesday's account, 'Wednesday got a second corner, which was beautifully placed by Kirkman, and with Hudson and McDonald hesitating about clearing, Robertson rushed up and scrambled the ball through.' In a fine day for the Wednesday left wing, Wilson notched a second goal in the dying seconds of the game.

The Wednesday fans were wildly enthusiastic about their new left-winger and urged the directors of the club to spend more money on signings of his quality in order that they could seriously challenge for the league title. The problem position for Wednesday initially appeared to be at centre-forward. George's former Motherwell team-mate, Jimmy Murray, started the season in that role but soon fell out of favour. A number of players were tried out before David McLean was signed from Preston and made the berth his own.

Wednesday certainly bettered their previous season's performance, thanks largely to a more settled side following their February signings. The club finished in an improved sixth place in a highly competitive league with 42 points, ten behind eventual champions Manchester United. George played in 35 of the 38 league games and scored seven goals.

ENGLISH FIRST DIVISION 1910/11

	Pl	*W*	*D*	*L*	*F*	*A*	*Pts*
1 Manchester United	38	22	8	8	72	40	52
2 Aston Villa	38	22	7	9	69	41	51
3 Sunderland	38	15	15	8	67	48	45
4 Everton	38	19	7	12	50	36	45
5 Bradford City	38	20	5	13	51	42	45
6 The Wednesday	38	17	8	13	47	48	42
7 Oldham Athletic	38	16	9	13	44	41	41
8 Newcastle United	38	15	10	13	61	43	40
9 Sheffield United	38	15	8	15	49	43	38
10 Woolwich Arsenal	38	13	12	13	41	49	38
11 Notts County	38	14	10	14	37	45	38
12 Blackburn Rovers	38	13	11	14	62	54	37
13 Liverpool	38	15	7	16	53	53	37
14 Preston North End	38	12	11	15	40	49	35
15 Tottenham Hotspur	38	13	6	19	52	63	32
16 Middlesbrough	38	11	10	17	49	63	32
17 Manchester City	38	9	13	16	43	58	31
18 Bury	38	9	11	18	43	71	29
19 Bristol City	38	11	5	22	43	66	27
20 Nottingham Forest	38	9	7	22	55	75	25

THE WEDNESDAY'S APPEARANCES AND GOALS 1910/11

	League		*FA Cup*	
	Apps	*Goals*	*Apps*	*Goals*
Bradley, M.	2	0	0	0
Brittleton, J.T.	32	1	0	0
Campbell, J.	13	1	0	0
Chapman, H.	18	11	0	0
Davison, J.E.	30	0	1	0
Dowling, M.	7	0	0	0
Glennon, J.E.	5	3	1	0
Holbem, W.	20	0	1	0
Kinghorn, H. McG.	8	0	0	0
Kirkman, S.	32	2	1	0
Lloyd, W.	16	0	1	0
McLean, D.P.	11	2	0	0
McSkimming, R.S.	29	0	0	0
Murray, J.M.	5	2	0	0
O'Connell, P.J.	10	0	1	0
Paterson, M.	14	2	0	0
Robertson, G.C.	35	7	1	0

Rollinson, F.	8	1	0	0
Spoors, J.	36	1	1	0
Stringfellow, F.	7	3	1	0
Warren, P.	3	0	0	0
Weir, W.F.	36	1	1	0
Wilson, A. McC.	38	9	1	1
Worrall, J.E.	2	0	0	0
Wright, P.L.	1	1	0	0

In the summer of 1911, Wednesday took part in their first continental tour. Orgryte, a Gothenburg team, were beaten 5-0, and a Swedish side were seen off 2-1. At Copenhagen, Wednesday had the honour of playing before the Crown Prince and Princess of Denmark and at the same time opening a magnificent new ground, owned by the Corporation. A Danish national team was defeated by 3-2 when the Prince handed silver scarf pins to the players.

A day or so afterwards a picked XI of Copenhagen was overcome 3-2, and the same result was arrived at when a third match with a national XI was played. The tour was a great success and the party was royally received everywhere. An anonymous detailed account by one of the party was printed in the *Green 'Un* on their return to Sheffield and is reproduced in full in the next chapter.

*(**Fig. 1**) Robert and Isabella, George's parents c1874.*

*(**Fig. 2**) The village of Menstrie around 1890. The Robertson family joinery premises are to the bottom left of the picture. The boy in the wheelbarrow may be George.*

*(**Fig. 3**) A Robertson family portrait from around 1893. George is on the extreme right, with his parents Robert and Isabella, older sister Mary and brothers Hugh (standing) and Robert (seated) and baby Helen.*

*(**Fig. 4**) A Menstrie Primary School group from 1894. George is third from the left in the second row from the top.*

*(**Fig. 5**) Another Robertson family group, from around 1901. George is on the left, with brothers Hugh (centre) and Bob (right). In front are sisters Mary and Helen (Nellie) and mother Isabella. George's father, Robert, died in 1897.*

*(**Fig. 6**) This is the earliest known photograph of George in football kit. This photograph is probably of a Menstrie Victoria line-up from the very early 1900s. George is the gangly youth on the extreme right of the players seated on the bench. George's brother, Hugh is also known to be in this photograph. The white building behind the team is Menstrie Mains Farm.*

(**Fig. 7**) *Motherwell FC 1906/07 George is seated on the extreme right of the front row. Back Row (left to right): W.H. Barrie (Secretary), T.J. Quirk (Director), McLean, Sneddon, W. White (Director), McDonald, McCallum, J. Fleming (Treas.), Rattray, A. McLaughlan (Chairman), W. Waugh (Asst. Trainer). Front Row (left to right): Reid, Richmond, Nicol, McNeil, Donaldson, Robertson.*

(**Fig. 8**) *George's Lanarkshire Cup winners' medal 1906/07.*

*(**Fig. 9**) Motherwell Team against Airdrieonians on September 11th 1909. George is the player cross-legged on the front bench. Jimmy Murray has the ball at his feet. (From left to right): Back Row: Wm. H. Barrie (Secretary), B.W. Gilmour (Director), W. Duffy (Director), T.J. Quirk (Chairman), C. Baillie (Director) Middle Row: S. Hill, John Johnston, D. Taylor, T. McDonald, J. Rattray, W. Downie, H. McNeil, A.B. Bowman (Director). Front Row: A. Sharp, James Johnstone, J. Gray, J. Murray, W. Lawson, G. Robertson, G. Miller (Trainer)*

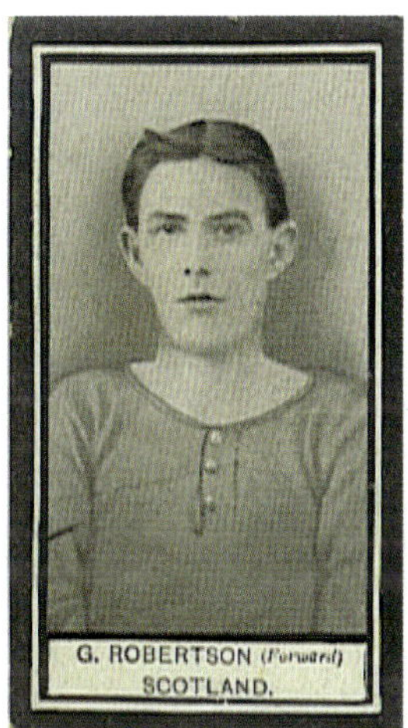

*(**Fig. 10**) George first appeared on a cigarette card after winning his first cap against Wales in 1910.*

*(**Fig. 11**) George Robertson from a postcard dated Motherwell 1909, possibly modelling a black and gold jersey which pre-dated the club's famous claret and amber shirts.*

*(**Fig. 12**) George with his first Scottish cap. Photo taken by the Furniss Studio when George first arrived in Sheffield.*

*(**Fig. 13**) Wednesday's Owlerton ground as it would have looked when George arrived.*

*(**Fig. 14**) The Wednesday team which beat Örgryte 5-0. Back Row: Lloyd (acting linesman), Campbell, Brittleton, Wilson, Davison, McLean, Paterson, Parramore (Trainer) Front Row: Kirkman, Robertson, Spoors, McSkimming, Weir.*

(Fig. 15) *A Wednesday squad from 1911. George is second from the right in the front row.*

(Fig. 16) *Some of the Wednesday squad on the beach at Saltburn – George is on the extreme right, with pipe in mouth.*

*(**Fig. 17**) Wednesday team training at the Alexandra Hotel, Saltburn before the cup tie with Middlesbrough. Back Row: Teddy Worrall, Ted Davison, Jimmy Spoors Middle Row: Tom Brittleton, Findlay Weir, Jimmy Campbell, Patrick O'Connell Front Row: John Davis (assistant trainer), Sam Kirkman, Ted Glennon, David McLean, Andrew Wilson, George Robertson, Ted Kinnear (trainer).*

SATURDAY, MARCH 2, 1912.

SCOTLAND'S TEAM AGAINST WALES.

(1) J. BROWNLIE, Third Lanark; (2) A. M'NAIR, Celtic; (3) J. WALKER, Swindon; (4) R. MERCER, Heart of Mid Lothian; (5) C. THOMSON, Sunderland; (6) J. HAY, Newcastle United; (7) G. SINCLAIR, Heart of Mid Lothian; (8) J. M'MENEMY, Celtic; (9) J. QUINN, Celtic; (10) R. WALKER, Heart of Mid Lothian; (11) G. ROBERTSON, Sheffield Wednesday.

*(**Fig. 18**) The* Evening Times *carried portraits of the Scotland team to face Wales in 1912.*

Welsh International v Scotland 3
March 2/3/12. Edinburgh

R T Evans
Lloyd Davies
J W Williams
J. J. Jones
Billy Meredith
Evan Jones
Ted Vizard
L Davies
Moses Russell
George Wynn
Ted Hughes
Billy Davies
Geo Latham

Wales 0

Charlie Thomson
Robert Walker
Jas McMenemy
John Walker
Geo L Sinclair
James Brownlie
James Quinn
George C Robertson
James Hay
Alex McNair
Robert Mercer
J McDowall Sec

Scotland 1
J. Quinn scored

(**Fig. 19**) *Autographs of the Welsh and Scots teams at the Tynecastle International on March 2nd 1912.*

(**Fig. 20**) *Home Scots and Anglo Scots teams at Firhill Park, Glasgow – Monday, March 11th 1912. George is in the middle row in the white shirt, fourth from the right.*

*(**Fig. 21**) The Wednesday squad at the start of the 1912/13 season. George is on the bench in the front row, second from the right.*

*(**Fig. 22**) George with a live owl mascot.*

(**Fig. 23**) *Owlerton was remodelled by football stadium architect Archibald Leitch, before being renamed Hillsborough.*

(**Fig. 24**) *A Wednesday team photograph from the start of the 1913/14 season. George is second from the right in the front row.*

*(**Fig. 25**) A Wednesday team photograph from around 1914 – George is in the front row second from the right.*

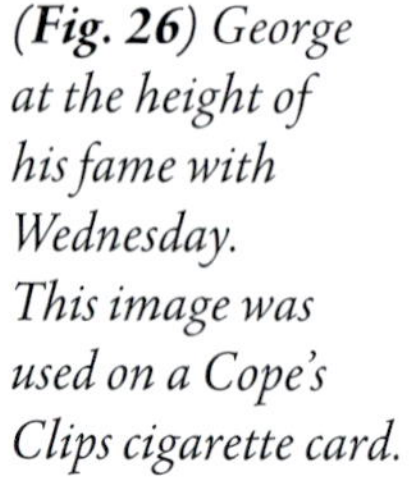

*(**Fig. 26**) George at the height of his fame with Wednesday. This image was used on a Cope's Clips cigarette card.*

*(**Fig. 27**) George (back row, second from left in coat and bunnet and clutching his pipe) with his East Fife team-mates.*

*(**Fig. 28**) East Fife's Bayview Park – the main grandstand was added just after George left the club in 1922.*

*(**Fig. 29**) George with sister Mary, mother Isabella, wife Jessie and probably George Junior. The photograph was probably taken in Scotland shortly before the family crossed the Atlantic.*

RHODE ISLAND DEPARTMENT OF PUBLIC HEALTH

Division of Vital Statistics

CERTIFICATE OF DEATH

City or Town No. 1474 | 95

1. PLACE OF DEATH
City or Town Providence St. and No. 5 Osborn Street
(If death occurred in a hospital or institution, give its NAME instead of street and number)
Length of residence in city or town where death occurred 15 yrs. ... mos. ... ds. How long in U. S. if of foreign birth? 15 yrs. ... mos. ... ds.

2. FULL NAME George Clark Robertson War Record — (Name of War)
(a) Residence: St. and No. 5 Osborn Street (If nonresident give city or town and State) City or Town Providence (Usual place of abode)

PERSONAL AND STATISTICAL PARTICULARS

3. SEX Male
4. COLOR OR RACE White
5. Single, Married, Widowed, or Divorced (write the word) Married
5a. If married, widowed, or divorced (if wife, FULL MAIDEN name) HUSBAND (or) WIFE Jessie Greig
6. DATE OF BIRTH (month, day and year) March 7, 1885
6a. If STILLBORN enter that fact here. Months of gestation
7. AGE Years 53 Months 2 Days 3 If LESS than 1 day ... hrs. or ... min.

OCCUPATION
8. Trade, profession, or particular kind of work done, as spinner, sawyer, bookkeeper, etc. Janitor
9. Industry or business in which work was done, as silk mill, saw mill, bank, etc. Insurance Co.
10. Date deceased last worked at this occupation (month and year) April 24, 1937
11. Total Time (years) spent in this occupation 4 Mo.

12. BIRTHPLACE (city or town) (State or country) Scotland

FATHER
13. NAME Robert Robertson
14. BIRTHPLACE (city or town) (State or country) Scotland

MOTHER
15. MAIDEN NAME (Full name) Isabel Campbell
16. BIRTHPLACE (city or town) (State or country) Scotland

17. INFORMANT Mrs. Jessie G. Robertson
(Address) 5 Osborn St. Prov. R. I.
(Relation to deceased) Wife

18. BURIAL ☒ CREMATION ☐ REMOVAL ☐ or OTHERWISE ☐
City or Town North Providence
Name of Cemetery Highland Memorial Park

19. Signature of Embalmer John Finlay 415 (License No.)
Funeral Director Carpenter-Jenks 31 (License No.)

20. FILED ... , 19 ... Local Registrar.

MEDICAL CERTIFICATE OF DEATH

21. DATE OF DEATH May 10, 1937 (month, day, and year)

22. I HEREBY CERTIFY, That I attended deceased from April 26 1937, to May 10, 1937
I last saw him alive on May 9 1937; death is said to have occurred on the date stated above at 8.35 A m.
The principal cause of death and related causes of importance were as follows: ‡ (See below) 107a
broncho-pneumonia Date of onset

Other contributory causes of importance:

Name of operation ‡ ... Date of ...
Was there an autopsy? ... What tests confirmed diagnosis? ‡ ...

23. If death was due to external causes (violence) fill in also the following:
Accident, suicide, or homicide? ... Date of injury ... , 19 ...
Where did injury occur? ... (Specify city or town, county, and State)
Specify whether injury occurred in industry, in home, or in public place.

Manner of injury ...
Nature of injury ...

24. Was disease or injury in any way related to occupation of deceased? no
If so, specify ...
(Signed) John E. Menzies M.D. (Degree)
(Address) 643 Elmwood ave.

‡ For more space use other side.

(**Fig. 30**) George's death certificate.

*(**Fig. 31**) George (back row second from left) at his son Robert's wedding – October 3rd 1931.*

*(**Fig. 32**) George's daughter Catherine Campbell Robertson. She was born in Providence in 1925.*

*(**Fig. 33**) George didn't live to see his grandchildren. Georgina, obviously named after him, was born on November 27th, 1937 in North Providence, Rhode Island.*

*(**Fig. 34**) The final photograph of George with Jessie (left) and Agnes in happy times relaxing near an amusement park.*

9

REPORT ON THE SCANDINAVIAN TOUR 1911 WEDNESDAY 17 MAY – THURSDAY 1 JUNE

THIS report was taken from the *Green 'Un* and is a contemporary account written by one of the players or club officials who took part in the tour. The identity of the correspondent is unknown.

WEDNESDAY'S TOUR

Interesting Record of the Matches

A SUCCESSFUL OUTING

(Specially Contributed)

Wednesday 17 May

We were a very happy party that left the Victoria Station at half past four on Wednesday afternoon, May 17th, for the first Continental tour ever undertaken by the Wednesday Club.

There were 20 of us all told, comprising four directors – Mr. A.J. Dickinson (hon. secretary), Mr. Herbert Nixon, Mr. J.H. Thackray and Mr. J.B. Gunstone, fourteen players – Davison, Spoors, McSkimming, Brittleton, Lloyd, Weir, Campbell, O'Connell, Kirkman, Paterson, McLean, Wilson, Glennon and Robertson and two trainers, Messrs C. Parramore and John Davis.

Wednesday 17 May to Friday 19 May

We reached Parkeston Quay, Harwich, shortly after 9.50, and at once went on board the Danish boat *Primula*, sailing at 10 o'clock. The sea was very calm so all slept fairly well and managed to put in an appearance at the first meal on Thursday morning.

It was an entirely different story to tell of the next meal though, and one could not help laughing as player after player got up hurriedly and left the dinner table for some quiet corner where he could suffer in silence. Only five of the fourteen players finished dinner, but they, too, were glad to get on deck again to feel the fresh air. But later in the afternoon some of these also suffered from mal de mer, and tea was not wanted.

After landing at Esbjerg at 11 p.m., Danish time, and getting once again on to terra firma, the feeling of sickness soon disappeared. We passed through the Customs, and then, after waiting some little time, commenced an eight hours journey by rail and ferry across Denmark. The scenery en route was beautiful, and time seemed to pass quickly, though we were somewhat tired out. Copenhagen was reached shortly after eight on Friday morning.

[The party travelled by rail and ferry from Esbjerg on the west coast of Denmark to Copenhagen and then on to Gothenburg. The smaller ferry crossings they faced have largely been replaced by bridges.]

Friday 19 May

We had plenty of time now for a good meal, and we stood in need of one, as some of the party had eaten little since leaving Harwich. After breakfast and a short rest, we left the Danish capital at eleven for Gothenburg. We proceeded through more delightful country to Elsinore [Helsingor, with its dramatic Kronborg Castle immortalised by Shakespeare in *Hamlet*] and then crossed in ferry to Halsingborg [Helsingborg] on the Swedish coast. Now began the last stage of our journey. The scenery again was charming, as for the greater part of the way we skirted the coast, and so had the sea on one side and country on the other.

We arrived at our destination shortly after half past six, after travelling for 49 hours since leaving Sheffield. None of us were sorry to leave the train, though the carriages were very comfortable indeed. The second-class carriages are fitted with every convenience, and can easily be converted into sleeping berths. The railways in Denmark and Sweden belong to the state.

We were met at Gothenburg by Mr. Hugo Levin, the secretary of the Swedish F A – a gentleman who never spared himself in his efforts to make our stay there enjoyable. Mr. Levin informed us that Bradford City were playing that evening against the Swedish combination – an International XI. We at once drove to the football ground in time to see the kick off. The English cup-holders played poorly against the ever-eager Swedes and lost 0-1. The spectators were very excitable, and one could often see some of them making kicks at imaginary balls. Needless to say they were delighted at beating Bradford, and especially as this was the first victory against an English League team. After the match we returned to our headquarters – Hotel Eggers – had late dinner and were soon in bed.

Saturday 20 May

The next morning was spent in looking round Gothenburg – a delightful town to holiday in, with many fine parks and avenues of trees, etc. We experienced no little difficulty when wanting to make purchases, as we could not understand them or they us.

After dinner we left for Trollhättan, about 45 miles away, and visited the magnificent waterfalls there. These are the largest falls in Europe and besides presenting a wonderful scene are used to supply the electric power all over Sweden. To describe the Falls is not in my province, and one must see them for one's self to realise their grandeur. In a conspicuous place is a large stone where previous Kings of Sweden have carved their names.

We also saw the very fine canal, with its many locks, which runs across the country, through charming scenery, into beautiful lakes to Stockholm.

Sunday 21 May

On Sunday we played the first game of the tour against the Örgryte club, a Gothenburg combination, and won rather easily by five goals to nil. Spoors (from a penalty), McLean, Kirkman, Wilson and Robertson scored the goals.

We do not favour Sunday football in England, and I think rightly so, but who can blame them on the Continent, after working six full days, that they regard Sunday as a day of recreation? Surely they need it.

Monday 22 May

The following morning we received a pleasant surprise when Fred Spikesley, who has always been regarded as one of the best wing men who ever kicked a ball for Wednesday and England, drove up to our hotel. He has accepted an invitation to become football coach in Stockholm, but, before commencing his duties, stayed a few days in Gothenburg.

After dinner we all went to Längediag [Långedrag] – a seaside place on the outskirts of Gothenburg, and Fred Spikesley came too.

Tuesday 23 May

On Tuesday we played our second and last game against the Swedish eleven, and won by two goals to one. Davie McLean scored both our goals. The Swedes showed some very good football, and were not easily beaten. The referee in these games was Mr. Charles Bunyan, the coach to the Örgryte Club, who belongs to Chesterfield. Many years ago Bunyan kept goal for Hyde and figured in that memorable match when Preston North End defeated them by 26-0.

At night we were the guests of the President of the Örgryte Club. Many toasts were drunk, and many complimentary things said of the Wednesday team. As a memento of our visit to Sweden we were kindly presented with neat little silver medals.

Wednesday 24 May

We were all up betimes the next morning, Empire Day, and left Gothenburg for Copenhagen at 10 o'clock. Mr. Dickinson could not come with us, owing to his having to be in London at the week-end for the League meeting, and he left by boat for Hull. Mr. Nixon now had charge of the party. We arrived in the Danish capital at half-past five, and at once proceeded to the Hotel Cosmopolite, and had dinner. The rest of the day was spent in sight-seeing. Copenhagen is a beautiful city, and a gay one.

Thursday 25 May

The following morning we again had a look round, and some of us went to the harbour to see the four American man-of-war boats which had recently come to Copenhagen.

At half-past one we commenced our first game against the Danish international eleven. We had the honour of playing before the Crown Prince and Princess of Denmark, [the crown prince's name was Christian and the princess's name was Alexandrine – he was crowned King Christian X the following year] and at the same time opening a magnificent new ground. The playing pitch seemed more suitable for cricket than football, and so did the weather.

There were about 7,000 or 8,000 spectators present – a very good attendance – and they saw a splendidly contested game. McLean soon scored for Wednesday, but the Danes quickly equalised with a brilliant goal. We again took the lead just to lose it again before half-time. In the second half our superior training told, and with Glennon scoring with a fine shot, we won by 3-2.

At the conclusion of the game both captains were presented to the Crown Prince, who congratulated them on the fine football shown.

The Prince then handed 11 silver scarfpins to each for their respective players.

Both teams and officials dined together at night. Toasts were drunk and laudatory speeches made, and altogether we spent a very happy evening. (Readers may be interested to learn that the Danes are coming over in October to play the English Amateurs on the Chelsea ground.)

Friday 26 May

Friday morning was spent in driving around the town sight-seeing. We rested after dinner and at 6.30 started our second game in Copenhagen against a picked eleven. Owing to minor injuries, McSkimming, Brittleton, Paterson and Wilson were unable to play, but we won again, with the same result as in the previous match, by 3-2. McLean, Kirkman, and Glennon were our goal-scorers. Our opponents again showed exceptionally clever football.

Saturday 27 May

Saturday morning was spent in shopping, etc. After lunch we motored to the Juborg [Tuborg] brewery, the largest lager beer brewery in Scandinavia, and were kindly shown round, inspecting every department. All were very much interested in what they saw, and the whole building was a model of cleanliness. We were all presented with a neatly got up book illustrating the different appliances etc. In addition to this we afterwards received a small medal and diploma making us members of the Juborg Society. While on the roof of the building, we saw the Danish King sail out to inspect the American fleet lying in the harbour.

From the brewery we proceeded to Hellerup, a pretty seaside suburb of Copenhagen, passing Queen Alexandra's Danish residence en route. After tea there, we were driven in landaus through the beautiful Forest at Klampenborg. We returned to our hotel after an enjoyable day, and feeling very grateful to the Danish officials for their hospitality.

Sunday 28 May

On Sunday, in very hot weather, we finished our programme by again beating the International team by the same result as in the other two games in Copenhagen 3-2. Kirkman had to stand down owing to an injury, so Lloyd filled the vacancy, otherwise we played the original team. The score stood one each at the interval, but shortly in the second half the Danes took the lead through a very fine goal, and played for a time as winners. Andrew Wilson eventually equalised, and soon after scored the winning goal with a very fine effort.

We played all three games on the fine new ground which belongs to the Corporation of the town. They have another ground in course of construction. Mr. Linthwaite was brought over from Leicester, and refereed in all the matches, giving great satisfaction.

We were again the guests of the Danish officials at dinner in the evening. Little speech making was indulged in, but we had a very pleasant evening together.

Sunday 28 May

Monday was spent by a good number in shopping, and taking a final view of the City.

Tuesday 30 May to Wednesday 31 May

Tuesday morning we were up for breakfast at seven, and then went to the station: bid good-bye to Copenhagen, and steamed out at 8.20 for home and England.

We had had a very enjoyable holiday indeed, and yet I think we all looked forward to getting home again. Re-crossed Denmark by the same route as we came. Though through being in through carriages we were saved a great deal of inconvenience, as our coach was shunted on to the ferries. We arrived at Esbjerg harbour about 4.30, and immediately went on board the *Primula*. Sailed at six – Scandinavian time – or five English time. The weather was brilliantly fine, the sea calm, so few thought of mal de mer. We had a delightful passage, and a great deal of time was spent on deck, looking out for passing ships – and England. There was a full attendance at meals, and no one was sick.

Wednesday 31 May to Thursday 1 June

We arrived at Parkeston Quay, Harwich, about 20 minutes to five Wednesday evening, too late to get a train back to Sheffield. We stayed the night at the fine hotel belonging to the Great Eastern Railway Co. and left at seven o'clock Thursday morning.

Sheffield was reached at 12.25, all feeling pleased after such a fine time, and glad to be back again. (By now the players have separated and gone to their respective homes).

It was no mean feat to return to Sheffield with a 100 per cent record from those tour matches. The Danish national side were no slouches having finished runners-up to Great Britain in the football tournament at the Olympic Games in London in 1908. The Danes finished runners-up again to the British team in the 1912 Olympics in Stockholm. From 1914 to 1919 the Danish team were ranked number one in the world based on the relative skill levels of individual players.

It must have been a very exciting trip for the players, the majority of whom would not have left British shores in their lives. By today's standards this would have been a gruelling programme for the modern player with five matches scheduled in a seven-day period. With no other goalkeeper in the party it would have been catastrophic if Teddy Davison had succumbed to injury.

Sadly Wednesday's anonymous correspondent did not provide us with team line-ups for any of the matches and unfortunately omitted the scorers of two of the goals against the Danish XI but the report is a wonderful account of a ground-breaking tour for the club.

MATCHES PLAYED IN SWEDEN AND DENMARK

Sunday 21 May v Orgryte (Gothenburg)
5-0 (Spoors [pen], McLean, Kirkman, Wilson, Robertson)

Tuesday 23 May v Swedish Select XI
2-1 (McLean 2)

Thursday 25 May v Denmark XI
3-2 (McLean, ?, Glennon)

Friday 26 May v Copenhagen Select XI
3-2 (McLean, Kirkman, Glennon)

Sunday 28 May v Denmark XI
3-2 (?, Wilson 2)

10

1911/12 – BEST OUTSIDE-LEFT IN BRITAIN

WEDNESDAY had high hopes at the start of the new season and 'Athleo' in the *Green 'Un* assessed all the signed players and was generally optimistic about their chances, although he seemed disappointed that there had been no 'sensational captures'. The success of the continental tour had moved Scandinavian onlookers to describe Wednesday as 'the best combined set of players that they had seen' and 'Athleo' felt that they had 'the build of a fine team'.

Owlerton was looking quite a picture with the stands having a fresh coat of paint and the playing surface in excellent condition. Wednesday listed 29 players for the start of the league campaign, eight of whom were Scots.

As in the previous season Wednesday made an indifferent start to the new league campaign. Preston North End were the visitors for the opening match on 2 September 1911 and left Sheffield with both points thanks to a second-half goal from inside-left Green.

The team may have struggled but George was in outstanding form in the match, creating many chances for his team-mates who all seemed to be unable to convert them into goals. The *Green 'Un* on 9 September was quick to recognise George's outstanding performance, 'Isn't Robertson a daisy? You can hear a sigh of satisfaction go up all round the Owlerton ground when the left-winger gets the ball. He had a tough nut to crack in Holdsworth (the Preston full-back) last week, and the trick by which he beat him suggested a combination of ballet-dancing and Maskelyne and Cooke.' Maskelyne and Cooke were famous late Victorian stage magicians.

Wednesday's next fixture took them to London on the following Monday where they went down tamely 3-1 to Tottenham at White Hart Lane with Andrew Wilson scoring his side's first goal of the season.

Wednesday earned their first point from a 2-2 draw with Bury at Gigg Lane on 9 September with all the goals coming in an exciting first half. Wednesday's marksmen were Sam Kirkman and David McLean who succeeded in beating Tom McDonald, George's former goalkeeping team-mate from his Motherwell days.

Wednesday's dismal home form continued when they suffered a 2-0 defeat to Middlesbrough the following Saturday although George was on the top of his game, 'Then brilliant work by Robertson raised Wednesday's drooping spirits. The home left-winger went through twice in great style, and his second centre passed right in front of goal, only a touch being needed to put Wednesday on level terms.'

Despite George's fine play Wednesday lacked a cutting edge in front of goal, 'Robertson was again the star of the line, and it must be galling for him to see all his fine work thrown away on colleagues who cannot accept the centres he puts across.' Alarmingly, this defeat saw Wednesday slip to the bottom of the table.

Notts County were the next team to take advantage of the struggling Wednesday outfit. Paterson made way for Glennon at inside-right in an effort to revitalise the forward line but the change made little difference as Wednesday slumped to a 1-0 defeat at Meadow Lane.

With only a single point to their name from their first five games the pre-season optimism seemed totally misplaced. Despite his team's poor results George's form was still impressive. The *Green 'Un*'s reporter was still singing his praises even after the loss to County on 23 September, 'Robertson might have got a cap last year had he not suffered from too much Charles Thomson. He's started in International form this term.'

Charlie Thomson was Sunderland's rugged Scottish centre-half and captain, who was notoriously difficult to get past. The reporter was not slow to compare George with one of Wednesday and England's great left-wingers, 'Fred Spiksley was at Owlerton last Saturday. Wonder what he thought of Robertson, the best outside left Wednesday have had since Fred himself ceased to scintillate.'

It wasn't until the sixth game of the season that Wednesday managed to record their first win, a 4-0 thrashing of Spurs at Owlerton on 30 September with the goals coming from Laurie Burkinshaw, Teddy Glennon, David McLean and Andrew Wilson.

If Wednesday fans thought their team were back on the rails then they were to be disappointed as they went down 3-1 away to champions Manchester United on 7 October with McLean on target for the Sheffielders.

A valuable point was earned in a 2-2 draw at home to a Liverpool side who were also struggling near the foot of the table. All the goals came in the second half with Glennon and Wilson on the scoresheet for the home side.

At this point in the season Wednesday's unpredictable results had them 19th and deep in relegation trouble. It was not until the ninth game of the league campaign that Wednesday managed their second victory, a hard-earned 3-2 win over Aston Villa at Villa Park on 21 October when Tom Brittleton, Glennon and Sam Kirkman were the second-half marksmen after Villa had led 1-0 at the interval.

With only one home win to their credit, Wednesday's form at Owlerton was giving cause for concern. Newcastle United were the next side to exploit that weakness with a 2-1 victory on 28 October. Wednesday's goal came from McLean who scored from the penalty spot in the second half.

Wilson's goal gave Wednesday a first-half lead in the Steel City derby game at Bramall Lane on 4 November but United's centre-forward Kitchen levelled the scores after the break and the match finished 1-1.

George's second-half goal, his first of the season, proved to be the winner in a vital 1-0 home success over Oldham Athletic on 11 November and helped lift Wednesday clear of the relegation places. That situation was only temporary as a second-half slump saw Wednesday lose 4-2 the following week away to Bolton Wanderers. The game was delicately poised at 2-2 at half-time with Kirkman and Wilson the Wednesday scorers but the home side dominated the second half, putting two more goals past Teddy Davison.

On 25 November George scored Wednesday's fourth goal, adding to earlier counters from Kirkman and McLean, who bagged a brace, in a satisfying 4-2 home win over Yorkshire rivals Bradford City. George's goal came early in the second half with Wednesday already 2-0 ahead. 'Following brilliant work by the home left wing Kirkman headed against the post and the rebound came to Robertson who scored,' wrote the *Green 'Un*.

George was having a fine match and laid on Wednesday's fourth goal after intense pressure from the determined home forwards, 'However, the home team would not be denied, and a great run and centre by Robertson was picked up in brilliant style by McLean, who crashed the ball into the net.'

Wednesday relaxed a little too much and allowed the FA Cup holders back into the match and they were able to pull back two soft goals.

For the first time in the season Wednesday were able to record back-to-back victories when Kirkman and McLean each scored in the first half to secure a good 2-0 away win against Arsenal on 2 December. McLean had clearly rediscovered his goalscoring touch as Wednesday recorded their third successive win with a 3-0 victory over Manchester City at Owlerton the following Saturday.

George always seemed to be able to turn on the style against City and he laid on the first two goals. The second in particular was typical of his wing wizardry, 'Glennon tricked Eadie and gave Robertson a beautiful pass. The winger went on and simply bewildered Henry, finishing with a centre which Glennon drove into the net. The crowd, now 12,000 strong greeted this further success very enthusiastically.'

After a sluggish start, the in-form McLean's brace of goals against City had pushed him into contention to top the First Division's list of scorers. Wednesday were beginning to find their best form now and the *Green 'Un* on 16 December was quick to praise the contribution of their Scottish forwards with some advice for the international selectors, 'McLean, Wilson and Robertson make up an Anglo-Scottish brigade which cannot be bettered at present.'

In the same piece the paper reported one Manchester critic's enthusiastic views on George. 'Best outside-left in Britain,' he murmured as George made circles round Henry.

Everton burst the Wednesday bubble at Goodison Park with a narrow 1-0 win on 16 December, the only goal of the game coming in the first half from Jefferis.

George had an outstanding match when Wednesday bounced back and put four goals past West Bromwich Albion at Owlerton on 23 December. His dazzling runs were a feature of the game and his goal, after 11 minutes, was quite spectacular, 'Robertson was standing on the halfway-line while Albion were pressing. The ball was slung out to him, and taking matters very coolly he ran right in, having outpaced the field, and from eighteen yards out he took careful aim and beat Pearson with a splendid drive which entered the further corner of the net.'

George suffered the curse of all pacey wingers, 'Robertson's speed was confusing not only the visiting backs, but the referee as well at this period, and twice in quick succession he was whistled offside when he had started from a legal position.'

Late on the Albion keeper made three great stops from the flying winger. The *Green 'Un*'s reporter had no doubt who the man of the match was, 'Wednesday's outside-left was still the leading figure in the game, and the visiting defenders grew very anxious whenever he got in close proximity to the ball.'

McLean, with another brace, and Glennon were Wednesday's other scorers as they cruised to a 4-1 win to take them to 13th, the highest place in the First Division they had attained this season.

Wednesday's next fixture took them across the Pennines for a Christmas Day match with Blackburn Rovers at Ewood Park. Neither side were in the mood to give away presents and the game finished goalless so, in the true spirit of Christmas, the points were shared.

Wednesday's resurgence was certainly bringing back the fans. The *Green 'Un* reported that there were 33,000 in Owlerton for the Sunderland match with around 10,000 stranded in the city centre waiting for cars which did not arrive. George's performance in the sensational 8-0 home win over Sunderland rates as one of the finest of his career.

Richard Sparling in his book, *The Romance of the Wednesday*, describes one of Wednesday's truly historic results:

> 'Boxing Day, 1911 will long be remembered by followers of Wednesday by reason of their 8-0 triumph over Sunderland at Owlerton. Such an event had not occurred in First Division football for three years. There was nothing to indicate such a sensation, for before the game the records of the two clubs were identical. However, as soon as the match began it was obvious that the home forwards were in great fettle. The goals were scored as follows:- After 4½mins. Kirkman; after 25 mins. Kirkman; after 30 mins. McLean; after 35 mins. Glennon; after 37 mins. McLean; after 40 mins. Glennon; after 43 mins. McLean; after 55 mins. McLean.
>
> 'Thomson the Sunderland pivot, having strained himself, was off the field very early, and retired altogether after 25 minutes. Wednesday, against the ten men, played wonderful football, and scored six goals in 18 minutes. They eased up in the second half, but they were always masters, and in any circumstances they would have won, so brilliantly did they play.
>
> 'Ten minutes from the finish, having had a magnificent shot saved by Scott (in goal), Robertson, who could not stop himself, collided with the goalkeeper, who had to be carried off. Scott was unconscious for some time in the dressing-room and had to spend the night in Sheffield Royal Infirmary. Holley went into the goal.
>
> 'The Wednesday players on that Boxing Day were:- Davison; Worrall and Spoors; Brittleton, Weir and Campbell; Kirkman, Glennon, McLean, Wilson and Robertson.'

Keith Farnsworth in his *Complete Record* also places this among his matches to remember and suggests that George's contribution to the game was immense. He wrote, 'George Robertson's name does not appear on the scoresheet, but the ex-Motherwell winger was as much of a hero as his fellow Scot, McLean. Robertson made four of Wednesday's goals; and five minutes from the end it was Robertson's determination which led to the collision which left the visiting goalkeeper dazed and unable to complete the match.'

The *Green 'Un* reported that George's late accidental clash with goalkeeper Scott caused him no little concern, 'Robertson was terribly distressed about Scott's accident, but the Scottish International's reputation as a gentlemanly player absolves him from all blame in the matter.'

George's tremendous form continued but the *Green 'Un* reminded George that he wouldn't have such an easy time if he was selected to play for Scotland against England, 'Robertson was in International form against West Bromwich and Sunderland, but he couldn't treat Crompton [Bob Crompton – Blackburn's English international full-back] as he served Smith, of West Bromwich, and Forster, of Sunderland.'

Wednesday's criss-crossing of the Pennines continued with another trip to Lancashire where Preston North End were defeated 3-2 at Deepdale. Another double from McLean and a goal from fellow Scot Wilson gave Wednesday a narrow but deserved victory. The win took them up to eighth in the table.

The much-awaited return fixture with Sunderland at Roker Park came on 1 January 1912. After the devastating crushing of the Wearsiders at Owlerton, Wednesday fans were, perhaps, hoping for another feast of goals but it was not to be. Sunderland were anxious to restore their dented pride and the Sheffielders could not match their stunning home form and the match finished goalless. George missed this game, with defender Findlay Weir unusually deputising on the left wing. After their good recent run Wednesday found themselves sixth in the table, their highest position for some time, and were beginning to be thought of as possible title contenders.

Wednesday were drawn away to Middlesbrough in the FA Cup first round on 13 January.

Coincidentally their next league match pitched them up against the same opposition at the same venue seven days later. The Owlerton management team decided to take the players away to prepare meticulously for both matches at the nearby resort of Saltburn. Some Sheffield City Libraries photographs of Wednesday players seeing the sights around Saltburn indicate that the squad was at the Alexandra Hotel from 2 January to 18 January.

A creditable 0-0 draw was achieved in a hard-fought match in the FA Cup tie at Ayresome Park and the replay was quickly scheduled for Thursday 25 January at Owlerton, five days after the sides were due to meet in the league fixture. On Saturday 20 January, Wednesday found themselves a goal behind at half-time after Eyre had given 'Boro the lead but a second-half goal from Andrew Wilson restored parity and the match finished level at 1-1.

Back in Sheffield, Wednesday were now concentrating on the cup replay and eagerly anticipating advancing to the second round of the competition. Those Wednesday fans who had been dreaming, fancifully, of perhaps achieving a league and cup double had their hopes dashed when Middlesbrough surprised them in the replay at Owlerton in front of a 30,000 crowd, winning 2-1.

The *Green 'Un* thought George was in 'sparkling form' in the replay, sending 'across sufficient centres to have won the match had Wednesday been playing against a side with an ordinary defence'. The prolific David McLean scored Wednesday's goal in the first half.

Two days later, what proved to be George's final goal of the season accompanied a McLean double when Wednesday were 3-0 winners over Notts County at Owlerton. Wednesday were 1-0 ahead at the break and the *Green 'Un* reported that the second period began in sensational fashion, 'After a little bit of brisk work in front of Worrall, Robertson started on a long run in which he cleverly evaded his men, swerved in for goal, and beat Iremonger with a lovely cross drive which sent the ball home just inside the post.'

Two weeks later, on 10 February, Wednesday saw off league champions Manchester United 3-0 at Owlerton with goals from Glennon, McLean and Wilson and were now in fifth place and poised to mount a serious title challenge.

The *Green 'Un* had words of advice for the Scotland selectors early in the New Year, 'Robertson will take a lot of beating when Scotland looks around for a left-winger.' The selectors must have been paying attention as the paper was delighted, on 17 February, to congratulate 'three Wednesdayites who have been chosen to play for the Anglo-Scots in the International trial match. Between them McLean, Wilson and Robertson ought to succeed in making things hum.'

That same day Wednesday faced Liverpool at Anfield and came away with a share of the points in a 1-1 draw. Both sides scored in the first half with Sam Kirkman getting the Wednesday goal.

Wednesday suddenly found themselves in fourth place as the title race hotted up. The *Green 'Un* heaped praise on the work ethic of the Wednesday left-wing pairing during the match against Liverpool, 'You couldn't find two better preachers of the gospel of work than Wednesday's left wing. Both Wilson and Robertson were among the defenders when Liverpool attacked most hotly.'

George was singled out for praise by Liverpool's full-back Longworth who voted him one of the most difficult men to tackle that he had faced. 'Robertson's close dribbling and push stroke repeatedly puzzled Liverpool's dashing defender,' wrote the newspaper.

George missed Wednesday's 2-0 win at Newcastle on 2 March while on international duty against Wales in Edinburgh when his stand-in Percy Wright was on target along with Teddy Glennon. The *Green 'Un* hadn't forgotten George though, carrying a photo of him in his first cap and stating that he got a new one today along with the message 'hope "Geordie" has shone at his brightest today'. Apparently Wednesday gave George the choice of playing for club or country and 'he thought he ought to take his cap. Most of his club colleagues agreed with him'.

The selectors were obviously unimpressed with George's international debut at Rugby Park in 1910 and it was to be another two years before his outstanding performances for Wednesday earned him a second chance in the Scottish team. Again the match was against Wales, this time at Tynecastle Park in Edinburgh and played before 31,000 spectators. Scotland were once again winners by a single goal, this time from Quinn in the 87th minute. George was again not at his best and he did not feature in the other two matches in the Home International Championship against Ireland and England.

The *Daily Record* was critical of the Scots forwards' performance, 'Quinn opened the game well, but he got few chances at close quarters. He was the best of the line. Sinclair did well, but he seemed to miss Walker, who, while earnest and at times clever on the ball, never seemed the man he was as an inside support. Robertson was not a striking success, and played below his Sheffield best.'

Elsewhere in the same paper, the SFA officials remarked that some changes would be necessary for the team to meet England, 'Mr Tom Gray, the secretary of St. Bernard's F.C., and a member of the S.F.A. Council, said he considered the two Scottish backs did extra well. At half Hay was bad in his placing, but Thomson did all right. With the exception of Robertson the forwards were poor, although for Quinn it must be said he worked extremely hard and made the most of the best opportunity he got.'

Scotland's team was James Brownlie (Third Lanark), Alex McNair (Celtic), John Walker (Swindon Town), Robert Mercer (Hearts), Charles Thomson (Sunderland) captain, James Hay (Newcastle United), George Sinclair (Hearts), James McMenemy (Celtic), James Quinn (Celtic), Robert Walker (Hearts), George Robertson (Sheffield Wednesday).

The second Steel City derby of the season took place at Owlerton on 9 March and once again finished all square at 1-1. Teddy Glennon's goal gave Wednesday a share of the points against city rivals United but that single point was enough to push them up into second place with only nine games remaining.

As news broke of Amundsen's triumph in the race to the South Pole, George, David McLean and Andrew Wilson travelled to Glasgow to take part in the Home Scots v Anglo Scots international trial match at Firhill. After the game local dignitaries and the press were struggling to reach a consensus in selecting a Scottish team to face England but the *Daily Record* felt that the travel-weary Wednesday players were not quite at their best.

George's old director from his Motherwell days, Sergeant Major Quirk, reckoned that the match was well contested and felt that two of the Wednesday players merited selection, 'I thought a good deal of the left wingers Wilson and Robertson. The Selectors saw nothing on the field to compare with them as a wing.'

Clyde and Celtic directors were like-minded as was influential senior *Daily Record* football reporter 'Bedouin'. The Home Scots were soundly beaten by the Anglos and McLean and Wilson each bagged a brace of goals but George did not catch the eye quite as much as his Wednesday colleagues.

In Glasgow the *Evening Times* reporter at the match praised Morton goalkeeper Bradford for an outstanding display despite conceding four goals. He was enthusiastic about the Wednesday players' contribution to the match, 'A spell of English football has taught McLean and Wilson the wisdom of the first time shot, and the pair gave such an exhibition as put them right in the running for the highest honours.

'As clubmates, they revealed excellent combination all through, and if Robertson did not entirely fulfil his share of the contract it was mainly due to the artfulness of McNair [Celtic's international right-back], who proved once more that he has no rival in the rounding-up business provided he is not asked to give away many yards.

'What we require are forwards who can keep open order, pass on the run and shoot early and often, and all these things the Sheffield trio did and did well.'

Sadly none of the Wednesday players were chosen for the international against Ireland in Belfast on 16 March but McLean and Wilson were selected to play against England at Hampden on 23 March.

Regrettably, after the drawn match in the Sheffield derby, Wednesday's form dipped a little, results became unpredictable and their slim title hopes began to fade. A 1-0 defeat away to lowly Oldham Athletic was disappointing but it was not enough to knock Wednesday from second place. A 2-1 win over bottom club Bury at Owlerton kept them very much in the title race when Teddy Glennon was the hero with a first-half double. On 23 March Wednesday were minus stalwarts McLean and Wilson (on international duty for Scotland against England in front of 127,000 fans at Hampden) and went down 1-0 at home to a strong-going Bolton side. This reverse was followed by a crushing 5-1 defeat by Bradford City at Valley Parade.

Despite Wednesday being well beaten, George had a good game although he was obviously seen as a threat and 'was rather roughly used'. He had to leave the field for a time for treatment but, fortunately, he was able to return and was still moving well and, 'even on the shocking ground showed great speed'. Wednesday were outclassed on the day and found themselves 3-1 down at the interval, their goal coming from Andrew Wilson although some authorities credit it as an own goal by City's left-half McDonald.

The team bounced back confidently the next week, disposing of Woolwich Arsenal 3-0 at Owlerton, and George was involved in the first goal after 15 minutes, 'The goal was the outcome of the Wilson-Robertson combination. Wilson made the opening in the first place, giving to Robertson, who shot. Roose, who was not clearing in the style which made him famous, again partially saved, and Wilson, rushing up, drove the ball into the net.'

Wednesday led 2-0 at the break with their other goal coming from Tom Brittleton. Glennon completed the scoring in the second half. George had another excellent game but let himself down late on by missing a 'sitter'. Although Wednesday were in fifth spot they still had a remote chance of capturing the title.

McLean's first-half goal earned his side a draw against front-runners Blackburn Rovers at Owlerton on Monday 8 April but Wednesday's tilt at the title was effectively over when this was followed by a shock 4-0 loss to Manchester City at Hyde Road on Saturday 13 April. Title contenders Everton inflicted another defeat, 3-1, in Wednesday's last home game of the season when Wilson was the scorer for the Sheffield side. This latest defeat pushed Wednesday down the table to sixth place and came in the week that the world began to learn of the enormity of the loss of life in the sinking of the *Titanic*.

The final game of the season gave Wednesday a chance to redeem themselves when they took on West Bromwich Albion at The Hawthorns. The match was a crucial one for the Sheffield side who were desperate to get back into the top five places which earned bonus payments from the Football League.

Wednesday had an early shock when West Brom had the ball in the net in the first minute only for the goal to be disallowed 'amidst a hostile demonstration' by the home fans. George was quickly into his stride, 'Robertson appeared to be in good form, and one great run by the Scot was cheered by the crowd. The winger put in a lovely centre, which was missed by the inside men.'

The *Green 'Un* was delighted to note that the team had returned to the form 'which made them hot candidates for the Championship at one time'. George 'was in the crowd's good graces very much, while the inside men were always doing something useful'. Wednesday finally won 5-1, their goals coming from a David McLean hat-trick and a double from Sam Kirkman. This win was enough to secure the vital fifth place, pipping Aston Villa on goal average.

Wednesday had a much more settled side in 1911/12, using only 18 players over the length of the season. Their points tally was reduced to 41, one less than the previous season, and they finished eight behind the eventual champions, Blackburn Rovers. Their disappointing results in the early part of the season and inconsistent form in the run-in probably cost them a chance of the championship.

McLean's goals were a vital component in Wednesday's good run. The Scot finished joint leading scorer with Hampton of Aston Villa and Holley of Sunderland with 25 goals.

George played in 36 of the 38 league games, missing one through injury and one when he gained his second Scottish cap, but he scored only four goals.

Again Wednesday were disappointing in the FA Cup. They held Middlesbrough to a goalless draw at Ayresome Park on 13 January but were bundled out 2-1 in the replay at Owlerton two weeks later, with McLean getting their only goal.

ENGLISH FIRST DIVISION 1911/12

	Pl	*W*	*D*	*L*	*F*	*A*	*Pts*
1 Blackburn Rovers	38	20	9	9	60	43	49
2 Everton	38	20	6	12	46	42	46
3 Newcastle United	38	18	8	12	64	50	44
4 Bolton Wanderers	38	20	3	15	54	43	43
5 The Wednesday	38	16	9	13	69	49	41
6 Aston Villa	38	17	7	14	76	63	41
7 Middlesbrough	38	16	8	14	56	45	40
8 Sunderland	38	14	11	13	58	51	39
9 West Bromwich Albion	38	15	9	14	43	47	39
10 Woolwich Arsenal	38	15	8	15	55	59	38
11 Bradford City	38	15	8	15	46	50	38
12 Tottenham Hotspur	38	14	9	15	53	53	37
13 Manchester United	38	13	11	14	45	60	37
14 Sheffield United	38	13	10	15	63	56	36
15 Manchester City	38	13	9	16	56	58	35
16 Notts County	38	14	7	17	46	63	35
17 Liverpool	38	12	10	16	49	55	34
18 Oldham Athletic	38	12	10	16	46	54	34
19 Preston North End	38	13	7	18	40	57	33
20 Bury	38	6	9	23	32	59	21

THE WEDNESDAY'S APPEARANCES AND GOALS 1911/12

	League		*FA Cup*	
	Apps	*Goals*	*Apps*	*Goals*
Brittleton, J.T.	29	2	2	0
Burkinshaw, L.	4	1	0	0
Campbell, J.	38	0	2	0
Davison, J.E.	38	0	2	0
Glennon, J.E.	32	13	2	0
Kirkman, S.	34	11	2	0
Lloyd, W.	6	0	0	0
McLean, D.P.	37	25	2	1
McSkimming, R.S.	25	0	0	0
O'Connell, P.J.	4	0	2	0
Paterson, M.	7	0	0	0
Robertson, G.C.	36	4	2	0
Spoors, J.	37	0	2	0
Warren, P.	2	0	0	0
Weir, W.F.	24	0	0	0
Wilson, A. McC.	37	12	2	0
Worrall, J.E.	26	0	2	0
Wright, P.L.	2	1	0	0

11

1912/13 – AN OWL ON THE WING

WEDNESDAY'S results and their top-five finish in 1911/12 showed that the team had the quality to challenge for the league title if they could manage to achieve just a little more consistency. The *Green 'Un* on 24 August assessed the current playing staff and updated readers on the arrivals and departures. 'Athleo' was concerned about cover in the full-back positions and the loss of experienced half-backs O'Connell (who moved to Hull City) and Weir who was still without a club. He noted that Paterson had returned to Scotland but that Campbell had remained and had now become one of the finest left-halves in England. 'Athleo' was not convinced that the team had what it takes to become title contenders but fancied that they may be a good bet for the FA Cup.

After the disappointing start to the last two seasons, Wednesday got off to a flyer in 1912/13, dropping only a single point in their opening five matches. They signalled their title aspirations in the opening game by defeating defending champions Blackburn Rovers 2-1 at Owlerton through David McLean's first-half brace.

Against Tottenham Hotspur at White Hart Lane on 7 September, defences were very much on top in the first half and the teams turned around with the scoresheet blank. The 35,000 fans were treated to a stirring second half with Wednesday coming out on top thanks to a 4-2 victory. Teddy Glennon gave Wednesday the lead three minutes after the restart from Sam Kirkman's pass but Middlemiss beat an unsighted Teddy Davidson to equalise for Spurs.

George put Wednesday back in front, 'It was a strong attack on the right which led to the trouble, and Glennon almost got the point with a shot which hit the bar. The ball dropped back to Robertson who banged it in the net without any formality.'

Sixteen minutes into the second period Tattersall drew the home side level again but six minutes later Glennon restored Wednesday's lead in a goalmouth scramble, 'Tottenham tired towards the finish, and a quick passing run by Robertson, McLean, and Kirkman saw the last-named score four minutes before the end.' They might have had a fifth goal but McLean's shot hit the upright a minute from time.

Wednesday led 2-0 at the interval when a McLean double and another goal from Kirkman gave them a satisfying 3-1 victory at Owlerton over the previous season's FA Cup conquerors, Middlesbrough. Three wins in a row had Wednesday second in the league table and the marked improvement on the start to the previous two seasons now saw them viewed as serious challengers for the championship.

Notts County were Wednesday's next victims as their impressive start to the season continued with a 2-1 win over the Magpies at Meadow Lane on 21 September. McLean was the Sheffielders' hero again, scoring his third double of the season. Wednesday slipped down to third place in the table after this match but only on goal average.

The winning run came to an end at Owlerton when they were held to a 3-3 draw by Manchester United on 28 September. The home side were 1-0 down at the break but a second-half penalty from McLean and goals from Kirkman and Wilson gave them a share of the points. McLean took his fine scoring form to an impressive seven goals in his first five games. Despite dropping a point to United, Wednesday still remained third in the table.

The following week, the title-chasing hopefuls suffered one of the most astonishing defeats in the club's history. Wednesday fielded a strong team but McLean and Glennon were missing from the line-up when they travelled to Villa Park, Birmingham. Aston Villa were one of Wednesday's principal rivals for top spot in the table and had won four and drawn one of their opening seven fixtures. A close-fought match was anticipated but the final scoreline, 10-0 to Villa, sent shockwaves around the league.

According to Richard Sparling, in his book *The Romance of the Wednesday*, the visitors apparently attacked more often than Villa but the home side seemed to score every time they bore down on Davison's goal. It was all downhill for Wednesday when Halse opened the scoring after only four minutes and by half-time they were trailing 6-0.

Sparling recalls that the Wednesday players could not believe the strength and accuracy of the Villans' shooting. Four more goals followed in the second period and English international centre-forward Harry Hampton helped himself to five of the total. This defeat brought Wednesday crashing back down to earth, an event which brought about significant changes for the club and indirectly shaped its future identity.

The Sheffield Wednesday official website history credits George with providing the club with their current nickname of 'The Owls'. It writes, 'Two other developments of this era, both taking place off the pitch rather than on it, were the adoption of an Owl as the club mascot [although the *Green 'Un* had for several years portrayed the club as the Owl of Owlerton] and the initial development of Owlerton (as it was still known) into a venue of national repute and prestige.

'Doubtless both events seemed merely incidental at the time but they have since irrevocably shaped The Wednesday's identity, remaining synonymous with the club until the present day. Most football fans, if asked to describe Sheffield Wednesday Football Club even now, will be quick to list "blue and white stripes", "The Owls" and "marvellous stadium" among their first responses.

'In the first instance, it was a player of the time – George Robertson – who presented the club with a mascot in the shape of an owl, in homage to The Wednesday's Owlerton home. For a fleeting period prior to that, the team's mascot had been The Wednesday Monkey [presented by English McConnell], which occasionally took to the field in a blue-and-white costume, but until this point the club's nickname had always been 'The Blades'; a reflection of Sheffield's world dominance over the steel manufacturing industry (Sheffield United, incidentally, followed a similar route by calling themselves 'The Cutlers' – but were quick to assume Wednesday's former alias once it had been discarded).'

Wednesday restored a little of their damaged pride on 12 October when Liverpool were beaten 1-0 at Owlerton. Percy Wright, standing in for the injured Glennon, got the solitary goal. Unfortunately that pride received another dent when Smith, Barber and a Worrall own goal gave Bolton Wanderers an easy 3-0 win at Burnden Park to push Wednesday down the table into seventh place.

An injury sustained in the Bolton match meant that George missed the derby game with Sheffield United at Owlerton on 26 October. Wright took over George's position on the left wing and Glennon, restored to the side after a three-game absence, scored what proved to be the winner in the first half.

Wednesday travelled to Newcastle on 2 November with Wright once again deputising for George on the left wing. A Higgins second-half strike sent the visitors home pointless as the early-season deluge of goals from McLean and company appeared to have dried up.

George returned to the Wednesday side, who seemed to have recaptured their sparkle, when Oldham Athletic were thumped 5-0 at Owlerton on 9 November. The goals came from Glennon, Kirkman with a double, and McLean, also with a pair, one of these being from the penalty spot.

Two goals in each half then earned Wednesday two valuable away points when Chelsea were defeated 4-0 at Stamford Bridge. Glennon with a brace, Wilson and McLean were the scorers.

A 2-0 home victory over Woolwich Arsenal, with goals either side of the interval from the Scots pair McLean and Wilson, was enough to elevate Wednesday to third place in the league. The *Green 'Un* was happy to report that George had returned to his best form in the victory over the Londoners. The arrival of George's owl (a wooden one according to Messrs Brodie and Dickinson) under the North Stand seemed to have coincided with a return to form in Wednesday's home matches. Apparently Wednesday officials were initially not keen on a change of nickname but after George's owl had taken its place under the stand and Wednesday won four games out of four, scored nine goals and conceded none, the nickname The Owls was hatched.

The last match of November saw Wednesday make the short trip to Valley Parade to take on Bradford City whose previous results had been somewhat unpredictable since their FA Cup win in 1911. The match finished in a disappointing goalless draw and Wednesday promptly slipped back down to fourth in the table.

Manchester City were enjoying their best run in the First Division since their promotion back into the top flight in 1910 and both sides were sitting on the 21-point mark when they met at Owlerton on 7 December. Teddy Davison had a relatively quiet afternoon as the Owls went all out for the win with the forwards, particularly McLean, giving a masterful display.

Despite constant pressure the match was goalless at half-time but six minutes after the break Andrew Wilson gathered a pass from McLean and got the goal that their fine play merited. George played well and enjoyed several fine runs, 'In one great dash against Henry, who, however, stopped him by giving him a very hard charge, and one could see Wednesday's left-winger feeling his ribs as he picked himself up.'

The *Green 'Un* reckoned he 'showed a more complete return to his old form than in any previous match, his speed being quite as marked as it was when he first came to Sheffield, while his command of the ball was delightful'. After 90 minutes Wilson's goal still separated the sides and the Owls leapfrogged City into second place.

Wednesday continued their winning ways when McLean's second-half goal at The Hawthorns earned his side a share of the points against West Bromwich Albion. McLean's 13th of the season on 21 December ensured that Wednesday and Everton went in level at half-time but a second-half goal from the Toffees silenced the Owlerton crowd as their favourites slumped to a 2-1 defeat and dropped back down to third in the table with the busy Christmas fixtures looming.

The Owls were due to play Sunderland at Owlerton on the morning of Christmas Day 1912. The year before, according to the *Green 'Un*, 'On Boxing Day it was Robertson who had most to do with Sunderland's [8-0] record defeat, and though he was not so good on Christmas Day, he scored one goal and gave McLean the opening from which the game should have been won.'

George's goal came after only 30 seconds and the 40,000 fans of both sides must surely have cast their minds back to Wednesday's spectacular win and thought, 'Could it happen again?' With Wednesday 1-0 to the good George laid on a great chance for McLean but the Owls' scoring machine missed the open goal and a chance to wrap up the points.

Before the game Sunderland's veteran centre-half and Scottish captain Charlie Thomson 'greeted Brittleton, McLean, Wilson and Robertson very cordially, and then proceeded to smash up any ideas they may have had about winning'. Sunderland's defence stood like a rock for the rest of the match and goals either side of the interval from Holley and Mordue earned their side both points and pushed the Owls down to fifth place. At the end of the match the Owls fans rated Sunderland the best team to visit Owlerton that season.

Given the result at Owlerton, there must have been an air of trepidation among the Wednesday players when they made the trip to Sunderland on Boxing Day for the return fixture. Happily the Owls were able to turn the tables with first-half goals from McLean and Kirkman giving them a deserved 2-0 win at Roker Park to reclaim third position in the title race.

During that congested festive period George managed to score against Tottenham again, this time at Owlerton on Saturday 28 December, in a 2-1 win. His goal, along with another from Laurie Burkinshaw, overturned a 1-0 half-time deficit and moved Wednesday up to second.

Three days later George was on top form in Wednesday's 3-3 draw with Derby County on 1 January 1913. Keith Farnsworth lists that New Year's Day match with Derby among his matches to remember. Before a crowd of 40,000, Derby, led by their legendary England striker Steve Bloomer, took the lead in the ninth minute with a goal by Barnes. Two further goals by Leonard left Wednesday 3-0 in arrears after 69 minutes and it could easily have been 4-0 as another was chalked off for offside.

But the *Green 'Un* wrote, 'Wednesday's revival began after 75 minutes when Robertson set up a goal for McLean, but it was not until six minutes from the end that McLean got the second following astute play by Campbell. A minute later, however, Robertson produced another flash of brilliance, and from his left-wing run and cross Sam Kirkman steered in a dramatic equaliser.' The crucial point gained from this remarkable comeback was enough to put Wednesday on top of the First Division.

Middlesbrough were beaten 2-0 at Ayresome Park on 4 January to keep the Owls ahead of the chasing pack in the title race. George added another goal to his tally in a goalmouth scramble to put the Owls ahead after ten minutes. Elliott had a chance to level the scores from the penalty spot but shot wide. The free-scoring McLean got the Owls' second and decisive goal after the break.

The weather intervened to postpone a number of league matches so Wednesday's attention then focussed on the FA Cup first round match on Thursday 16 January when they hosted Grimsby Town in front of 26,442 fans on a snow-covered Owlerton pitch. The Second Division side were still in contention at half-time and were only 2-1 down but three second-half Wednesday goals extinguished any hopes they had of a comeback. McLean stole the show with four on the day while Tom Brittleton, with a rare strike, was also on the mark for the Owls.

George missed Wednesday's 3-1 win over Notts County at Owlerton on 18 January after sustaining an injury against Grimsby. McLean and Wilson put the Owls 2-0 up at the break and Glennon completed the scoring in the second half to keep them at the top of the league table.

However, George returned to take his place in the team for the trip to Manchester United on 25 January. Wednesday went 2-0 down at Old Trafford to two goals early in the first half. The Owls hit back and George 'tested Beale with a great shot, which the keeper put behind for a corner'. Later, 'Wilson gave Robertson a glorious opening. The winger made a fine shot which looked a goal all over, but at the finish the light ball rose sharply and just cleared the bar.'

George was once again 'playing very finely and some of his centres should have borne fruit' but, in the absence of the free-scoring McLean, his colleagues' finishing left much to be desired. Jimmy Spoors had the misfortune to miss a second-half penalty but despite this defeat Wednesday still stood proudly in first place in the title race.

Wednesday were drawn away to Chelsea in the second round of the FA Cup on 1 February. A crowd of 36,606 saw a hard-fought contest at Stamford Bridge which ended in a 1-1 draw with both goals coming in the first half through Chelsea's inside-right Whittingham, with McLean again on target for the Owls. In a one-sided replay at Owlerton on 5 February, Wednesday comprehensively demolished the Pensioners 6-0 with a hat-trick from McLean, one from the penalty spot, a pair from Wilson and a single from Kirkman.

Title-chasers Aston Villa were the visitors to Owlerton on 8 February and Wednesday held them to a 1-1 draw in a bad-tempered match in which the Scottish left-sided triangle of Campbell, Wilson and Robertson all caught the eye with Wilson getting the Owls' goal. The local papers were quick to recommend the trio to the Scottish selectors and noted, 'Robertson's speed was a source of danger to the Villans over and over again.'

Wednesday's championship aspirations took a knock when they were beaten 2-1 by Liverpool at Anfield on 15 February, when McLean scored yet again for the Owls. Sadly this result knocked them off the top rung of the ladder, where they had sat proudly for six weeks, and pushed them back into third place.

Following Wednesday's outstanding performance in the cup replay against Chelsea, the *Green 'Un*, on 15 February, was eagerly anticipating the clash in the third round away to Second Division side Bradford Park Avenue and many pundits were tipping the Owls as potential winners of the trophy. The paper carried a cartoon showing the importance of the Caledonian contingent in each side – Bradford had seven Scots players and Wednesday five.

The *Green 'Un* even carried a poem singing the praises of each of the current Wednesday players and harking back to the club's previous FA Cup triumphs.

HERE'S TO WEDNESDAY (CUP WINNERS 1895-6, 1906-7 and ----) By 'WAB.'

'By gum!' said the Sheffielder filled with elation
'I've just now been looking at t'names of the teams
Who's left in the Cup : and the best combination –
The club that I fancy the most in the nation –
Is owd Sheffield Wednesday, the club of my dreams.'

'I've eyed 'em this term and admired their footer
I've noticed what's in 'em – both fire and grit.

They've put the best sides in an adjective flutter,
And made some of t'others look utterly utter
No wonder to look at each man bit by bit.'

'Wee Davison – ox in a teacup – the goalie,
A quality tabloid, tho' little he's great.
With Worrall and Spoors, both assisting him wholly ;
Brawny Tom Brittleton, aye heart and solely.
McSkimming and Campbell as halves are first rate.'

'Then there's the for'ards – the fear of each tenter !
Kirkman and Glennon, the boys on the right ;
McLean the sharp-shooter, our goal-scoring centre
Auld Andrew Wilson, alongside as mentor ;
Robertson, fast and elusive as sprite.'

'I know there's some gradely stuff in t'competition.
And I know there's some others who're making a noise,
And thinking they're in a Cup-winning position ;
But I'll tip owd Wednesday now (with your permission) –
So here's health and jolly good luck to the boys!'

'We don't bear the others a ha'porth o' malice,
We've done it on Grimsby, our friends from the port ;
And just 'ousted' Chelsea. And now for the Palace –
Via Bradford! We think that we'll capture that chalice !
'(And the wish in this case is the dad to the thought !)'

Too much belief in the publicity or perhaps an element of complacency brought about Wednesday's downfall as Bradford unceremoniously dumped them out of the FA Cup with a 2-1 scoreline. Kirkman was the Owls' marksman as Bradford ended Wednesday's dream of a league and cup double at Park Avenue, the winning goal coming five minutes into the second half.

The cup dream may have been over but the league championship was still a very real possibility, although that too began to look less likely when Wednesday were held at home by fellow title contenders Bolton Wanderers. McLean scored from the spot to put Wednesday 1-0 up at the break but second-half goals from Smith and Feebury for Bolton and Glennon for the Owls saw the match finish level at 2-2. Despite dropping a point Wednesday found themselves back on top of the table as results elsewhere went in their favour.

On 1 March George and McLean were the scorers when Wednesday won the Sheffield derby 2-0 at Bramall Lane. George opened the scoring after good work by Tom Brittleton who, 'made a very fine centre just in front of goal. The ball fell almost at Robertson's feet and although he took a second or so to steady himself Hufton was unable to get at him, and he just pushed the ball into the net.'

On the same day the paper castigated the Scottish selectors for leaving George out of the Scottish team to play Wales alongside his team-mates Campbell and Wilson, 'The Scottish selectors have had the idea that George Robertson is not so good as Englishmen think, for in his two International runs against Wales he has not done so well… For all that he is the best outside-left in England and Scotland cannot afford to do without him.'

George's team-mates Jimmy Campbell and Andrew Wilson played in the match against Wales which finished in a goalless draw in Wrexham.

George was selected to play for Scotland against Ireland on 15 March, the day Wednesday were due to play Oldham at Boundary Park. Wilson and Jimmy Campbell turned down Scotland in order to help their club out but Wednesday were beaten 2-0 through two highly controversial penalties. Wednesday's defeat saw them slip from the top of the league down to fourth place.

Little did George know, as he crossed the Irish Sea to represent Scotland, that he was about spark off a serious incident in Dublin from which he would consider himself lucky to escape with his life.

12

THE IRISH INTERNATIONAL INCIDENT AND THE LEAGUE TITLE RUN-IN

GEORGE was recalled to the Scottish team for the second home international in 1913, against Ireland at Dublin's Dalymount Park on 14 March, displacing Templeton who had played in the first game against Wales. George was joined in the Scotland team by two former Motherwell team-mates, Willie Reid and the captain Donald Colman, who later achieved football immortality by introducing the dugout when he was trainer at Aberdeen. The 30th full 'A' international between Scotland and Ireland was moved to Dublin to financially help the Irish Football Association.

At last George turned on the style and helped Scotland to a fiercely-contested 2-1 win. He was considered one of Scotland's top performers on the day.

In fact, many reporters were adamant that the first-half goal he had disallowed, presumably for offside, was perfectly good and the officials got it hopelessly wrong. All the goals came in the first half as Reid and Bennett put Scotland two ahead with McKnight reducing the arrears just before half-time.

Scotland's team was James Brownlie (Third Lanark), Donald Colman (Aberdeen) captain, John Walker (Swindon Town), Robert Mercer (Hearts), Thomas Logan (Falkirk), Peter Nellies (Hearts), Alex Bennett (Rangers), James Gordon (Rangers), William Reid (Rangers), James Croal (Falkirk), George Robertson (Sheffield Wednesday).

It was the events at the close of this encounter that led to a near riot in Dublin, with the Scottish team initially besieged in the dressing room by over 1,000 angry fans, Swindon full-back John Walker assaulted by one of the ringleaders at the team's hotel and their departure from Dublin on the SS *Tiger* considerably delayed.

Andrew Ward, in his history of Scottish international sides, *Scotland – The Team*, describes the events:

> 'Arthur Adams blew his whistle to end the game in Dublin and the stage was set for some of the most unruly scenes in the history of international football. Players fought to keep the ball as a souvenir. Scotland's George Robertson reached it first, but a spectator, Patrick Gartland, knocked the ball out of Robertson's hands and Ireland's Andrews grabbed it.
>
> 'In the struggle which followed, Gartland was knocked over and feared badly injured. Rumours that Robertson had broken the spectator's leg spread through the Irish crowd who were already incensed by Scotland's second goal – there were universal pleas for offside when Alex Bennett scored – and frustrated by Ireland's failure to save the game after dominating the second half.
>
> 'An angry mob gathered outside the dressing room and began smashing windows. For an hour, the Scotland team were virtual prisoners. Referee Adams, busy preparing for his bath, opened a French window to find a huge Irishman rushing past him brandishing a wooden stake. Fortunately the Irishman contented himself with damaging the bath.
>
> 'George Robertson was arrested and taken to the police station. The Irish F.A. agreed to meet the costs of the injured man, who dropped charges, but the mob pursued the Scottish players to their hotel where full-back John Walker was attacked outside.'

According to 'Bedouin' in the *Daily Record*, the Scottish team were only able to escape from the dressing room when a plucky young Irishman, possibly a police officer, wearing George's kit, sprinted away as a decoy; a very brave man indeed.

The *Daily Record* report states that George, 'emerged in the company of the two R.I.C. men and the three S.F.A. officials. Wearing a soft hat, light trousers, and heavy overcoat, and sporting a walking stick, the man who once delighted Motherwell football people managed to escape. His disguise was complete. The other man ran the gauntlet dressed in football pants, jersey and boots. About 150 policemen were about, and 1000 people hanging around.'

Mr A.M. Robertson of the SFA was reluctant to talk of the events following the game. He praised the pressurised Scots for their grit and added, 'I have yet to learn why that goal scored by Robertson was disallowed.' Bradford City's Irish manager Peter O'Rourke thought that Ireland were unlucky not to draw but 'thought that Robertson's goal was a good one'.

Thanks to Richard McBrearty at the Scottish Football Museum at Hampden I was able to view two contemporary unnamed newspaper reports which looked at the international from different viewpoints. The first deals exclusively with the events of the match itself. The reporter considered the Scottish side an experimental one and not really up to the task of beating an Irish team which had recently beaten England for the first time in 32 years:

> 'If the Scots were inclined to take a gloomy view of the situation they did not allow their feelings to interfere with their play, and when Reid ran through and scored a pretty goal after 15 minutes' play the Irishmen got a shock from which they did not recover for some time, and before their halves regained confidence Croal passed to Robertson, and the Sheffield player went ahead and scored one of the finest goals ever seen in an International match.
>
> 'Unfortunately, the referee gave the player offside , which rather pleased the crowd, as the claim for a penalty kick against a Scottish player had just previously been negatived... At this time Croal and Robertson were showing beautiful combination, and the former was about to add a second goal when [former Wednesday player] Warren got up and put behind for safety. The corner kick was nicely placed by Robertson, and after Logan's failure with a header he recovered and passed to Bennett who hooked the ball into the net well out of Scott's reach.'

The Scots' performance was considered to be well below par. The reporter awarded pass marks to some of the players, 'Nellies was the best of three fair halves, Reid and Robertson most impressive in a moderate attack.'

The second report dealt exclusively with events after the game and was entitled, 'SCOTCH FOOTBALLERS MOBBED – Rowdy Scenes in Dublin – A DISLOYAL BAND'. It wrote:

> 'A scene discreditable to the sport of Dublin occurred just after the close of the Association football match between Scotland and Ireland in the Irish capital on Saturday.
>
> 'The final whistle had scarcely died away when there was a scramble among the players to secure the ball to keep as a memento of the occasion. This practice is still in vogue in minor International

> matches, the commonsense example of the Scotland v. England game, which dictates that the ball be given to the winning captain, or tossed for in the event of a draw, being too mild for the ardent Celtic temperament. Robertson, of Sheffield Wednesday, obtained possession, when one of the spectators, who had gone on the field of play, knocked the ball from the Sheffielder's grip.
>
> 'His name is said to be Patrick Gartland, an attendant at the Dublin College of Science. In the subsequent scramble he fell to the ground, and at first it was thought that his leg was broken.
>
> 'Thereupon a rush was made at Robertson, who had the utmost difficulty in rejoining his comrades in the dressing room allotted to the visiting team. Scarcely had he reached shelter than the windows were smashed, and several players had narrow escapes from falling glass. The Scots then took refuge in the Irish players' room, the windows of which were protected by wooden shutters. As it happened, the protection was flimsy, for one individual smashed glass and wood with a long pole, and others attempted to make their way into the room.
>
> 'Fortunately a large staff of police had been on duty while the match was in progress. These were hastily summoned, and with their assistance most of the Scottish players and officials boarded a conveyance, and were followed all the way by a small crowd, mainly boys. Arrived at the hotel, the visitors had to run the gauntlet of another section, and Walker (Swindon) and one or two other players sustained sundry kicks and bruises.'

A 'ring-side' view of events following the international in Dublin was recorded by 'John O' Groat', the football correspondent of the *Weekly Record*, a sister paper of the *Daily Record*, which specialised in sporting matters. His report conveys the anxiety felt by the Scottish players and George in particular.

'John O' Groat' was with members of the Scottish team as they made their escape from Dalymount Park back to their hotel. He was also there at the Imperial Hotel when George was brought in by Irish Football Association officials. Despite George's state of nervous collapse 'John O' Groat' was able to carry out a brief interview with the distraught player.

When he learned that reports of the riot were likely to reach the English and Scottish newspapers George's first concern was for his family – his wife Jessie in Sheffield and his mother in Menstrie and he pleaded with the journalist to wire home to reassure them of his safety.

MORE LIGHT ON THE DUBLIN 'DONNYBROOK' HAS THE SCOTTISH TEAM GOT SUFFICIENT CREDIT FOR THE VICTORY

[By 'John O' Groat']

'I may have done some unwise things in my day, but I believe I crowned them all when over at Dublin for what Peter Nellies calls the never-to-be-forgotten international. In the midst of a jostling and irresponsible crowd, I watched the melee, and was not sorry, I may tell you, to get out of it. I heard the pavilion windows being crashed in; I heard the infuriated Dubliners shout for Robertson to be brought out that they may deal with him; I listened to an excited clergyman in one breath denounce what he called the "dastardly action," and, in the next, appeal to the sportsmanship of the Dubliners. Can you imagine how relieved I was when I reached the outskirts of that crowd?

'But after that came what I consider my venturesome, if not foolish action. As I reached the street, several of the Scottish and Irish players were getting into a waiting conveyance. I was invited to join, and, without thinking, jumped in. No sooner seated than I regretted what I had done. The howling mob round the brake threatened all sorts of things. And they looked fit for anything.

'John Walker was the last man to get in, and his appearance seemed to further incite the hooligans – for that is the word which best describes them. Walker sat down on the floor of the conveyance, and we started on our perilous journey to the Hotel Metropole. The Dublin police had all probably gone home for tea, for not one could be seen anywhere about.

'If the horses had been in league with the rioters they would not have moved at a slower pace. Jamie Brownlie urged the driver to use his whip, but that gentleman probably did not hear. It was an easy matter for the crowd to keep pace with us. They continued to shout for Walker, and as his comrades were inclined to think he had been mistaken for Robertson they urged him to stand up and let himself be seen. The Swindon back did so, and lifted his cap from over his eyes.

'No sooner had he done so than a missile of some sort whizzed past his chin. No more standing up for John. He got down on the floor at once. Several attempts were made to sprag the wheels of the brake, but without effect, although it would have taken very little to bring the four Belgians to a standstill.

'At last the hotel was reached, and just as we were all considering that we would soon be safely housed, greater trouble than ever loomed up. You will have read by this time, no doubt, of how the players were attacked as they fought their way into the hotel, and of how such Irish players as Val Harris and Frank Thompson went to their assistance. I watched the melee, and would not care to see the like again.

'When all had got through I crossed the street to the Imperial Hotel, where the Irish party were putting up. I had interviews with most of the Irish players and officials, and all deplored the regrettable occurrence.

'While I was in the Imperial, George Robertson arrived in the company with several of the I.F.A. officials. Never have I seen a man in such a state of nervous collapse. I entered into conversation with him, but he could scarcely speak. The tears were in his eyes. "Do you think this will get into the Scottish or English papers tonight?" he asked me. I replied that it was more than likely. His thought were of home, and at his request I sent a wire to his wife at Sheffield, and another to his mother at Menstrie, in Clackmannanshire, of which village he is a native.

'We chatted for a time, and latterly he became more composed. It was pathetic, almost, to hear him ask later on if the crowd was away. "If they had got at me," he said, "I would have been done for." Early in the evening Robertson and Walker went quietly away to the boat by which we were to travel home, and there the remainder of the party joined them later on. It was an eventful day. I will not belabour the subject. More will be heard of it from the legislative side; that was evident from the attitude taken up by the S.F.A. Council at their meeting on Tuesday evening.

'More than seems necessary has been written regarding any luck Scotland had in this game. My own opinion is that Ireland were fortunate not to be beaten more emphatically, and the referee most decidedly erred in giving Robertson offside when the Sheffield man scored the best goal of the match. What luck was there in that, might I ask? In the first half Reid, Croal and Robertson had the Irish defence at their mercy, and goals might have come at any moment.

'Then again, we were carrying a right-wing combination which was not a success, and that not altogether the fault of the selectors, for although they chose Alec Bennett, it was through no fault of theirs that James Gordon had to occupy his third position in International fixtures. And this versatile Ranger was certainly not a success as a forward. Neither do I agree with those critics who have been so severe on John Walker. I grant you the Swindon man was robust, but give me a robust back every time so long as he is fair – and John Walker was that.

'The annual "farce" at Cathkin Park on Monday evening did not disclose much that would be of assistance to the Selectors. I was well pleased with the display of Donnachie, the Oldham left-winger, who does not require to learn much in order to become a first-flight man on the other side of the field. Taylor showed great recovery power, at left-back, but that was the best part of his play, for his returns found the touch very often. Next week I will nominate a team which I believe can win at Stamford Bridge.'

'John O' Groat' contradicts other reporters of the period by suggesting that Scotland were unlucky not to have won more decisively. He agreed with many that the referee erred in giving offside against George, whose goal he considered the best of the match.

The *Green 'Un* caught up with George on his return to Sheffield and he made it clear that he considered himself lucky to have got out of Dublin alive, 'When he was waiting for the crowd to go away from the front of the pavilion he thought that his last hour had come, and he was fearful about the experiment of dressing him up as an Irishman, a ruse which worked all right at the finish. He is of the opinion that he was the handsomest Irishman in Dublin last Saturday night, but is not anxious to play the part again.'

Excerpt from SFA Minute Book, 18 March 1913

'Item 169:- Match versus Ireland. Decided to delay fixing the venue for 1913-14 meantime. Irish FA to be asked what steps they are taking to deal with the leaders of the disturbance at the finish of the International match at Dublin on 15th March 1913, particularly with regard to the clergyman who fomented the regrettable scene and the individual who broke the window of the referee's room and assaulted J. Walker at the door of the hotel.

'Item 170:- International Matches. With a view to prevent the unseemly scramble by the players for the ball at the finish of the International and other matches the delegates were instructed to bring the matter before the International Board.'

Excerpt from SFA Minute Book, 15 April 1913

'Item 199:- Match versus Ireland. Irish FA expressed deep regret for the unfortunate disturbance at Dublin on 15th March 1913 and stated all information possible will be got with a view to comply with terms of a letter from the Scottish FA To allow fixtures to be made up the venue for next season's match was asked for. Decided to wait until report of Inquiry is received before fixing venue.'

Excerpt from SFA Minute Book, 27 May 1913

'Item 5:- Match versus Ireland. The following reply was received

> from the Irish FA In reply to yours of 17th April, I am instructed to inform you that the Committee of Inquiry into the unfortunate trouble at Dublin on 15th March have reported that, after most careful and diligent inquiry, they are unable to get any evidence to implicate any person or persons with the trouble. Your Council can understand how difficult it is to get witnesses in a matter of this sort and they feel that they have no other option but to allow this matter to drop.
>
> 'They wish to express their deep regret at the unfortunate occurrence and hope your Council will feel assured that they have done all they could to bring the offenders to justice. The Irish FA was thanked for the letter. It was decided to play the International match versus Ireland, in Ireland, on 14th March 1914.'

No disciplinary action was taken against George following the events in Dublin; indeed the whole affair appears to have been swept under the carpet. This may be in part because of the dire financial straits that the Irish FA was in at the time. The association was keen to have Scotland play their international fixtures in Ireland so it could benefit from the gate receipts.

Back on league business, Wednesday crossed the Pennines on Friday 21 March to defeat Blackburn Rovers through Wilson's goal 20 minutes after the start. They entertained Chelsea at Owlerton the following day when George was in 'very bright form' against the Londoners and he got the second of three goals as the Pensioners were beaten by the odd goal in five. After 25 minutes, 'Fine work by all the forwards ended in Robertson taking a pass from McLean and shooting into the net from 20 yards range. It was a splendid shot, and quite unstoppable.' Wilson and Kirkman were the other scorers for the Owls who led 2-1 at the break.

That same day the *Green 'Un* remarked, 'Robertson played a fine game for Scotland at Dublin on Saturday, and was the best forward on the field at Glasgow in the Trial game on Tuesday, and from all accounts his cap against England is a certainty.'

Andrew Wilson was also selected to represent Scotland and he and George would make up the left wing against England at Stamford Bridge where they would be opposed by their Wednesday team-mate Tom Brittleton. Brittleton anticipated a difficult afternoon, saying of George, 'That his equal cannot be discovered.'

A contemporary account of the Home Scots versus Anglo Scots match which was used to help select the team to face the Auld Enemy at Stamford Bridge suggests that George was among the Anglos' better performers on the day. The match was disappointing and finished goalless. It is interesting to note that 15,000 people turned up to watch the trial, at Third Lanark's Cathkin Park, providing gate receipts of £300.

The Home Scots' line-up was J. Brownlie (Third Lanark), captain, A. M'Nair (Celtic), J. Dodds (Celtic), R. Mercer (Heart of Midlothian), J.L. Logan (Rangers), P. Nellies (Heart of Midlothian), W. Templeman (Airdrieonians), J. King (Partick Thistle), J. Robertson (Falkirk), J.A. Croal (Falkirk), A. Smith (Rangers).

The Anglo-Scots' team was K. Campbell (Liverpool), captain, J. Walker (Swindon), D. Taylor (Burnley), G. Halley (Bradford Park Avenue), R. Torrance (Bradford City), J. Campbell (Sheffield Wednesday), J. Donnachie (Oldham Athletic), J. M'Lachlan (Aston Villa), D. M'Lean (Sheffield Wednesday), A. Wilson (Sheffield Wednesday) G. Robertson (Sheffield Wednesday).

George put the Owls 1-0 ahead at the break away to Derby County on Monday 24 March. Wednesday ran out easy 4-1 winners as George added another goal in addition to a McLean double in the second half. He was in great form five days later as Wednesday convincingly beat Arsenal 5-2 to storm back to the top of the table. Wilson, McLean with two, Kirkman and Glennon got the goals. While George was involved in the international match against England, Wednesday thrashed Bradford City 6-0 at Owlerton when all the forwards (Kirkman, Glennon, McLean, L. Burkinshaw and Wright) got on to the scoresheet, with McLean getting his customary double.

The title race was now a gripping contest between Wednesday and Sunderland with only four games remaining.

Despite the well-publicised problems at the end of the Irish match, George must have impressed sufficiently as he was selected for the next international, played against England in front of 52,000 spectators at Stamford Bridge on 5 April.

George had a reasonably good game as Scotland went down to a 1-0 defeat. He was paired on the left wing alongside his Wednesday team-mate Andrew Wilson and the duo were directly opposed by Wednesday's right-half Tom Brittleton. It was a big day for the Wilson family as Andrew's brother David, the Oldham wing-half, was making his international debut.

'Bedouin' in the *Daily Record* complained that centre-forward Reid, George's former Motherwell team-mate, was neglected, 'On the left, Robertson and Wilson played well to each other, and worked with tremendous energy, but they were not regardful of the benefit of slipping the ball into the centre. Wilson had one of the best shots of the match.

'I am not going to condemn the team wholesale, for with the slightest bit of luck, they ought to have drawn the match. I saw no evidence of weakness in the English defence. As in many past contests, Crompton and Pennington [the full-backs] were stalwarts in defence.

'McCall [England's centre-half] was lucky in once saving the situation when Hardy was drawn out of goal, and Pennington another time when he was in the way of a ball that was going through when Andrew Wilson, Robertson and Reid crowded and sorely beset a defence that for the moment was utterly mystified.'

The only goal of the game came when keeper Brownlie saved a shot and was charged into the net by England's centre-forward Harry Hampton in the 37th minute.

The *Daily Record* sought the views of celebrity spectators: "England's goal was one in a million," said Mr Archd Leitch, the well-known football architect, who is always to the fore when Scotsmen visit England. "Hampton caught the goalkeeper at the psychological moment. I must honestly say I thought the better team won, although Scotland had hard lines not to equalise."

The *Evening Times* blamed the Scottish forwards for not getting at least a draw. Wilson was unlucky when his shot hit the bar and George, according to the *Times*, missed a sitter late on which would have tied the game. The English press had a different view of this incident and credited goalkeeper Hardy for saving a 'cannonball' shot from the Scottish winger.

The *Green 'Un* thought, 'Robertson and Wilson were the best of the Scottish forwards, although Robertson was the only success, and he made sufficient openings to win the game surely.' The reporter felt that George didn't get as much of the ball as he should have.

Scotland's team was James Brownlie (Third Lanark), Alex McNair (Celtic), John Walker (Swindon Town), James Gordon (Rangers), Charles Thomson (Sunderland) captain, David Wilson (Oldham Athletic), Joseph Donnachie (Oldham Athletic), Robert Walker (Hearts), William Reid (Rangers), Andrew Wilson (Sheffield Wednesday), George Robertson (Sheffield Wednesday).

For the match against England the *Evening Times* carried portraits and brief notes on the English and Scottish players. This is George's entry:

> 'George Robertson (Sheffield Wednesday), outside-left, makes his first appearance against England, although he has had international experience against both Wales (1910 and 1912) and Ireland (1913).

> His grand display against the "disthressful" country probably accounts for his inclusion today, though he is not likely to forget his experience at the close of the match, when he was the "hero" or the "victim" – you can choose your word – of a little affair which is engaging the attention of the "powers that be" on both sides of the Channel.
>
> 'He served his football apprenticeship with Yoker Athletic before adhibiting his signature to a Motherwell form, for which club he showed such conspicuous ability that it was not long before the English talent spotters were on his track. Sheffield Wednesday were successful in inducing him to change his allegiance, and in conjunction with Andrew Wilson he has had a large share in bringing his club to the prominent position it occupies to-day.
>
> 'With his club-mate to back him up, the erstwhile Motherwell flier will not want for support, and we look forward to this combine proving a happy and successful one in Scotia's interests.'

Wednesday appeared to have let their league title chance slip when they could only draw with Manchester City at Hyde Road on 12 April. The Owls were 2-0 down with 18 minutes to go when 'a fast movement between Wilson and McLean led to the ball being put across the goal and, with [City defenders] Goodchild and Fletcher getting mixed up, Kirkman was able to tap the ball to Robertson, who scored'.

In a frantic finish, Teddy Glennon equalised with seven minutes remaining to keep Wednesday's hopes alive although they had now slipped into second place behind Sunderland. Sadly Wednesday's chances virtually disappeared two days later when they were beaten 2-1 at home by Newcastle with McLean the Owls' scorer from the penalty spot.

Although it was still mathematically possible for them to take the title it would now depend upon the correct permutation of results elsewhere. In the end it was not to be. In their penultimate game Wednesday beat West Bromwich Albion 3-2 at Owlerton. A goal from Glennon and a brace from McLean had the Owls 3-1 ahead at the break and, although the Throstles pulled a goal back in the second period, the home side held on for the win and the essential two points.

Wednesday's final fixture of the season took them to Goodison Park for a clash with mid-table Everton in a match that they simply had to win to have even the remotest chance of claiming the title.

Although the Owls crashed to a 3-1 defeat, George had the distinction of scoring their last goal of the season after, 'Andrew Wilson struck the crossbar with a fast drive and George netted the rebound.'

With the other teams involved in the title race still having outstanding matches the final placings were still in doubt until late April. Wednesday's defeat in Liverpool and Sunderland's 3-1 defeat of Bolton at Burnden Park on 26 April secured the league title for the Roker Park side. Wednesday came so close to carrying off the championship, just stumbling at the final couple of hurdles. In the event they actually finished in third place with 49 points for the season, one behind Aston Villa who won their final game against Sheffield United at Villa Park on 28 April to leapfrog the Owls.

For the second season in a row David McLean was the First Division's leading goalscorer, this time on his own, with 30 goals from 36 appearances.

This season was undoubtedly George's most successful in English football although he did have a spell in October and November 1912 when his form shaded and he was rested for two matches to recharge his batteries. He played in 33 of the 38 games, notching a personal record of ten goals – largely singles, apart from a double in the 4-1 away win over Derby County at the Baseball Ground in March.

ENGLISH FIRST DIVISION 1912/13

	Pl	*W*	*D*	*L*	*F*	*A*	*Pts*
1 Sunderland	38	25	4	9	86	43	54
2 Aston Villa	38	19	12	7	86	52	50
3 The Wednesday	38	21	7	10	75	55	49
4 Manchester United	38	19	8	11	69	43	46
5 Blackburn Rovers	38	16	13	9	79	43	45
6 Manchester City	38	18	8	12	53	37	44
7 Derby County	38	17	8	13	69	66	42
8 Bolton Wanderers	38	16	10	12	62	63	42
9 Oldham Athletic	38	14	14	10	50	55	42
10 West Bromwich Albion	38	13	12	13	57	50	38
11 Everton	38	15	7	16	48	54	37
12 Liverpool	38	16	5	17	61	71	37
13 Bradford City	38	12	11	15	50	60	35
14 Newcastle United	38	13	8	17	47	47	34
15 Sheffield United	38	14	6	18	56	70	34
16 Middlesbrough	38	11	10	17	55	69	32
17 Tottenham Hotspur	38	12	6	20	45	72	30
18 Chelsea	38	11	6	21	51	73	28
19 Notts County	38	7	9	22	28	56	23
20 Woolwich Arsenal	38	3	12	23	26	74	18

THE WEDNESDAY'S APPEARANCES AND GOALS 1912/13

	League		*FA Cup*	
	Apps	*Goals*	*Apps*	*Goals*
Brelsford, C.H.	2	0	0	0
Brittleton, J.T.	34	0	4	1
Burkinshaw, L.	5	2	0	0
Campbell, J.	38	0	4	0
Davison, J.E.	38	0	4	0
Glennon, J.E.	34	12	4	0
Kirkman, S.	36	10	4	2
Lloyd, W.	1	0	0	0
McLean, D.P.	36	30	4	8
McSkimming, R.S.	36	0	4	0
Miller, J.	8	0	0	0
Robertson, G.C.	33	10	4	0
Spoors, J.	36	0	4	0
Wilson, A. McC.	37	9	4	2
Worrall, J.E.	36	0	4	0
Wright, P.L.	8	2	0	0

13

1913/14 – BADLY DAMAGED

BEFORE the start of the new season the *Green 'Un* reported on 'the wonderful transformation' that had taken place during the summer at Owlerton and was confident that when the works were complete, 'Wednesday will have an enclosure fit to rank with the best in the country. The old Olive Grove stand has gone, and in its place there towers one of the greatest structures on any football ground. The new stand, built to the designs of Mr. Archie Leitch, the famous football architect, will not be finished for the opening match on September 6, but I understand that 3,000 seats will be ready for the public very shortly. The enclosure in front of this huge stand will hold nearly 11,000 spectators, and when the ground is full that side will present a wonderful sight.'

Leitch began his programme of ground improvements with the South Stand, the clock face from which still adorns the ground to this day. The first home match of the season was officially the first to be played at Hillsborough as the directors had decreed that Owlerton be renamed after the Parliamentary Constituency which included the ground.

Before the start of 1913/14 the *Green 'Un* listed Wednesday's 27 signed players, their positions, birthplaces, heights and weights. George was listed as an outside-left, born Menstrie, height 5ft 9.75in and weight 12st 0lb.

One significant omission from the list of players was the name of David McLean. McLean held out for a better deal after his scoring exploits the previous season and returned to his home-town team Forfar Athletic when Wednesday refused to offer him more than a one-year contract. The *Green 'Un* speculated on who might replace him in the side with the versatile Laurie Burkinshaw or his brother Jack, signed in the close season from Swindon, emerging as favourites.

Wednesday made a winning start when Teddy Glennon's first-half goal was enough to give them a 1-0 victory over Bolton Wanderers at Burnden Park on 1 September. Manchester United were the first visitors to enjoy Wednesday's new facilities when the partially-opened stand was first used on 6 September but the visitors spoiled the celebrations by defeating the Owls 3-1. The match was level at 1-1 at half-time, with new centre-forward Jack Burkinshaw opening his account for the home side, but United upped their game in the second period and added two more goals.

Things began to look bleak for Wednesday when they went down 3-0 to Burnley at Turf Moor the following week and slipped down the league table to a lowly 17th position. The Owls' unpredictable September form continued when they managed to overcome Preston North End 2-1 in a bad-tempered affair at Hillsborough.

A goal from Andrew Wilson saw the sides go in level at the break but a second-half penalty from Jimmy Spoors gave Wednesday the win.

On Monday 22 September, Oldham Athletic visited Hillsborough and made off with both points with a 2-1 win. Glennon had the Owls ahead at the interval but second-half goals from Walters and Cook from the penalty spot gave the visitors the victory.

It was clear that Wednesday were struggling without McLean. They were creating chances but Jack Burkinshaw lacked the goalscoring instinct that the Scot had provided the previous season.

Goals from Hall, Hibbert and Low at St James' Park earned Newcastle United the points on 27 September as Wednesday suffered a second defeat in seven days. Andrew Wilson was on target for the Owls and George had a nightmare of a game. The *Green 'Un* commented that he had 'his worst game since coming south'.

He bounced back the following week in an eventful 4-1 home win over Liverpool. With Wednesday leading 2-1, 'Robertson rushed through and shot hard against [goalkeeper] Campbell's knees. When he tried to secure the rebound, both players came down together, and Robertson had to be attended to by the trainer before he could get up. Robertson had apparently cut his head, and he retired to the dressing room, but Wednesday, despite the handicap, continued on the attack until the winger returned after an absence of five minutes.'

He seemed unaffected by his injury, 'Robertson's knock on the head didn't appear to have done him any harm, and, in fact, he was more like his old brilliant self when he returned. He led several raids, and one of these, two minutes from the finish, brought success, for after the Liverpool goalkeeper had half saved a curious drive by Kirkman, [Laurie] Burkinshaw rushed in and kicked the ball out of Campbell's hands into the net.

'Immediately after this Robertson scored the most brilliant goal of the game. He sprinted through like lightning to take a pass from Burkinshaw, beat two men in his stride and then from 30 yards drove the ball hard and high into the net, the final whistle coming immediately afterwards.'

George's poor form at the start of the season led the *Green 'Un* scribe to remark that if he could play like that after a head knock perhaps his colleagues should give him a 'dint on the cranium' before each game. The paper reckoned that George's goal was one of the most brilliant scored at Owlerton for a long time. Wilson and Kirkman were Wednesday's other scorers. The victory over the Merseysiders propelled Wednesday up to a more comfortable 12th in the league standings.

George missed the Owls' 2-0 defeat by Aston Villa at Villa Park on 11 October through the injury sustained in the Liverpool match. He was back for the next home game against Middlesbrough the following week when he scored the opener after eight minutes in a 2-0 win.

The *Green 'Un* wrote, 'Glennon, who was playing a fine, vigorous game in the centre, whipped the ball out to his left wing, where Robertson immediately made use of his speed, and swerving inward, put in a great shot, which was beating Davies, all the time going away from him and finding a haven in the farther corner of the net.'

The reporter was delighted at George's return to form, claiming, 'The whole line went with a rare swing from start to finish, the "star" performer being Robertson, who was nothing short of brilliant.' Jack Burkinshaw got Wednesday's other goal four minutes after George's score.

George's smart runs were a highlight of Wednesday's play in the Sheffield derby at Bramall Lane, which the Owls won 1-0 with a goal from Glennon, but he was injured in a scramble when Glennon and United's Brelsford nearly came to fisticuffs and, as a consequence, missed the next four games. The win over United took the Owls up to ninth place in the league, the highest spot they had occupied since the first day of the season.

Without George, Wednesday went down 3-1 at home to Derby County on 1 November with left-back Jimmy Spoors their scorer. Jack Pickering deputised for George for the second time as goals from Sam Kirkman and Andrew Wilson, either side of the break, helped Wednesday to a 2-1 away victory against Manchester City on 8 November. Wednesday's inconsistent form continued when Bradford City visited Hillsborough a week later and ran out comfortable 3-1 winners. The Owls' scorer was Andrew Wilson.

Wednesday were 2-0 down at half-time to Blackburn Rovers at Ewood Park on 22 November but second-half goals from Wilson and Kirkman were not enough to prevent them being beaten by the odd goal in five.

George's return to action came in a fiercely contested match against Sunderland at Hillsborough on 29 November. Sunderland led through a goal by Mordue after 20 minutes but Wednesday threw everything at them in an effort to grab the equaliser, 'In a fierce attack…Robertson got badly damaged, and although he remained on the field he was limping so badly that he was unable to make a run.'

Wednesday's chances were looking even more remote when Teddy Glennon was laid out after a clash with a Sunderland defender and had to be assisted to the dressing room. He was able to return later but with a severe limp, thus effectively reducing Wednesday to nine fit players and two walking wounded.

Half a minute from the interval, George, despite his injury, turned the game, 'In the course of a Wednesday attack, Robertson lobbed the ball in the goal from near the touch-line. There was a tremendous swerve on the ball, which curled into the net at the far corner just as Butler thought it was going out.' Wilson's second-half goal gave Wednesday a hard-earned 2-1 win.

George's injury gave Percy Wright another chance to shine on the left wing when the Owls travelled to Goodison Park to face Everton on 6 December. Wilson's goal was sufficient to earn Wednesday a share of the points in Liverpool.

George scored for Wednesday on his return to first-team action against West Bromwich Albion at Hillsborough on 13 December although it could not stop the team going down 4-1 to the Throstles. Wednesday were one down after a minute and were soon reduced to ten men when Wilson sustained a fractured cheekbone. They equalised when Jack Burkinshaw 'passed across the front of the goal. Miller scraped the ball to Robertson, who with a tremendous effort got to the leather and banged it past Pearson. Robertson injured himself as he shot, and had to be attended to before play was restarted'. George was able to continue but was obviously not fully fit. With Wednesday effectively reduced to nine fit men they conceded three second-half goals to the Birmingham outfit.

At this stage of the season, with the congested holiday period approaching, Wednesday were hit by a number of serious injuries to key players; Kirkman, Glennon, Wilson and George – almost the entire forward line. They were reduced to bringing in some of their untested young reserve players and, in desperation, had even tried out

Scottish right-half Jimmy Miller at centre-forward. George was out for a total of six weeks with a serious knee injury with Wright continuing to deputise for him in his absence.

Against Tottenham Hotspur at White Hart Lane on 20 December, Wednesday's much changed forward line managed to earn them a share of the points with Wright on the scoresheet for the Owls in a 1-1 draw. Wednesday were still in the capital on Christmas Day when Wright scored again but on this occasion Chelsea ran out 2-1 winners to plunge the Owls deep into relegation trouble.

Back on home turf on Boxing Day, Wednesday gained revenge on the Pensioners with a handsome 3-0 win. Jack Burkinshaw put them ahead in the first half and brother Laurie added a second after the break before Jimmy Campbell completed the scoring. The Owls' third game in three days saw them slip back down to 16th in the league when Manchester United were 2-1 winners at Old Trafford. Jimmy Spoors got the Owls' goal from the penalty spot.

Jimmy McGregor, standing in at centre-forward for the injured Glennon, gave the Owls a first-half lead against Bolton at Hillsborough on 29 December but, unfortunately, Lillycrop levelled for the Trotters after the break and the points were shared.

If the Wednesday directors thought that the New Year might provide better fortune they were rudely awakened when Wednesday were humbled 6-2 by Burnley at Hillsborough on 3 January 1914. Goals from Tom Brittleton and McGregor were the only bright spots in the match for the 25,000 Wednesday fans.

Clearly things weren't going too well in the league campaign and the directors perhaps hoped that a good FA Cup run would salvage something from a miserable season. Wednesday disposed of Second Division side Notts County 3-2 in the first round at home on 10 January and were drawn away to another Second Division outfit, Wolverhampton Wanderers, in the second round. Wednesday's goals against County came from Brittleton and the Burkinshaw brothers.

During this dark period only one win was achieved from eight league matches and Wednesday were sliding, inexorably, towards the foot of the table. Wednesday's directors, in desperation, decided to re-sign proven goalscorer David McLean. McLean made his first appearance of the season against Preston North End at Deepdale on 17 January but even the return of the talismanic centre-forward could not prevent another embarrassing defeat as the Owls were slammed 5-0 by their fellow strugglers. Wednesday were now 18th, one spot above the relegation places.

George made a brief return to the front line, although not fully fit, in the goalless draw at home in the league match with Newcastle United on 24 January, and it was reported, 'For Wednesday it must be said that they had many chances wasted by Robertson, who was fearfully weak, and seemed to be afraid to trust himself to go within a yard of an opponent.'

Wednesday pressed home many attacks and during one of these, 'Robertson ran full tilt into one of the Newcastle defenders, and fell so heavily that he seemed badly damaged. After a short delay he was taken behind the goal, and Wednesday resumed with ten men.'

Another three-week absence through injury gave young Jimmy Gill a chance to make a bid for George's left-wing spot.

The *Green 'Un* of the period carried a regular feature on the various positions of the football field. On 24 January George was interviewed regarding the skills required of a left-winger and some of the techniques he used to beat an opponent.

HOW TO PLAY THE GAME
Scotland's Tricky Winger on Dodges for Forwards

XII. – OUTSIDE LEFT : BY GEORGE ROBERTSON (WEDNESDAY)
(Interviewed by 'Athleo')

Most Scots are supposed to be golfers, and to take up the game early: but I never tackled it in earnest until last year. The reason is for the greatest part of my life most of my spare time has been given over to football. I was born in a little village some five miles from Stirling. Football was there our one great relaxation from work, from schooldays onwards.

We played the game all day if we had the chance. What is more, I have often played football at night, when the moon was bright; just as you read of Queen's Park men of old doing. The love for the game seemed to be in our blood. We could never have too much of it.

I smile nowadays when I hear English trainers saying that they mustn't allow their men to have much ball practice, for fear of them getting sick of the game. I have yet to learn what it is to be 'fed-up' with football. In the old days we played cheerfully at every opportunity, in season and out of it; as soon as work was done in the summer, away we went to the green with the ball, and there was just as much fun as on a sharp winter afternoon.

Laying the Foundation

When I have had a good day in a League match now, it often occurs to me that my success really dates back to those kickabouts on the village green. It was there I laid the groundwork of my game, and learnt the art of controlling a lively ball. I believe it would do English professional football no harm if the men were allowed to have more ball practice. It is quite a job to get a ball out on a League club's premises.

I quite admit that some very clever wingers partly spoil their game by wasting time in doing tricks. But that is a matter of bad judgement, which might easily be remedied as the result of a little straight talking. It is a very much harder matter, however, to put a knowledge of ball control into a player who is denied the necessary opportunities of practising it.

There is nothing like practice for bringing a youngster on. Speaking for myself, I have followed three special lines of practice. The first was to sprint hard down a short track or strip of turf, turn as quickly as possible, and then sprint back without a stop. This helps one to turn and start sharply, and I need hardly say that sharpness is one of the great things on the football field; particularly in the case of a winger, who if he can get away the least bit before an opponent, may lead a raid which will yield a goal.

How to Practise

The second thing was to take out a ball alone and dribble it round the field. It isn't exactly as easy as lying in bed on a cold morning, but it gives a man a fine grounding in ball control. He acquires something of that intimacy of touch with the ball which you see in a good billiard player. He learns to twist and turn his feet round the ball until he is almost able to grasp it with them, and to judge the strengths of his kicks to a nicety.

My third great item of practice was to go out with one other player and run up and down the field, giving and taking long swinging passes. In this way I mastered the art of centring on the run. A smart dash along the field is not much use unless you can finally part with the ball to advantage. Centres need to be placed to the men who can use them best, and should not be too fast. It is only by good practice that you can learn to drop the ball across with this precision of pace and direction.

So much for training in the game itself. But while speaking of centres, I would say that I generally like to run right up to the line before putting a ball over. Some wingers think this is harder than centring slightly forward, or square, but I find it easier, besides which it is a sure method of keeping all the others fellows on-side. I might add that I do not consider it the best game for the other forwards to follow a winger in a line. No man can be sure of dropping a ball in to the inch, and if the inside men are positioned on slightly different lines there is a much better chance of one of them getting it exactly as he would like it.

Some Tricks

It is advisable for a winger to occasionally practise taking flag-kicks and free-kicks from an advanced position. There is always danger in a well-placed flag-kick, and I believe in dropping the ball slightly to that side of the goal which is furthest away, because there is generally a bit more room there than plum it in the goal-mouth. The ball should come down about seven yards from the goal-line. If it is any nearer the average good goalkeeper will get it nine times out of ten.

Now comes the question of how to beat the opposition. Well, the main thing is to try and make him think you are going to do exactly what you aren't.

I am not really so very fast as some of my friends imagine, and one reason why I often get the ball in front of an opponent is that I succeed in deceiving him as to my pace. We are both going for the ball. As far as he can tell from my action, I am going all out. As we approach the ball it seems odds on him getting it. Unless he is simply content to kick into touch, he doesn't want to get the ball too soon, or I shall have time to pull up and embarrass him in his effort to part with it. He feels sure the ball is his and eases off the very least shade. At that moment my stride lengthens, I nudge the ball forward the fraction of a second before he can touch it, and he is beaten.

It Comes Off

He wasn't beaten for speed. He made an error of judgement – in which, of course, I had gladly assisted him. This is one of the simplest tricks by which a winger can beat an opponent, but I consider it quite one of the most important. Nobody knows, unless they have worked it as often as I have done, how frequently it comes off.

You mention that trick of taking a ball past an opponent who has stationed himself within a few inches of the side-line. Well, it is done in this way. An opponent taking up that position is generally content to stick one leg out towards the touchline, and as he has left practically no room to get past him on the outside, he feels certain that you will only try to beat him on the inside. Consequently he sets himself ready for a tackle there. All you have to do is to feint with your body as if you meant to try and pass in the inside, but touch the ball over his foot, or between his legs. Then swiftly follow it either along the line, or if need be run a few inches outside the line. He has deceived himself as to your intentions, and he cannot tackle you in time. Of course that kick ahead of yours must be dead accurate, or the ball will go where it's no use to you or anybody else for the moment. But I have beaten two opponents in succession in this manner.

Fooling an Opponent

I'd much rather go out with the ball and show you a few tricks than try to explain them here. But there is another which can be described; and which comes in very useful. That is to check the ball in one's run and then go on with it without an appreciable stop. An opponent, say, is running shoulder to shoulder with me, and waiting for his chance to kick the ball. I make just an ordinary run up to a point; then suddenly, when I have nudged the ball forward with my left foot, instead of letting it go on I wrap my right foot round the side, and check it just for an instant. My left foot drives it on again practically at once, but that tiny check has either caused my opponent to lose a stride, or he has gone plunging across my original path, and I am free to come inside him.

When a winger is away with the ball, he should do all he can to keep his would-be tackler at his back.

A winger naturally depends on his inside man for a great deal, and the better understanding the pair have the better for their team. It is an excellent plan to change positions with each other in the course of a run, as long as it is not overdone. Most of my own footwork is done with the right foot, a fact which I think helps me a good deal in deceiving opponents.

It is a good business for a winger to have a pop at goal now and then, but not too often.

The second round of the FA Cup took Wednesday to Molineux on 31 January to face Wolverhampton Wanderers. David McLean's first goal since his return to Wednesday's ranks put the Owls in front at the interval but a second-half goal by Howell ensured that the tie would go to a replay at Hillsborough.

Wednesday were still hovering around the bottom of the table but four wins and a defeat during February saw them halt the downward slide, move up a place and advance to the fourth round of the cup. The replay saw Wolves defeated 1-0 on 4 February through Sam Kirkman's first-half goal. The match was marred by the collapse of a newly-built wall which caused injury to around 70 people. The Wolves keeper fainted at the sight of the injured spectators and took no further part in the match. Wednesday were rewarded with another home tie in the third round when they were drawn against Southern League side Brighton & Hove Albion.

In the First Division, goals from Jack Burkinshaw and McLean gave Wednesday a narrow 2-1 win over Liverpool at Anfield on 7 February after they trailed 1-0 at half-time. Aston Villa did not show any love towards the Owls when they defeated their hosts 3-2 on St Valentine's Day. Wednesday's goals came from Andrew Wilson either side of half-time.

On Tuesday 24 February, the Owls eased into the fourth round of the FA Cup by defeating Brighton 3-0. Albion put up an excellent first-half showing, keeping their First Division hosts to a goalless draw after 45 minutes, but second-half goals from McLean, Gill and Jack Burkinshaw saw the Owls progress. Wednesday were so impressed by the performance of David Parkes, the Brighton centre-half, that they moved quickly to sign him.

George missed the Sheffield derby against United at Hillsborough on 28 February when the Owls completed the double over their city rivals, winning 2-1. The returning Ted Glennon put Wednesday in front in the first half and McLean scored what proved to be the winner in the second period. This crucial victory raised Wednesday up to 17th in the table. Although still not clear of danger, the return to goalscoring form of the re-signed McLean gave hope that the Owls could pull away from the relegation zone.

Wednesday's FA Cup run came to an end at Hillsborough on 7 March when they were eliminated in the fourth round by high-flying Aston Villa in front of around 57,000 fans. Edgley's goal in the first half separated the sides as the Owls' only hope of any silverware disappeared.

Having missed the entire cup campaign, George returned to the team again for the midweek match away to lowly Derby County on 11 March. The fixture finished with the scores level at 1-1 and George appeared somewhat lacklustre. He then played out all but one of the remainder of the season's games although not with the same dash as in previous campaigns.

Wilson gave the Owls a first-half lead against the Rams but Moore levelled the match in the second half. The point gained, however, was good enough to push Wednesday a couple of places up the table to 15th.

Against Manchester City at Hillsborough the following Saturday he did exhibit flashes of his old pace and crossing ability although the *Green 'Un* reporter was not convinced of his complete recovery, 'Robertson failed to reveal his best form, except for a short period in the early stages. Like Glennon he appeared to lack confidence in his injured leg.'

The 2-2 draw against City appeared to have pulled Wednesday clear of relegation worries but two successive defeats plunged them back down to third from bottom with only six games remaining.

Wednesday were 2-0 down at half-time to Middlesbrough at Ayresome Park on Wednesday 18 March. They did manage to get on the scoresheet through McLean and Wilson in the second half but three further Boro goals saw them well beaten, 5-2. A 3-1 defeat by Bradford City at Valley Parade on 21 March had Wednesday's fans worrying again as they slipped back down to 18th, one above the relegation places. Andrew Wilson got the Owls' goal in the first half.

David McLean's return to the fold had brought with it the anticipated goals, and seven goals from the Scot in the last ten games were instrumental in finally securing Wednesday's First Division status.

McLean was on the mark along with Laurie Burkinshaw and Wilson as eventual champions Blackburn Rovers were beaten 3-1 at Hillsborough on 28 March. McLean scored in the first half against Sunderland at Roker Park on 4 April and Wednesday held out for a crucial win which kept them 16th as the season drew towards a close.

George did display some flashes of his old form towards the end of the campaign. The *Green 'Un* noted, 'The Sunderland folk were rather premature in their programme on Saturday last. They remarked: "Robertson, of Sheffield Wednesday, has fallen off form terribly this season, and is not a patch on what he was as a left-winger."

'The Wearsiders wouldn't say that after the match, for Robertson was the man who gave them a world of trouble. As a matter of fact, he did much better than he has done for a long time. So much for prophecy!'

The newspaper was convinced that George simply lacked confidence, 'Robertson was within an ace of his best form at Roker Park on Saturday. The touch-line runs for which he was famous were in evidence again, and altogether he was more like his old self than he has been for a long time. He is as good as ever, if only he would think so.'

Wednesday found themselves a goal adrift at the break in the penultimate home game of the season against Everton on 11 April. McLean scored both the Owls' goals in the second half as the match finished level at 2-2. Wednesday then dropped back down to 17th as Derby were relegated to the Second Division.

Worryingly the Owls slumped to a 2-0 defeat to Oldham Athletic at Boundary Park as they battled with Preston, Spurs and Liverpool to avoid the second relegation place. Jack Burkinshaw got the goal which secured the vital point at The Hawthorns against West Brom to ensure that the Owls would play First Division football in 1914/15.

George missed the match in Birmingham but returned to action when Spurs were Wednesday's opponents in the final league game of the season at Hillsborough on 25 April. With the threat of relegation over, the Owls relaxed and signed off with a comfortable 2-0 win through second-half goals from Wilson and McLean.

On Thursday 30 April George played on the left wing as Wednesday fielded an almost full-strength team against local rivals United in a charity match at Hillsborough in front of 5,000 fans. On this occasion United got the better of the hosts, winning 2-0.

George's numerous injuries, especially the severe one to his knee, limited his appearances in 1913/14 as the club slumped to a disappointing 18th in the First Division with only 34 points. George played in only 22 of the 38 games and scored four goals. He missed the Owls' entire FA Cup run through injury.

ENGLISH FIRST DIVISION 1913/14

	Pl	*W*	*D*	*L*	*F*	*A*	*Pts*
1 Blackburn Rovers	38	20	11	7	78	42	51
2 Aston Villa	38	19	6	13	65	50	44
3 Middlesbrough	38	19	5	14	77	60	43
4 Oldham Athletic	38	17	9	12	55	45	43
5 West Bromwich Albion	38	15	13	10	46	42	43
6 Bolton Wanderers	38	16	10	12	65	52	42
7 Sunderland	38	17	6	15	63	52	40
8 Chelsea	38	16	7	15	46	55	39
9 Bradford City	38	12	14	12	40	40	38
10 Sheffield United	38	16	5	17	63	60	37
11 Newcastle United	38	13	11	14	39	48	37
12 Burnley	38	12	12	14	61	53	36
13 Manchester City	38	14	8	16	51	53	36
14 Manchester United	38	15	6	17	52	62	36
15 Everton	38	12	11	15	46	55	35
16 Liverpool	38	14	7	17	46	62	35
17 Tottenham Hotspur	38	12	10	16	50	62	34
18 The Wednesday	38	13	8	17	53	70	34
19 Preston North End	38	12	6	20	52	69	30
20 Derby County	38	8	11	19	55	71	27

THE WEDNESDAY'S APPEARANCES AND GOALS 1913/14

	League		*FA Cup*	
	Apps	*Goals*	*Apps*	*Goals*
Bentley, H.	1	0	0	0
Brelsford, C.H.	4	0	1	0
Brittleton, J.T.	30	1	5	1
Burkinshaw, J.D.L.	31	6	3	2
Burkinshaw, L.	14	3	2	1
Campbell, J.	32	1	5	0
Davison, J.E.	36	0	5	0
Gill, J.J.	5	0	3	1
Glennon, J.E.	20	4	2	0
Kirkman, S.	24	3	3	1
Lamb, J.W.	2	0	0	0
McGregor, J.	6	2	0	0
McLean, D.P.	15	9	4	2
McSkimming, R.S.	32	0	5	0
Miller, J.	22	0	1	0
Monaghan, J.	2	0	0	0
Nicholson, H.	3	0	0	0
Parkes, D.	10	0	0	0
Pickering, J.W.	4	0	0	0
Robertson, G.C.	21	4	0	0
Spoors, J.	37	3	5	0
Streets, G.H.	2	0	0	0
Wilson, A. McC.	31	15	5	0
Worrall, J.E.	25	0	4	0
Wright, P.L.	9	2	2	0

14

1914/15 – LACKING RESOLUTION

WITH the ground improvements at Hillsborough now complete, the new capacity of the ground was estimated at between 75,000 and 80,000. Whether there would be any football or any fans present to fill the ground was in doubt as Europe teetered on the brink of war.

Despite some reservations the football season kicked off at the beginning of September. The first major casualty as far as Wednesday was concerned was the loss of three players to the draft including Scottish international half-back Jimmy Campbell. Before the start of the league campaign Wednesday had splashed out £1,975, almost twice their previous transfer record, for the highly-regarded Clyde full-back Jimmy Blair who promptly injured himself in a motorcycle accident.

George began the new season quietly as Wednesday made a winning start with a 3-2 home victory over Middlesbrough at Hillsborough on Tuesday 1 September. Sam Kirkman put the Owls in front at the interval and two goals from veteran inside-forward Andrew Wilson in the second half clinched the victory.

Local bragging rights were achieved with a 1-0 triumph over Sheffield United in the Steel City derby at Bramall Lane on 5 September with Wilson the Owls' marksman in the first half. The point gained in the goalless draw away to Newcastle United on 9 September took Wednesday to the top of the table. This came at a cost as George sustained a recurrence of his serious knee injury which was to keep him out of the side for 12 matches. Initially Jimmy Gill took George's place in the side but after two matches he gave way to the more experienced Alf Capper.

The previous season's runners-up Aston Villa were beaten emphatically 5-2 at Hillsborough on 12 September when Wednesday led 4-0 after 45 minutes. David McLean helped himself to a hat-trick and Glennon and Wilson completed the scoring to keep Wednesday on top of the table. Liverpool inflicted Wednesday's first defeat of the season when they won 2-1 on 19 September at Anfield with McLean again on the mark for the Owls.

Wednesday bounced back in style with a 6-0 thrashing of newly-promoted Bradford Park Avenue at Hillsborough with McLean bagging his second hat-trick in a fortnight, including one penalty. Kirkman, Glennon and Capper, on his first-team debut, got the other goals and the win reinstated the Owls as league leaders.

However their topsy-turvy form saw them slump to third place when they were beaten 5-2 by Oldham at Boundary Park on 3 October. McLean, with his eighth goal in four games, and Wilson were the scorers for the unpredictable Owls.

Ted Glennon's second-half goal was enough to earn both points when Manchester United visited Hillsborough the following week. McLean then kept up his remarkable scoring record with another two goals when Wednesday defeated Bolton 3-0 at Burnden Park on 17 October, Glennon the other Owls scorer.

McLean's 11th goal of the season gave Wednesday a 1-1 draw with title contenders Blackburn Rovers at Hillsborough as the Owls continued to occupy second spot in the table. They maintained that position on 31 October with a good 2-1 win over Notts County at Meadow Lane. McLean scored from the spot and the teams went in level at the interval but Wilson got the vital score after the break.

Sunderland upset Wednesday's title challenge with a 2-1 win at Hillsborough on 7 November when Capper, filling in for George on the left wing, got the Owls' only goal. Wednesday were now back in third place as a host of teams fought tooth and nail for the lead in the title battle.

Ted Glennon's brace either side of half-time gave Wednesday a 2-1 home win over fellow challengers Manchester City on 14 November. Then neither side could break the deadlock at The Hawthorns when Wednesday travelled to take on West Bromwich Albion but the point gained was enough to push the Owls back into second place. High-flying Everton visited Hillsborough on 28 November, the week after they thrashed Sunderland 7-1 at Goodison Park with centre-forward Parker scoring a hat-trick for the Toffees. Parker went one better against the Owls by scoring all his side's goals in a 4-1 win with two in each half, one coming from the penalty spot. McLean got Wednesday's solitary counter as the Owls dropped back to fourth place. In George's absence Wednesday won six, drew two and lost four of their league matches.

George made his return to the first team on 5 December in the goalless draw against Chelsea at Stamford Bridge. The *Green 'Un* remarked, 'Capper gave place to Robertson, now reported as recovered from his long knee trouble.'

Wednesday's forwards were in good form and George was looking lively, 'A beautifully judged square pass by Wilson set Robertson going, and he finished one of his old-time runs with a fine high shot, which Molyneaux managed to beat away.'

The Owls had now slipped to fifth place and remained there following a hard-fought 3-3 draw with Bradford City at Hillsborough on 12 December when Wilson, Tom Brittleton and McLean scored to give their side a share of the spoils. McLean grabbed another brace seven days later in a good away victory over a Burnley side containing David Taylor, George's erstwhile Motherwell colleague, at left-back. Jack Burkinshaw scored the other Owls goal and this win hoisted them one rung up the ladder to fourth.

The matches on Christmas Day and Boxing Day pitted Wednesday against struggling Tottenham Hotspur home and away. Wednesday narrowly won the Hillsborough encounter 3-2. Burkinshaw and McLean gave the Owls a 2-0 lead at half-time and Wilson got what proved to be the winner as Spurs mounted a second-half comeback. Wednesday's trip to the capital proved to be a fruitless one as they were humiliated 6-1 by a rampant Spurs at White Hart Lane with McLean's goal the only bright spot on a miserable Boxing Day.

Fortunately Wednesday were able to put this reverse behind them and welcomed in 1915 with a good 2-1 win over Newcastle United at home with the ever-dependable McLean and left-half Harry Bentley, with his first goal for the club, on the scoresheet. George was able to keep up his good record in derby games against Sheffield United on 2 January in a typical fiercely-contested contest at Hillsborough which finished with honours even at 1-1, with Wilson increasing his tally for the season to nine.

The *Green 'Un* reporter was happy to see 'The Robertson of Old', noting that George 'sparkled in several good runs and centres' and did very well although he missed a glaring opportunity after United's equaliser.

On the following Saturday Wilson's second-half goal was enough to seal victory for the Owls over Manchester United at Hillsborough in the first round of the FA Cup as Wednesday began their latest quest for the coveted trophy. Wednesday then secured a valuable away point at Villa Park on 16 January when Aston Villa were held to a goalless draw. The Owls were now second in the league on goal difference.

Despite beating Liverpool 2-1 at Hillsborough on 23 January, with goals from McLean and Kirkman, Wednesday slipped down to third place in one of the most keenly-contested title races seen for many a year.

Before the FA Cup second round against Wolverhampton Wanderers at Hillsborough on 30 January the *Green 'Un* expressed concern over George's condition after his long lay-off, 'Robertson doesn't seem to make the amount of improvement expected, though he is very earnest.'

George was prominent in the match although not displaying quite his old dash. He took this opportunity to record his first goal of the season and first ever in the FA Cup in the 2-0 win. George's goal was a beauty, 'The home defence, in a word, was at full stretch for a time, but at length Kirkman got a move on, and finished a fine run with a splendid centre, which Wilson purposely allowed to pass him so that Robertson, unmarked, could try his luck. The latter sent in a superb shot, which was going away from Peers all the time, and eventually entered the far corner of the net, high up.'

Ted Glennon, at centre-forward in place of the injured McLean, scored the Owls' second goal after 40 minutes to seal the victory.

In heavy conditions at Hillsborough on 6 February there was evidence that George was beginning to recapture some of his old sparkle. Wednesday were considered unlucky to only draw 2-2 with Oldham Athletic and George was quickly into his stride in the match, 'Parkes eventually brought the ball down the middle, and putting it forward to Glennon that player turned it straight out to Robertson. The result was a capital dribble by the winger and a very fine shot which Matthews got to under the bar.'

'J.H.S.', the *Green 'Un*'s reporter at the match, was pleased to report, 'Robertson is finding a very great deal of his old form.'

Manchester United gained revenge for their FA Cup exit at Wednesday's hands when they scored twice in the second half to beat the Owls 2-0 at Old Trafford on 13 February. Despite this reverse Wednesday remained in third spot with 12 league games remaining.

Wednesday were eliminated from the FA Cup in the third round at Hillsborough the following Saturday, going down 2-1 to Newcastle United with McLean the scorer for the home side. According to the *Green 'Un*, 'Robertson played in patches.'

Back on league duty, this patchy form continued over the next few weeks although the *Green 'Un*'s reporter could detect hints of George's international class in some games. On 27 February, in the 1-1 draw against Blackburn Rovers at Ewood Park, 'Robertson did several good things' as Ted Glennon's goal gave the Owls a share of the points. Only goal difference separated the top sides but Wednesday slipped to fourth place as competition for the title hotted up.

An astonishing result was achieved in a rearranged match on Monday 1 March when Wednesday ran riot against Bolton Wanderers, winning 7-0 at Hillsborough with seven different players getting their names on the scoresheet. Wednesday attacked from the kick-off and Bolton keeper Edmondson kept his team in the game with good early saves from Brittleton, Robertson, Parkes and Wilson. Bolton were handicapped when left-back Feebury had to go off injured and eventually retired after a brief spell back on the field.

The floodgates opened after 15 minutes when David Parkes scored his first goal for the club in a goalmouth scramble. It was 3-0 by half-time as Glennon added a second goal from a header and Gill scored from close range after being set up by Glennon.

A second-half altercation between Thomas of Bolton and Spoors saw the Wednesday right-back being kicked in the face by the Bolton player. Spoors retaliated and fists flew before the referee intervened but treated the pair leniently with only a cautionary word.

George added a fourth goal almost on the hour-mark with a low drive and five minutes later Wilson made it 5-0. All the forwards were on the scoresheet when right-winger Capper made it 6-0 after 73 minutes and left-half Harry Bentley completed the scoring with ten minutes remaining. This impressive showing finally put the Owls back on top of the table.

Wednesday remained in top spot after fighting out a goalless draw with Notts County at Hillsborough on 6 March when George showed 'a great deal of good form'. They then lost 3-1 to Sunderland in a very hard game at Roker Park on 13 March with George the scorer of the Owls' goal. Wednesday were 1-0 down in the first half and quickly lost another goal early in the second. Thirteen minutes into the second period, 'Wednesday reduced their arrears, and the goal was of a soft order from the home point of view, though cleverly got by Wednesday. The ball was taken up by Wilson and Robertson, and with the latter in charge, Scott ran well out, but Robertson cleverly lifted the ball over his head and scored. The sight of the ball trundling into the empty goal looked rather ludicrous.'

The race for the league title was an impossible one to call with almost all the top ten still in with a realistic chance of carrying off the silverware provided they could maintain their form in the remaining eight matches. Despite the loss to Sunderland, Wednesday were still top of the pile but slipped down to second place after a disappointing

1-1 draw away to Bradford Park Avenue on St Patrick's Day when Glennon scored a second-half equaliser for the Owls.

On 20 March Wednesday lost 4-0 away to Manchester City although George was considered the best forward on the field in the first half but noticeably faded out of the game in the second. Wednesday were now in fourth place and their title hopes appeared to be slipping away.

George was rested for the match against West Bromwich Albion at Hillsborough on 27 March which finished goalless and further dented each side's title hopes. The *Green 'Un* reporter was convinced that George simply lacked confidence. On 3 April he wrote, 'Robertson has had a very brief rest, but sufficient to spoil his run of appearances. Perhaps he will come into his old form some day, but, as far as we can see, all he lacks at present is resolution.'

Everton were beaten 1-0 at Goodison Park that same day to push the Owls back into second place and revive hopes of another run at the league title. George played well and was involved in the goal which came after 14 minutes from Sam Kirkman, 'Robertson made a long run in chase of Thompson, a throw in coming to Wednesday near the corner flag. Robertson centred, and Kirkman dashed across, and with a wonderful hard right foot shot crashed the ball into the net, Fern having no chance.'

With many of the top teams facing each other in the last four matches it was clear that any side who put together a strong final run-in would have a good chance of snatching the championship, but Middlesbrough overcame Wednesday 3-1 at Ayresome Park on 5 April to virtually kill off any hopes the Owls had of carrying off the prize. Wilson's goal gave them brief hope but sadly it came to naught.

George's good wing play and accurate crosses were a feature of Wednesday's 3-2 victory over Chelsea at Hillsborough. After McLean had equalised Croal's early goal George almost put the Owls in front, 'Wednesday were struggling hard to secure a lead and a very clever piece of work by Robertson, who, after losing the ball, regained it very smartly brought Molyneaux out for a supreme save, Robertson driving in a magnificent shot from the corner flag and the goalkeeper just managing to touch it over the crossbar.'

The sides were level at 1-1 at half-time but another goal from McLean and one from Wilson in the second half gave the home side both points.

Bradford City were 1-0 victors at Valley Parade when Wednesday were reduced to ten men, Alf Capper having to leave the field because of injury. George was 'prominent' in the match but his colleagues were unable to take advantage of the many chances he set up. 'Wanderer' for the *Green 'Un* thought that Wednesday were, at least, worthy of a share of the points.

The season fizzled out in a disappointing manner with a dull goalless draw against Burnley at Hillsborough when George's old Motherwell team-mate David Taylor managed to contain the Owls' attack.

The 1914/15 season saw Wednesday recover from their lowly 18th place the year before. With eight games remaining they were top of the table but with just two wins and three draws they managed only seven points from a possible 16 to finish three points behind champions Everton.

In one of the most competitive seasons in the history of the Football League only six points separated Bradford City in 11th place from the eventual winners and the destination of the championship was in doubt right to the very last match.

Again injury took its toll on George who was absent for a period of 12 weeks after playing the first three games of the season. He did recover to make a total of 25 league appearances but his goal tally was reduced to a meagre two.

George had to wait until 1 March to open his account in the 7-0 demolition of Bolton Wanderers. His only other goal came in the club's 3-1 defeat by Sunderland at Roker Park on 12 March.

He managed to shake off his injury problems in time to take part in Wednesday's FA Cup campaign when the club were luckily drawn at home for the first three rounds and he was finally able to break his scoring duck in the competition with a goal in the 2-0 victory over Wolves in the second round.

ENGLISH FIRST DIVISION 1914/15

	Pl	W	D	L	F	A	Pts
1 Everton	38	19	8	11	76	47	46
2 Oldham Athletic	38	17	11	10	70	56	45
3 Blackburn Rovers	38	18	7	13	83	61	43
4 Burnley	38	18	7	13	61	47	43
5 Manchester City	38	15	13	10	49	39	43
6 Sheffield United	38	15	13	10	49	41	43
7 The Wednesday	38	15	13	10	61	54	43
8 Sunderland	38	18	5	15	81	72	41
9 Bradford Park Avenue	38	17	7	14	69	65	41
10 West Bromwich Albion	38	15	10	13	49	43	40
11 Bradford City	38	13	14	11	55	49	40
12 Middlesbrough	38	13	12	13	62	74	38
13 Liverpool	38	14	9	15	65	75	37
14 Aston Villa	38	13	11	14	62	72	37
15 Newcastle United	38	11	10	17	46	48	32
16 Notts County	38	9	13	16	41	57	31
17 Bolton Wanderers	38	11	8	19	68	84	30
18 Manchester United	38	9	12	17	46	62	30
19 Chelsea	38	8	13	17	51	65	29
20 Tottenham Hotspur	38	8	12	18	57	90	28

THE WEDNESDAY'S APPEARANCES AND GOALS 1914/15

	League		FA Cup	
	Apps	Goals	Apps	Goals
Bentley, H.	32	2	2	0
Blair, J.	18	0	2	0
Brittleton, J.T.	24	1	2	0
Burkinshaw, J.D.L.	7	2	1	0
Capper, A.	24	4	1	0
Davison, J.E.	38	0	3	0
Gill, J.J.	6	1	0	0
Glennon, J.E.	30	9	3	1
Kirkman, S.	27	4	2	0
McLean, D.P.	33	22	2	1
McSkimming, R.S.	35	0	2	0
Parkes, D.	29	1	3	0
Robertson, G.C.	25	2	3	1
Spoors, J.	36	0	3	0
Wilson, A. McC.	38	13	3	1
Worrall, J.E.	16	0	1	0

15

WARTIME FOOTBALL – PLAYING EXTRAORDINARILY WELL

THE war raging in northern Europe eventually put paid to league football as many players volunteered or were drafted into the armed forces or essential war work. Jason Dickinson in *One Hundred Years at Hillsborough* states, 'Wednesday were denied the services of Jimmy Blair, Bob McSkimming, George Robertson and David McLean, all of whom returned to their native Scotland.'

Jason and John Brodie's superb 2005 publication *The Wednesday Boys* revealed that George worked in a munitions factory during the Great War.

From the 1915/16 to 1918/19 seasons Wednesday took part in the regional competitions which were set up at the time. Wednesday played in Midland Section (Principal Tournament) which ran from September through to the following February. This was followed by a Midland Section (Subsidiary Tournament) which ran from March until the end of April or beginning of May.

George missed all of the matches during 1915/16 but did return to represent Wednesday in three games in September and October of 1916/17 in the Principal Tournament.

The *Green 'Un* of 23 September 1916 was delighted to see George and another old campaigner, Sam Kirkman, return to Wednesday's ranks against Hull City, 'Then the promised appearance of George Robertson was pleasing, for neither of these players had appeared since the end of the 1914/15 season.'

The forwards were in good form with 'every one of them doing well, and Kirkman and Robertson playing extraordinarily well considering how long it is since either of them took part in serious football'. Wednesday won the match 2-1 with goals from Islip and Glennon.

The paper was still talking about the pair the following week, 'I saw two prime favourites of olden times in tip-top form, and fairly rose at Robertson and Kirkman for the good work they did. Robertson in his last season or two, thanks to illness never gave us much of the sparkle which marked his earlier play, but on Saturday he seemed imbued with quite his old fire, and got in some sparkling centres, and one shot only missed the angle of the goal by the breadth of a hair.'

Wednesday were well beaten 5-1 by Nottingham Forest on 30 September and the *Green 'Un*'s man at the match complained that the ball never went to the wings, 'And Robertson hardly took part in the game in the second half.' Cawley got Wednesday's consolation goal.

George's final game in this competition was at Hillsborough against Barnsley on 7 October when Wednesday returned to form and won comfortably by 3-0 with two goals from Glennon and another from Cawley.

George appeared again for Wednesday in the Subsidiary Tournament for a local derby against Sheffield United on 14 April 1917. The bright start to the day gave way to a heavy shower of sleet which cleared up just before the contest was due to get under way. Wednesday were quickly on the attack. George did manage to get in one good shot which was cleared by full-back Sturgess before the Owls took the lead through Tom Brittleton. Teddy Glennon doubled their advantage before the interval but almost halfway through the second half United pulled one back through Simmons but Wednesday held on to win 2-1.

George was absent again for 1917/18 and 1918/19 and little did he know that it would be another two and a half years before he would next don Wednesday's famous blue and white stripes.

Although *The Wednesday Boys* suggests that George returned to Scotland and worked in a munitions factory during the Great War it is possible that he remained in the Sheffield area. He was able to play four games for Wednesday during 1916 and 1917 and was certainly in the city when his second son, George Clarke Robertson Junior, was born on 19 April 1918 at the family home at 122 Dixon Road. The boy's birth certificate reveals that George was then working as a shell machinist.

THE WEDNESDAY'S APPEARANCES AND GOALS 1916/17

	Principal		*Subsidiary*	
	Apps	*Goals*	*Apps*	*Goals*
Atkins	2	0	0	0
Bell, H.	1	2	1	1
Birch, A.	3	0	4	0
Brittleton, J.T.	24	0	4	0
Brelsford, B.	2	0	1	0
Brelsford, C.	30	0	6	0
Brelsford, T.W.	22	2	2	0
Buddery, H.	6	0	2	1
Burkinshaw, J.D.L.	13	4	5	1
Capper, A.	14	1	4	0
Cawley, T.E.	22	3	0	0
Clarke	5	0	1	0
Cooper, A.	7	0	1	0
Cowham, J.	3	0	0	0
Firby, G.	1	0	2	0
Gill, J.J.	2	0	0	0
Glennon, J.E.	24	9	5	3
Harrop, J.	19	0	4	0
Jones, W.	12	2	3	0
Kirkman, S.	7	4	1	0
Lowe, E.	2	0	0	0
Lyall, J.	19	0	0	0
Islip, E.	14	2	2	0
McGregor, A.W.	3	0	1	0
Oldacre	2	2	0	0
Robertson, G.C.	3	0	1	0
Roulson	1	0	1	0
Spoors, J.	7	0	1	0
Thorpe, E.	15	0	6	0
Watson, W.	3	0	0	0
Wilson, A. McC.	24	3	5	3

Goals were clearly at a premium with only one Wednesday player reaching double figures during the one wartime season that George made his four appearances for the club. Teddy Glennon was the Owls' top scorer in 1916/17 with 12 goals. Even the usually dependable Andrew Wilson could only manage six goals over the two tournaments.

16

1919/20 – PALPABLE INEFFICIENCY

GEORGE made his return to the club in 1919/20 when Wednesday remained loyal to many of the players they had on their books prior to the conflict. Pre-war stalwarts such as Jimmy Spoors, Tom Brittleton, Bob McSkimming, Jimmy Campbell, Sam Kirkman, David McLean, Teddy Davison, Alf Capper and Jimmy Gill were all retained and took part in several games.

Around 29,000 spectators were present on a perfect afternoon at Ayresome Park on 6 September 1919 to see George, now 34 years old, make his return to the Football League. 'Free Lance' was there for the *Green 'Un* and reported that Middlesbrough would field the announced 11, and, 'Wednesday the same team which drew at Old Trafford with one exception. The exception was a notable one, the old favourite George Robertson turning out at outside-left. Everyone was anxious to see a repetition of his old form.'

Middlesbrough were two up at the interval and George had made little impact on the game. Wednesday were hard pressed and George got little of the ball although just after the break, 'We had a brief glimpse of Robertson shortly afterwards, who centred across the goal. But there was no comrade up at the time to defeat Williamson.' Middlesbrough added another in the second half to complete Wednesday's misery.

George made his return to Hillsborough the following week as Wednesday went down 3-1 to Manchester United. He was not impressive and sat out the next five games before reappearing on the left wing away to Blackburn Rovers on 18 October. Rovers ran out 1-0 winners and George played reasonably well enough to be selected for the next match against Manchester City at Hyde Road.

Here he formed a new left-wing partnership with Arthur Price and caught the eye of the *Green 'Un*'s man at the match, 'Price and

Robertson got on well together and I think Price will help Robertson to recover his confidence. They displayed sparkling harmony at times.' Despite this harmony Wednesday went down 4-2 and the pair were destined never to play together again.

George was absent for the next six games before being recalled for the match against Sunderland at Roker Park on 13 December. This was to be his final appearance for the club and ended with the home side winning 2-0. Wednesday never looked like scoring and lots of injuries were picked up by both sides in a bruising contest. The final comment from the *Green 'Un* on George's playing career was the brief summary, 'Robertson and Capper were practically passengers.' George played only five games in this final season and finished on the losing side on each occasion.

The Wednesday Boys recalls, 'His long-standing knee injury meant he played only a handful of games in wartime soccer and The Owls paid for an operation on the offending joint in 1919 in the hope of finally curing the problem. However it seemingly was not a success as amazingly in November 1919 he was given 14 days' notice to terminate his engagement due to his "palpable inefficiency"!'

Wednesday's loyalty to their pre-war favourites, many of whom were carrying injuries, and constant changes of personnel in an effort to find a winning blend, eventually cost them their place in the top flight of English football. They made a disastrous start to the campaign, winning only three of their opening 20 fixtures, and never rose above second from bottom in the table.

The club had failed to find a settled side and, in desperation, had tried out a total of 39 players, buying several new faces in a frantic search for a prolific goalscorer to help turn their fortunes around. Wednesday finished bottom of the First Division, winning only seven games during the entire season. They collected only 23 points, 13 fewer than the other relegated side, Notts County.

The *Green 'Un* of 29 May 1920 had got wind that 29 players were to be released by the club and speculated who they might be. This followed on from the announcement of the transfers of Brittleton, Parkes, Burkinshaw, Lamb and Campbell and the placing on the transfer list of Spoors, Kirkman and McSkimming. The following Saturday, 5 June, the club published the list of retained, transferred and released players. George's name appeared in the latter category.

George had made a total of 163 league appearances for Wednesday, scoring 30 goals, with one goal in ten FA Cup matches while a further four appearances were made in the Midland Section tournaments during wartime. He also won three caps for Scotland while with the Sheffield club.

Beside the list of retained, transferred and released players, the *Green 'Un* carried the fifth part of a feature on the career of that distinguished Wednesdayite, Tom Brittleton. The former England international recalled some of the great Wednesday players he had played alongside in his long career and George was worthy of a mention under the heading 'Men with "Knees"':

> 'There's a couple of forwards I would like to include in my list in addition to those I have mentioned. They are Georgie Robertson and Frank Bradshaw. Frank Bradshaw was a grand forward, with any amount of ability, and just as Robertson is probably leaving Wednesday on account of knee trouble, so did Frank. Wednesday will never hear the last of Frank Bradshaw's knee trouble! He's playing yet, and is one of the great guns of The Arsenal, though he is a full-back nowadays. "Braddy" is a credit to Sheffield football, for he is a Sheffield lad, and they tell me he learnt a lot on the Crookesmoor Recreation Ground when a lad at school. Anyway, he did Wednesday a lot of good.
>
> 'What Robertson will do I don't know, but before the war he was a very fine left-winger, and earned his International honours by sheer brilliance. I never saw Fred Spiksley, but when old cronies used to talk to us there was always an argument as to whether George at his best was the equal of Fred. I cannot say, but if Spiksley was his superior, then he must have been a wonderful player, the like of which you do not come across in football nowadays.
>
> 'His style of play is so well remembered that there is no need for me to say more about Georgie!'

Although they lost 26 of their league games Wednesday were not really thrashed in any of those matches so clearly the dearth of goals was the principal reason for their relegation.

Jimmy Gill, once George's understudy, was the top scorer for the Owls with a mere eight goals. Fletcher Welsh, the free-scoring centre-forward bought from Raith Rovers in an effort to turn around Wednesday's fortunes, was the next-highest scorer with four.

Once again Wednesday scored no goals in the FA Cup, going out in the first round to non-league Darlington at Hillsborough after a goalless encounter at Feethams. The Quakers won the replay 2-0.

ENGLISH FIRST DIVISION 1919/20

	Pl	*W*	*D*	*L*	*F*	*A*	*Pts*
1 West Bromwich Albion	42	28	4	10	104	47	60
2 Burnley	42	21	9	12	65	59	51
3 Chelsea	42	22	5	15	56	51	49
4 Liverpool	42	19	10	13	59	44	48
5 Sunderland	42	22	4	16	72	59	48
6 Bolton Wanderers	42	19	9	14	72	65	47
7 Manchester City	42	18	9	15	71	62	45
8 Newcastle United	42	17	9	16	44	39	43
9 Aston Villa	42	18	6	18	75	73	42
10 Arsenal	42	15	12	15	56	58	42
11 Bradford Park Avenue	42	15	12	15	60	63	42
12 Manchester United	42	13	14	15	54	50	40
13 Middlesbrough	42	15	10	17	61	65	40
14 Sheffield United	42	16	8	18	59	69	40
15 Bradford City	42	14	11	17	54	63	39
16 Everton	42	12	14	16	69	68	38
17 Oldham Athletic	42	15	8	19	49	52	38
18 Derby County	42	13	12	17	47	57	38
19 Preston North End	42	14	10	18	57	73	38
20 Blackburn Rovers	42	13	11	18	64	77	37
21 Notts County	42	12	12	18	56	74	36
22 The Wednesday	42	7	9	26	28	64	23

THE WEDNESDAY'S APPEARANCES AND GOALS 1919/20

	League		*FA Cup*	
	Apps	*Goals*	*Apps*	*Goals*
Armitage, L.	3	0	0	0
Bentley, H.	17	1	0	0
Binney, C.	12	1	2	0
Birch, A.	21	0	2	0
Blair, J.	25	0	2	0
Brelsford, T.W.	10	0	0	0
Brittleton, J.T.	31	2	1	0
Burkinshaw, J.D.L.	18	0	1	0
Campbell, J.	23	1	2	0
Capper, A.	21	0	1	0
Cooper, A.	3	0	0	0
Davison, J.E.	20	0	0	0
Eggo, R.M.	4	0	0	0
Edmondson, J.	14	2	0	0
Gill, J.J.	27	8	2	0
Harvey, E.L.	9	0	0	0
Harvey, W.H.T.	19	1	1	0
Kirkman, S.	6	0	0	0
Lamb, J.	3	0	0	0
McKay, C.	12	3	2	0
McIntyre, J. McG.	9	1	0	0
McLean, D.P.	3	0	0	0
McSkimming, R.S.	16	0	2	0
O'Neill, H.	7	0	0	0
Parkes, D.	8	0	0	0
Pearson, S.	2	0	0	0
Price, A.	19	2	1	0
Reed, P.	11	0	2	0
Robertson, G.C.	5	0	0	0
Shelton, G.	9	0	0	0
Spoors, J.	18	1	0	0
Stapleton, W.	19	0	0	0
Sykes, W.J.	2	0	0	0
Taylor, C.S.	7	0	0	0
Taylor, W.	2	1	0	0
Welsh, F.	9	4	0	0
Whalley, J.W.	5	0	0	0
Wilson, A. McC.	1	0	0	0
Wilson, G.	9	0	0	0

17

1920/21 – A FINAL FLOURISH WITH THE FIFERS

FOR years my father had believed that George's football career was over when he was released by Wednesday but it appears that was not the case.

The publication of *The Wednesday Boys*, that splendid book of Wednesday players' biographies, revealed that George still had a passion for the game and wished to continue playing, 'He then returned North of the Border and after signing for Junior side East Fife he played in their first ever Scottish League game, against Bathgate Thistle in August 1921. After ending his playing career George emigrated to Canada where he returned to his original capacity as teacher.'

Again there is a very clear suggestion that George had no intention of resuming his career as a baker and many football authorities erroneously suggest that he had trained as a teacher, possibly during his time in Sheffield. *The Wednesday Boys* states, 'It was said he did not transfer to Wednesday because the club impressed him but because Sheffield could boast a University!'

There is no documentary evidence to support this theory. A quick check with Sheffield University confirmed that George's name does not appear on the list of alumni. His colleague Jimmy Murray, with whom he transferred from Motherwell, was an unregistered teacher in Scotland and there was probably an element of confusion over their occupations at some time.

East Fife were not, of course, a junior side. When George joined them they had applied, unsuccessfully, on a number of occasions for membership of the Scottish League but had been denied entry. They were then competing in the Central League which could boast a number of teams that could compare favourably in terms of wages and playing ability with many of the Scottish League outfits.

The Methil-based side were founded in 1903 and were anxious to quickly progress to the top flight of Scottish football. Their application to join the Scottish League was ultimately successful and they joined the newly formed Second Division in 1921/22.

I am deeply indebted to passionate East Fife fan and historian Jim Corstorphine who diligently researched one of the local newspapers, the *Leven Advertiser and Wemyss Gazette*, for references to George.

He explains the dearth of information available, 'The great difficulty in researching East Fife around this time [before Scottish League entry], though, is that all the reports appear not in the sports section, but in the "Local News – Methil" section. There is therefore no actual mention of George signing for East Fife in the *Leven Advertiser and Wemyss Gazette*.'

More recently the *Mail for Leven, Wemyss & East Fife* became available to researchers and Jim quickly found the date of George's arrival at East Fife under an article headed 'INTERNATIONALIST FOR BAYVIEW':

> 'George Robertson, the Motherwell youth who distinguished himself in the ranks of Sheffield and represented Scotland in the international against England, signed for East Fife on Saturday night. George is a contemporary of Andrew Burton's and is equally speedy. He made his mark as a left winger and, as such, will be highly acceptable at Bayview. The crowd honours George Wilson and his great record, but sadly admits that "Doddy" cannot shift himself as a winger needs to do after beating the opposition.
>
> 'Robertson has the advantage there and his presence should be an ever ranking thorn in the defence of any opposition. By this master stroke Mr McLean (East Fife Manager) has made the East Fife van one of the most dangerous in the Central League, an attack to be treated with deference by any club likely to be encountered in the Scottish ties. Robertson is to turn out on Saturday versus Armadale.'

The Saturday night when George signed would have been 16 October 1920. The article refers to Andrew Burton, who was a distinguished player who played for Motherwell in 1904, moved to Bristol City in 1905, then on to Everton before ending his career with East Fife.

George Wilson, known as 'Doddy', was another distinguished player who was capped six times for Scotland. He also played for Hearts, Everton and Manchester City before ending up at East Fife.

The article also confirmed that George's debut was against Armadale in a Central League match at Bayview on 23 October 1920.

East Fife lost 2-1 in front of a crowd of around 4,000, although the *Leven Advertiser and Wemyss Gazette* said 3,000.

The *Mail for Leven, Wemyss & East Fife* reported on the game and began, 'Ninety minutes of gruelling football opened with excellent play from Robertson, who twice played accurate squares into goal.' It concluded, 'Robertson, though done before the finish, gave a great display.'

The *Leven Advertiser and Wemyss Gazette* report on 28 October, referring to the Central League match against Armadale, also mentions George's contribution, 'Burton and Robertson were the better wing, but both fell away after the interval. Robertson gave glimpses of First League football in his perfect squaring, but it is evident he lacked training.'

It is uncertain if George played in the first match against Inverness Caledonian in the Scottish Qualifying Cup a week later, as the newspaper report is very brief and makes no references to players. In the match report of the replay, which appeared in the following edition of the *Leven Advertiser and Wemyss Gazette* on 11 November, however, George is mentioned, 'Close on time Robertson gave a glimpse of the art which made him a famous international player by popping in the third.'

The *Mail for Leven, Wemyss & East Fife* on 20 November had more detailed coverage of the match, 'Burton and Robertson had the Caley backs beaten times without number and slipped the ball across to Moffat till it became clear the centre wanted no easy chances.'

The pair combined to set up the opener, 'Neal and Allan were doing better but it was Burton and Robertson who took down the ball to square it to the waiting, if offside, centre. Moffat did the trick. The winning goal had still to come and it was a magnificent one. Robertson slipped the leather to Burton near midfield. Andrew saw Rhind closing on him, and feinted to return the ball to the winger.

'Rhind made to intercept this but Andrew had swerved inside, saw a clear field for a hit, and after taking four strides let volley at the net, almost bursting the meshes. The coup de grace was applied by Robertson, and East Fife qualified to meet Alloa by 3-1.'

The *Mail*'s reporter summed up proceedings, 'The left wing had a thrilling day – a little more practice and they will become the finest combination in the League.'

Among the 'Football Notes' elsewhere in the paper it was recorded, 'George Robertson is not responding to the training as East Fife hoped he would.' I suspect that this refers to a recurrence of his knee injury which had robbed him of much of his celebrated speed.

The next reference to George was when the player pool was announced for the Qualifying Cup quarter-final second replay, played at Central Park, Cowdenbeath, on 27 November. However, he is not mentioned in the match report.

It would appear that George was either out of favour or injured until the start of 1921, when he played against Falkirk 'A' in a goalless Central League match at Bayview on New Year's Day. The *Leven Advertiser and Wemyss Gazette* match report states, 'Robertson raced through from mid-field and squared from the goal-line for Moffat to head over. Robertson agreeably surprised everybody by his smart play, his runs being a feature of the game, which certainly should not have ended in a no-scoring draw.'

The *Mail for Leven, Wemyss & East Fife* on 5 January 1921 confirmed George's contribution to this game, 'Methil right wing had become a peril: they got that ball across the field instanter, and brought Robertson into action. Slow he may be but George can still lob a ball directly across the goal mouth. Not once but half a dozen times, did he glance these inviting shots to his inside men.'

And George was not averse to having a go himself, 'A thriller was Robertson's own essay at scoring – a first timer, which rose dead for the top corner, where Allan bravely caught it over the head of a crowd.'

On 3 January, George scored the third goal in a 3-1 Central League victory against St Johnstone at Bayview. No team is listed in the *Leven Advertiser and Wemyss Gazette*, but the report does mention that East Fife fielded a 'scratch eleven'. The *Mail for Leven, Wemyss & East Fife*, reporting on the same game, mentions that George had an outstanding solo run.

On 29 January George was on the left wing in the 3-0 away defeat to St Johnstone. The *Mail for Leven, Wemyss & East Fife* reporter remarks on his well-taken corners.

George sparked an East Fife revival in the game against Bathgate on 26 February. East Fife were struggling and ready 'to accept a second consecutive home defeat, and the crowd was beginning to drift away home when the fire got into the Methil heels. Robertson swung over a fine ball, and it was netted twelve minutes from time'.

George certainly didn't feature in any of the Scottish Cup ties played in February 1921, which included the club's first competitive meeting with Celtic, and his next mention is in the match report for the 3-0 Central Cup victory against Lochgelly at Bayview on 10 March, which states, 'Robertson was not well supplied with the ball, but when it came he showed masterly touches.'

George is also mentioned in the report for the 2-1 Central League win against Stenhousemuir two days later, 'Robertson ought to have got more of the ball, and time and again O'Donnell would have been better to pass to his unmarked partner instead of giving it to McLaren. The centre played a fine game and had both goals, although credit for the first really goes to Robertson.'

His next reference is in the goalless Central League match against Alloa Athletic on 31 March, which confirms that the Robertson still playing occasionally for East Fife IS George, 'Burton and Robertson formed the better wing, although things did not come off just as Andrew [Andrew Burton] expected. Robertson had the best effort of the game, and showed his old mastery in manipulating the ball. He had wormed his way through and beaten Orrock, when the left-back intervened just as Geordie was on the point of driving into goal.'

Just a week later comes confirmation that George is sometimes dropping back into the midfield when the match report for the East Fife v Dunfermline fixture states, 'In a moderate mid-line, Lamb and Robertson were the best.'

There is no further mention of George until the start of the following season, when he played almost exclusively at left-half for the club.

George is known to have played ten times for East Fife in 1920/21 but it is impossible to say exactly how many appearances he made that season. It is clear, however, that he was by no means a regular starter.

In their final season in the Central League, East Fife managed to finish in fifth place despite being the lowest scorers of the 18 teams. Their prominent position is largely due to their good defensive record, especially at their Bayview home.

In addition to finishing well up the league, East Fife were proud winners of the Qualifying Cup, beating Bo'ness 3-1 at Cowdenbeath's Central Park in front of 18,603 fans on 18 December 1920. George did manage to score in the 3-1 win over Inverness Caledonian in the fifth round replay during the competition but he does not appear to be among the 13 players photographed with the trophy which suggests he did not appear in the final.

Winning this prestigious trophy represented the greatest moment in the ambitious club's history at that time. The team was welcomed home at Methil Station by huge crowds and some players were carried shoulder-high along the High Street with the trophy.

The Scottish Qualifying Cup was a football competition played in Scotland between 1895 and 2007. During that time, apart from a brief spell in the 1950s, it was the only way for non-league teams to qualify for the Scottish Cup.

The Qualifying Cup was open to all full member clubs of the Scottish Football Association, who were not members of the Scottish Premier League or Scottish Football League. In June 2007 the Scottish Football Association announced a new format for the Scottish Cup from 2007/08 that would allow all full member clubs direct entry into the competition and consequently the Qualifying Cup competition was scrapped.

The Qualifying Cup was introduced in 1895 to make the number of entries into the main Scottish Cup more manageable and reduce the number of mismatched ties in the early rounds. Until 1930/31 it was played as a single national competition, although ties were often drawn on a geographical basis so that the final would often be between the best teams in the north and south.

From 1931 there were separate competitions for the north and south, and additionally in 1946/47 and 1947/48 there was a midlands competition. There was a brief hiatus for three seasons between 1954/55 to 1956/57 when all clubs were given direct entry into the Scottish Cup and the Qualifying Cup was not contested.

The Central League proved highly successful and attracted good crowds, meaning that some of the players were paid better wages than their Scottish League contemporaries. In order to prevent a mass migration of players from the Scottish League to the Central League, the Scottish League offered membership to 16 of the Central League teams in addition to Vale of Leven, Johnstone, Forfar Athletic and Arbroath, at the start of the 1921/22 season. So after many failed applications to join, East Fife finally managed to achieve Scottish League status.

CENTRAL LEAGUE 1920/21

	Pl	*W*	*D*	*L*	*F*	*A*	*Pts*
1 Bo'ness	34	21	7	6	66	34	49
2 Hearts 'A'	34	22	4	8	84	36	48
3 Cowdenbeath	34	20	6	8	64	37	46
4 Dunfermline Athletic	34	16	7	11	65	52	39
5 East Fife	34	13	12	9	33	37	38
6 Bathgate	34	13	11	10	58	37	37
7 St Bernard's	34	11	12	11	48	42	34
8 Stenhousemuir	34	15	4	15	51	56	34
9 Alloa Athletic	34	9	15	10	50	56	33
10 St Johnstone	34	13	6	15	44	51	32
11 Falkirk 'A'	34	10	10	14	41	52	30
12 Broxburn United	34	12	5	17	44	58	29
13 Clackmannan	34	13	3	18	39	57	29
14 East Stirlingshire	34	10	8	16	44	60	28
15 Armadale	34	10	7	17	44	51	27
16 King's Park	34	9	9	16	39	51	27
17 Dundee Hibernian	34	10	7	17	39	52	27
18 Lochgelly United	34	11	5	18	39	73	27

18

1921/22 – BACK IN THE SCOTTISH LEAGUE

GEORGE appeared in the left-half berth in the friendly against Cowdenbeath at Bayview on 15 August 1921 and again in East Fife's first ever Scottish League match at home to Bathgate, a 2-1 defeat, on 20 August. The *Mail for Leven, Wemyss & East Fife* reported on the Bathgate match and suggested that the half-backs performed well, dominating the Bathgate forward line, 'Bathgate came through the mill in the second half. Ross, Wightman and Robertson had the quintette on toast.'

The next match that George is known to have appeared in was on 1 October when he played in a 2-2 draw with Johnstone (the team from the Renfrewshire town, not St Johnstone) at Bayview. The *Leven Advertiser and Wemyss Gazette* match report states, 'Robertson played well in the first period, but lacked training.'

The *Mail for Leven, Wemyss & East Fife* report suggested that George had lost some of his shooting ability, 'Nearly 4,000 spectators witnessed a breezy start. Robertson, following up Cant, got a dead certainty put to his foot, but the half skied the ball most curiously.'

There is a suggestion in the paper that George was tried at full-back in one or two games for East Fife's junior team but it seems that he was not performing particularly well at this time and frustration was beginning to show.

In the home game against Bo'ness on 29 October the *Mail for Leven, Wemyss & East Fife* remarked, 'Robertson was the one weakness, and that by his rough tactics rather than weak play.' It appears that he questioned the referee, spinning the official around to remonstrate with him.

His form appears to have returned a few weeks later. Against Alloa Athletic on 12 November at Recreation Park, the *Leven Advertiser and Wemyss Gazette* report states, 'Robertson was outstanding in the mid-line.' The *Mail* praised the back division and indicated that George had headed a corner narrowly over the Wasps' bar.

George appeared at left-half in the games away to Armadale and Cowdenbeath but was not mentioned in the *Mail*'s match reports. However, against Arbroath at Bayview on 10 December, he comes in for some praise from the *Advertiser*'s reporter when again playing at half-back, 'After a shaky opening, however, Robertson came into his game, and it was he who, practically single handed, disposed of the Arbroath attack all the second period.'

George was injured in this match in a clash of heads with Arbroath's right-half, Stirling. The *Mail*'s man at the match wrote, 'Stirling and Robertson came into collision with their heads. Both were injured, and Stirling had to be carried off.' It is worth mentioning that at this time East Fife were in third place in their league and handily placed for promotion.

George appeared in the 1-0 defeat to Vale of Leven at Millburn Park on 24 December, and also in the 'Game of Accidents' at Lochgelly where the Methil Men lost 3-1 to the home side in a hard-fought contest which saw both sides reduced to nine men each at one point through injuries.

A succession of winless games saw East Fife slide down the table as form dipped during the winter months. George is next mentioned in the 2-0 home defeat by Alloa on 14 January 1922 when the *Mail for Leven, Wemyss & East Fife* criticised the wing-halves, 'Ross and Robertson were scarcely able for the smart tactics in use against them.'

George was able to raise his game when his former club visited Bayview in the first round of the Scottish Cup. The headlines on the *Mail for Leven, Wemyss & East Fife*'s report tell the sad story, 'East Fife's Luck Hopelessly Out'; 'Motherwell's Gift Goals'; 'Methil Half Back Failure'; 'A Day of Disappointment'; although their reporter rated George as an improvement on his colleagues in the half-back line. Ironically it was Tennent on the Motherwell left wing, George's old position, who was in outstanding form and was among the goals which eliminated the Fifers.

The *Mail* on 15 February noted the absence of Stewart and Robertson as East Fife's fortunes continued to decline. George is next mentioned in the 2-0 victory over local rivals Raith Rovers in the Wemyss Cup and in a tough 2-2 draw with St Johnstone where, according to the *Mail*, the halves did well.

During the rest of the season he is listed at left-half in team sheets for the Scottish League games against St Johnstone, Dundee Hibs, Vale of Leven, Arbroath and then his final mention in the *Mail* is in the 3-0 defeat of Dunfermline at Bayview in the semi-final of the Fife Cup. In none of these reports are there any remarks on his performance.

Although the last game of the league season was against Clackmannan at Bayview on 29 April, George didn't actually leave East Fife until June when he was one of several players released by the club at the end of the season.

The *Mail for Leven, Wemyss & East Fife* on 14 June regretted his departure, 'Robertson is not re-signed, and the line is weaker by his absence.'

George is known to have played in 18 of East Fife's fixtures during that 1921/22 season.

East Fife's first season in the Scottish League saw them finish well down the Second Division table in 12th place. Alloa were runaway winners of the league with East Fife's local rivals Cowdenbeath finishing in the runners-up spot.

SCOTTISH LEAGUE SECOND DIVISION 1921/22

	Pl	*W*	*D*	*L*	*F*	*A*	*Pts*
1 Alloa Athletic	38	26	8	4	81	32	60
2 Cowdenbeath	38	19	9	10	56	30	47
3 Armadale	38	20	5	13	64	49	45
4 Vale of Leven	38	17	10	11	56	43	44
5 Bathgate	38	16	11	11	65	41	43
6 Bo'ness	38	16	7	15	57	49	39
7 Broxburn United	38	14	11	13	43	43	39
8 Dunfermline Athletic	38	14	10	14	56	42	38
9 St Bernard's	38	15	8	15	50	49	38
10 Stenhousemuir	38	14	10	14	50	51	38
11 Johnstone	38	14	10	14	46	59	38
12 East Fife	38	15	7	16	55	54	37
13 St Johnstone	38	12	11	15	41	52	35
14 Forfar Athletic	38	11	12	15	44	53	34
15 East Stirlingshire	38	12	10	16	43	60	34
16 Arbroath	38	11	11	16	45	56	33
17 King's Park	38	10	12	16	47	65	32
18 Lochgelly United	38	11	9	18	46	56	31
19 Dundee Hibernian	38	10	8	20	47	65	28
20 Clackmannan	38	10	7	21	41	75	27

It is not known where George and the family lived on their return to Scotland. We will have to wait until the release of the 1921 Census in 2021 to see if they returned to the family home in Menstrie or found somewhere a little closer to East Fife's ground in Methil. The Census will also provide details of any other job George had outside his football career.

George would have been 37 years old when released by East Fife. It was not unusual for players at that time to continue to play even into their 40s but given his age and his niggling knee problems he probably decided that he would not be able to find a position with another league club.

George had to make a crucial decision about what to do with his life following the end of his football career. Unlike so many of his contemporaries he did not go into football management or become a publican. Instead he chose to make a new life for himself and his family across the Atlantic.

19

BUTCHER, BAKER OR CANDLE-STICK MAKER?

SO what happened to George after he left Scotland? The two branches of the family lost touch with each other and there was no address for George among the papers and photographs I inherited from my grandmother. The last known images of George are in a set of small photographs sent home to the family in Menstrie in the 1930s. A few of these photographs are of George's son Robbie's wedding day but, unfortunately, they are not dated and give no indication of where they were taken. Thankfully they did identify the individuals concerned although Robbie's in-laws were not named.

Jason Dickinson and John Brodie, in their excellent *The Wednesday Boys*, maintain that George emigrated to Canada where he 'returned to his original capacity as teacher'. Tony Matthews, in his unreliable *The Men Who Made Sheffield Wednesday*, states erroneously that George was born in Stonefield, Lanarkshire, in 1884 and died in Scotland in 1962. He also suggests that George may have been in the army in the First World War.

The International Federation of Football History & Statistics website has an entry for George which states that he was born in Stonefield as early as 1870 (if that were the case he would have been 52 when he hung up his boots!) and that 'he had studied and become a teacher, but in the 1920s emigrated to Canada, where he died in 1943'.

Douglas Lamming's *A Scottish Soccer Internationalists' Who's Who 1872–1986* is also adamant that George was 'a schoolmaster by profession', and 'he was reported to be living in Canada in the mid 1920s'. Even the most recent book of Scottish players' biographies, *Scotland's Who's Who – International Players 1872–2013*, by Paul Smith, perpetuates the myth that George was born in Stonefield and ended up teaching in Canada.

The Wednesday Boys and both Lamming's and the IFFHS biographies are adamant that George was a teacher. I can find no evidence for this and suspect that they have somehow confused George's profession with that of his former team-mate Jimmy Murray, who joined Wednesday from Motherwell at the same time.

Murray's biographical notes in the *Green 'Un* reveal that, before joining Wednesday, he was an unlicensed teacher while George's biography makes it clear that he was a baker by trade during his time with Motherwell. Some biographies have even suggested that George chose to go to Sheffield because the city had a university; Tom Reaney of Sheffield University, however, was able to rubbish that idea by confirming that George's name does not appear among the university alumni.

Lamming and other authorities are also convinced that George, whatever his occupation, settled in Canada but my father's recollection was that some of George's memorabilia was posted to his family somewhere in Rhode Island, USA.

Separating fact from fiction and finding out where and when George died has occupied much of my time for the best part of 20 years. To help identify individuals I started by gathering together all of the available birth and marriage certificates for known members of the immediate family. I knew from the family photographs that George and Jessie had three children, Robert – known as Bobby or Robbie – George Jr. and Catherine, who was much younger than her two brothers.

Robert Robertson was born at 4.30am on 9 February at 2 Findlay Street, Motherwell. George's address at the time of his marriage in 1908 was 6 Findlay Street so it is not clear if Robbie was born in the family home or in that of a neighbour. Just to confuse things a little further, George's occupation on his first-born son's birth certificate is given as works despatch clerk. The arrival of George and Jessie's first child came while he was in the form of his life with Motherwell and just about to appear in the Scottish League trial match. This extra mouth to feed may have been a deciding factor when the opportunity arose to transfer to full-time football with The Wednesday.

George Clarke Robertson Jr. was born in his parents' home at 122 Dixon Road, Sheffield, on 19 April 1918. On his birth certificate both father and son have their middle name spelled with an 'e' at the end. This certificate confirms the biographical note in *The Wednesday Boys* that George worked in a munitions factory during the First World War although the address given on the certificate suggests that he may not have returned to Scotland during the war but remained at home in Sheffield. The birth certificate describes George senior as a shell machinist. It is possible that he had been excused active service because of his serious knee injury.

Armed with all the available dates of births and marriages I began to search through all of the available on-line databases to try to pin down where and when George died. Not knowing where and when George had crossed the Atlantic meant that I was clutching at straws from the outset. I think when I started I read somewhere that Robertson was the third most common name in Scotland. Let me assure you it is extremely common not only in Scotland but throughout most of the English-speaking world, especially in areas where Scots have settled.

To cut a long story short, years of fruitless and expensive searching followed. I regularly bought into new family history databases as they became available and pursued literally thousands of George Robertsons from Alaska to the Gulf of Mexico. I really thought I had found him in Florida with a George C. Robertson who died in 1964 and shared our George's date of birth but it proved to be a false dawn.

I even enlisted the help of BBC Radio Scotland's genealogical programme *Digging Up Your Roots* who broadcast an appeal on my behalf on 22 February 2009. Unfortunately there was no reaction to the broadcast and I began to despair of ever making any progress. The Glasgow and West of Scotland Family History Society was kind enough to print an appeal for information in its October 2010 newsletter but this too elicited no response.

My big breakthrough came when one genealogical database made available on-line the 1930 US Federal Census. I got lucky very quickly and found George, Jessie, Robert, George Jr. and young daughter Catherine at 5 Osborn Street, Providence, Rhode Island, confirming that my father's memory was spot on and all the football biographies were well wide of the mark. The Census contained another surprising piece of information – George's occupation was listed as house painter.

The Census indicates that George and his family arrived in the USA in 1922 (Jessie and the two boys actually arrived in 1923) and that George was the owner of the Osborn Street property which was then valued at around $10,000. Also in the family home were wife Jessie, sons Robert (20) and George (12), and daughter Catherine (5) who, the document confirms, was born in Rhode Island. Earlier documents reveal that the family had previously lived at 72 State Street, Providence.

The Census shows that the family were still considered aliens but that George had applied for naturalisation papers. The area they lived in was a cosmopolitan one. Their neighbours on one side were an Armenian family while on the other side were a Swedish couple with their locally-born daughter. Along the street at number one was another Scottish family, the Morrisons.

At last I knew now where to concentrate all my efforts to trace individual family members. Having not had any lucky searching for George I decided to change tack by searching for his and Jessie's children on various genealogical databases. Before long I found, in Cranston, Rhode Island, the death of a George C. Robertson in 2002 who seemed to fit the bill in terms of date of birth for George Jr. Luckily on the same database I found the death date for a Jessie Robertson in Providence who shared the same birth date as George's wife.

While I was waiting for copies of the two death certificates from Rhode Island Department of Health I did a trawl of ships' passenger lists to determine when and from where George and his family sailed to the USA. The search for the family of four proved fruitless and frustrating until I accidentally came across a party of three Robertsons, Jessie, Robert and George, sailing from Liverpool to Boston on the 8,391-ton Cunard vessel *Andania*, master E.T. Britten, departing on 3 March 1923 along with 972 other passengers bound for Halifax, Nova Scotia, and Boston. They shared a cabin and their ticket indicates that they were destined for Boston.

That they were definitely our family was confirmed by their last UK address which was listed as 21 Ochil Road, Menstrie, George's mother's home. Jessie (35) was described as a housewife, Robert (9) was a scholar and George (4) was simply listed as 'child'.

The fact that Robert's age was given as (9) set alarm bells ringing; he, according to his birth date, should have been 13 years old at the time of their departure. Did George and Jessie's first-born die and did they re-use the name Robert for a second boy?

The 1930 US Census was clear that Robert was 20 years old so there was clearly an error on the ship's passenger list. Or was there? One possible answer is that Jessie may have given Robert's age as (9) so that he could travel over cheaper. Children over the age of 12 were required to pay full fare.

As George was not with his family on board the *Andania* I made the assumption that he had travelled over earlier to establish a home for them in Rhode Island. The 1930 US Census stated that George had settled in the US in 1922 so I checked passenger lists for any George Robertson with a similar birth date heading for the same area of the USA in that year. Only one strong candidate emerged although he was not listed as baker, professional footballer, teacher or house painter but joiner.

Given the Robertson family origins I feel sure that this is our man although his last UK address was given as c/o Cunard Coy., Liverpool. I suspect that he was in temporary lodgings in the city while he made the arrangements for his voyage.

This George Robertson departed from Liverpool on 4 October 1922 on board the 8,526-ton Cunard vessel *Ausonia*, skippered by Captain G. Horsburgh, bound for Boston and New York. George's ticket showed him as travelling to Boston.

After an anxious wait of a few weeks Jessie and George Junior's death certificates duly arrived from Rhode Island. These were the first American death certificates I had seen and I was delighted to find that they are even more detailed than their Scottish counterparts and provided great details of where and when the deceased was buried and even the name of the undertaker involved – an absolute boon for the amateur genealogist.

Jessie died on 21 April 1969 in the Belvidere Nursing Home, North Providence, of hypostatic pneumonia. She was 82. Importantly her death certificate gave her marital status as widowed, indicating that George had predeceased her. So I now knew that George had died sometime between the mid-1930s and 1969.

George Junior's death certificate revealed that he had died of pneumonia as recently as 8 December 2002 in the Philip Hulitar Inpatient Center in Providence. He was 84. George Junior had worked as a jeweller with Herff-Jones Inc. and was survived by his wife Leona A. Bernier. He had also served in the US Navy in the Second World War.

Although different undertakers had dealt with the interments, crucially both Jessie and George Junior were buried in the Highland Park Memorial Cemetery in Johnston, Rhode Island, just to the north-west of the city of Providence.

As these developments were taking place I submitted a brief biographical note on George's career to the Central Scotland Family History Society Newsletter and this was published in the spring edition in March 2011.

My next step was to contact the Highland Memorial Park Cemetery to see if George was buried alongside Jessie and George Junior. Within days of each other I received fulsome details of the burials of the Robertson family members in the cemetery from Linda Manuppelli, the cemetery administrator, and from Central Scotland Family History Society member Lizbeth Holt in nearby Connecticut who had sought out exactly the same details from Ms Manuppelli on my behalf.

Both enclosed burial card details for George Senior as well as Jessie and George Junior. George and Jessie were buried side-by-side in the

Resthaven section of the cemetery while George Junior was at rest in the Memory section. From George Junior's burial card it emerged that Leona A. Bernier was his second wife. He had made provision for his first wife Anna to be buried in the plot he had purchased but she had been cremated.

At last, after nearly 20 years of wondering, I had a date and place of death for my great uncle. George apparently died of broncho-pneumonia on 10 May, aged only 52. I immediately applied to the Rhode Island Department of Health for George's death certificate but there was a complication – certificates from the period around 1937 were not held by the Department of Health but were located in the State Archives Division.

I quickly redirected my application and within a couple of weeks I received the officially stamped copy of the certificate. And there was a further twist; George's occupation was listed as, not baker, works despatch clerk, professional football player, joiner, or house painter, but janitor in the offices of an insurance company where he had been employed for only four months.

George's death was confirmed as being at 8.35am on 10 May 1937 at his home at 5 Osborn Street, Providence. He had been ill with broncho-pneumonia for two weeks.

That is not the end of the story however. In a general search for the name George C. Robertson I came across an entry on the New England Soccer Hall of Fame website indicating someone of that name was inducted into the Hall of Fame in 2001.

I wrote to the organisation and received a very cordial letter from Joseph Sousa, the chairman of the Screening and Awards Committee. Joseph was able to pass on George's résumé submitted to the Hall of Fame on 18 April 2001. Clearly this was not my great uncle but George Junior who had followed in his father's bootsteps and played inside-left for his junior and senior high school teams between September 1931 and June 1936 before joining the Acorn Athletic Club for two years.

Between 1939 and 1940 he played for a team called Modern Ice Cream before joining Fairlawn Rovers of Fairlawn, Rhode Island, in 1941. George represented Rovers for two seasons before serving in the US Navy between 1943 and 1946. He returned to play with Rovers for another six seasons after his tour of duty in the Navy.

George's résumé also indicates that he played for teams in Albany and the Bronx, New York. He mentions his father's professional career and international honours and that his brother, Robert, also played soccer professionally although he does not reveal where.

That Robertson footballing gene extended beyond George's immediate family. George's nephew (my uncle), John McLaren Paterson, represented Scotland against England, Northern Ireland and Wales in 1939 as a schoolboy and played at Junior level before being called up. Thanks to Ceri Stennett of the Welsh FA, I was alerted to John's pen portrait in the programme for the Wales v Scotland schoolboy international match played at Ninian Park, Cardiff on 1 April 1939. It makes mention of his distinguished uncle:

> 'Paterson, J., Goalkeeper (Clackmannan) 5ft 8½". Product of Alloa Academy and captain of the "Wee County" team. Although his chief hobby is goalkeeping, he is also a first class centre-half and frequently plays in that position. He is a nephew of the one-time famous George Robertson, Sheffield Wednesday and International left winger.'

To bring this whole tale to a conclusion I set out to determine what had happened to the other members of the Robertson family. I have been unable to find a death certificate for Robert, George's eldest son, but I have managed to track him to several addresses in the Providence area through information supplied on Jessie's death certificate and cemetery details.

The 1930 US Federal Census reveals that Robert was involved in the manufacture of jewellery (Providence was a major centre for jewellery and silverware manufacture). A few of the photographs sent from Rhode Island were clearly of Robbie and his bride Bertha on their wedding day and another small photograph is of a young toddler labelled Georgina and is dated August 1939.

I made the assumption that Georgina was the daughter of Robbie and Bertha and focussed my search for Robbie's wedding and Georgina's birth between 1930 (when Robbie was listed as single in the Census) and around 1938 when Georgina was likely to have been born.

Eventually I was able to obtain a copy of the marriage certificate of Robert Robertson and Bertha Harling Hirst. The couple shown in the pictures I acquired were married on 3 October 1931 by Episcopal Minister Robert Meadus in Providence. Bertha was a mill operative and was born in Wales on 21 June 1908. She was the daughter of English-born parents Harold Hirst and Mary Hannah Hill who lived at 51 Peckham Avenue, North Providence. Robbie was aged 21 and worked in the jewelry (American spelling) trade. The witnesses at the wedding were William Haggart and Mildred S. Schofield.

Sadly George never got to see his granddaughter as Robbie and Bertha's daughter Georgina (named in memory of her late grandfather) was born at 5.50am on 27 November 1937 at the couple's home at 250 Fruit Hill Avenue, Providence. On Georgina's birth certificate her father's occupation has changed from jewelry (sic) worker to dye house hand, working for a bleach company.

Robbie, by this time a press operator in a machine shop, and wife Bertha appear in the newly-released 1940 US Federal Census living at 57 Lismor Avenue, Providence, with their two-year-old daughter Georgina. Jessie was still living at 5 Osborn Street at the time of that Census along with son George Junior, now 21 and working as a bench hand in jewelry manufacturing, and daughter Catherine, aged 15.

So somewhere across the Atlantic today there are probably now several generations of Robertsons who may or may not be aware of the life and exciting times of their once celebrated forebear. I would be happy to hear from them and pass on my knowledge of George's life and the history of the Robertson family.

BIBLIOGRAPHY

Motherwell Times match reports 1906–1910

The Football & Sports Special (*Green 'Un*) match reports 1910–1920

Mail for Leven, Wemyss & East Fife match reports 1920–1922

The Romance of the Wednesday 1867–1926, Richard A. Sparling, (re-printed 1997 by Desert Island Books)

Wednesday, Keith Farnsworth, Sheffield City Libraries, 1982

Sheffield Wednesday, A Complete Record 1867–1987, Keith Farnsworth, Breedon Books Sport, 1987

A Scottish Soccer Internationalists' Who's Who 1872–1986, Douglas Lamming, Hutton Press Ltd, 1987

Scotland – The Team, Andrew Ward, Breedon Books, 1987

One Hundred Years at Hillsborough, Jason Dickinson, The Hallamshire Press, 1999

Scotland – The Complete International Football Record, Richard Keir, Breedon Books, 2001

Sheffield Wednesday 1867–1967, Nick Johnson, Tempus Publications, 2003

On That Windswept Plain, James K. Corstorphine, published by the author, 2003

'Well Again, Graham Barnstaple and Keith Brown, Yore Publications, 2004

The Wednesday Boys, Jason Dickinson and John Brodie, Pickard Communication, 2005

Engineering Archie, Simon Inglis, English Heritage, 2005

Motherwell Legends, Graham Barnstaple, Yore Publications, 2009

The Football League – Match by Match (Seasons 1909/10 to 1919/20), edited by Tony Brown, SoccerData Publications, 2010

Sheffield Wednesday, The Complete Record, John Brodie and Jason Dickinson, DB Publishing, 2011

Scotland's Who's Who – International Players 1872–2013, Paul Smith, Pitch Publishing, 2013

I am very grateful for the interest shown in my early research by John Litster, editor of the *Scottish Football Historian*, who serialised George's story in editions 103-106, autumn 2007 to summer 2008.

PHOTO CREDITS

1. Author's Collection
2. Author's Collection
3. Author's Collection
4. Author's Collection
5. Author's Collection
6. Robert Robertson (George's nephew)
7. Keith Brown
8. Author's Collection
9. Author's Collection
10. Keith Brown
11. Author's Collection
12. Author's Collection
13. Photograph reproduced from www.picturesheffield.com with permission. Copyright John Higginbotham
14. Photograph reproduced from www.picturesheffield.com with permission. Copyright John Higginbotham
15. Getty Images Ref: 79660996
16. Photograph reproduced from www.picturesheffield.com with permission. Copyright John Higginbotham
17. Photograph reproduced from www.picturesheffield.com with permission. Copyright John Higginbotham
18. Image courtesy of the *Evening Times*
19. Author's Collection
20. Photograph reproduced courtesy of the Scottish Football Museum, Hampden
21. Photograph reproduced from www.picturesheffield.com with permission
22. Author's Collection
23. Image courtesy of Simon Inglis & Sheffield Wednesday FC
24. Getty Images Ref. 79660997
25. Photograph (v01151) reproduced from www.picturesheffield.com with permission. Copyright John Higginbotham
26. Photograph: Getty Images Ref. 79663986
27. Photograph: Fife Cultural Trust (Methil Heritage Centre) on behalf of Fife Council
28. Author's Collection
29. Author's Collection
30. Reproduced courtesy of Rhode Island Archives Division
31. Author's Collection
32. Author's Collection
33. Author's Collection
34. Author's Collection

ACKNOWLEDGEMENTS

I AM indebted to Graham Barnstaple and Keith Brown for their advice on matters relating to Motherwell Football Club. Keith was especially kind in allowing me to draw on images from his own extensive collection of Motherwell memorabilia.

The staff at Motherwell Heritage Centre were always helpful during my trawl through all the *Motherwell Times* match reports.

Thanks to Andrew Drake and his Wednesday Historian website for providing valuable, previously unknown, facts on George's time with The Wednesday.

I owe a huge debt to Jim Corstorphine, passionate East Fife fan and dedicated historian, for guiding me towards the best sources to research in the Methil area to enable me to complete the story of George's football career with East Fife.

Thanks to the staff at Methil Heritage Centre for their assistance in helping me locate photographs of George with his East Fife team-mates.

Thanks also to Simon Inglis and to Trevor Braithwait, director of communications at Sheffield Wednesday FC, for permission to reproduce the image of Archibald Leitch's drawing of Owlerton/Hillsborough.

Special thanks to Richard McBrearty and his colleagues at the Scottish Football Museum at Hampden for access to their newspaper archives, SFA Minute Books and taking interest in this publication.

Thanks to the staff in the Local Studies Department of Sheffield Central Library and Sheffield City Archives for their advice and assistance during my visit to the city.

Thanks too, to the people of Sheffield (especially the blue and white half) for taking George to their hearts and making him so welcome.

Many thanks to John Higginbotham for making available six photographs from his collection. The people of Sheffield owe him an enormous debt for rescuing such a large part of Wednesday's history.

Thanks to Tom Reaney of Sheffield University for searching for George's name among the university alumni.

The staff at the Department of Health and State Archives Division in the State of Rhode Island for providing birth, marriage and death certificates of George's family to help complete this story.

Thanks to Central Scotland Family History Society for publishing a biographical note on George and especially member Lizbeth Holt for all her efforts on my behalf in Connecticut and Rhode Island.

Huge thanks to Linda Manuppelli, cemetery administrator, Highland Memorial Park Cemetery, Johnston, Rhode Island, for finally revealing George's last resting place and providing many clues for further research on the Robertson family in Rhode Island.

Menstrie team photograph from George's nephew, Robert Robertson.

Robertson family photographs and medals from my late father Robert Campbell Paterson who set this whole quest in motion and sadly never lived to see it completed.

POSTSCRIPT

SO after nearly 20 years of searching I have, at last, brought George's story to something like a conclusion by discovering where he settled and where and when he died. In the process I have also managed to scotch the myths that he was born in Stonefield, Lanarkshire, and that he became a teacher and migrated to Canada.

I am delighted to be able to reclaim George for the 'Wee Coonty' of Clackmannanshire; his birth certificate, the Census returns for 1901 and 1911, and various newspaper articles in the Sheffield and Glasgow press all make mention that he was born in my home village of Menstrie.

The 1901 Census, his marriage certificate and the pen portrait of George in the *Green 'Un* when he signed for The Wednesday all confirm that he was a baker by trade and not one official document lists George's occupation as teacher. Even after leaving the UK his ship's passenger list gives his occupation as joiner and the 1930 US Census describes him as a house painter.

There is absolutely no evidence to support the theory that he settled in Canada. Ticket number 11,599 for the Cunard liner *Ausonia* shows that he was bound for Boston and the 1930 US Census confirms that he had lived in Providence, Rhode Island, since his arrival in the United States in 1922.

Recently I discovered a copy of the Motherwell Football Handbook for Season 1937-38. This small book lists all Motherwell's capped players but ignores the club's first two caps before the Great War, James Murray and his team-mate, George.

Later in the booklet a small paragraph makes mention of George's passing but, as has become customary, the report is confused and inaccurate.

In May news was received in Menstrie of the death at Providence, Ontario, of John Robinson (54), the former well-known Motherwell winger. "Jinky," as he was familiarly called up Fir Park way, was a native of Menstrie, and played for Motherwell, Sheffield Wednesday, and East Fife. He was capped for Scotland for Scotland as an outside left against England and Ireland in 1913, and against Wales in 1910 and 1912.

No wonder he was difficult to track down. At least they got his birthplace right. Never knew that he was nicknamed Jinky!

The final word goes to the *Mail for Leven, Wemyss & East Fife* on 27 October 1920 which makes reference to George's troubles at the end of his international match with Ireland in 1913. Since this information could only have come from George himself it is likely to be the most reliable account of the events which sparked the research for this publication:

> 'George Robertson, who appeared for East Fife on Saturday, has the Irish and English national caps. Playing in the former, he was the lucky player in capturing the ball at the sound of the whistle. A spectator let drive at the ball and caught Robertson's fingers. Naturally, George spoke out to the fellow. In a minute the crowd was furious at the report that he had assaulted a spectator, and they made to give him a rough handling.
>
> 'By this time the players had reached the pavilion. The crowd watched on. An Irish Jarvey came out by a side door and slipped away among the spectators. The crowd waited in vain. George was the Jarvey.'

'Naturally, George spoke out to the fellow.' Aye, right!

Iain Paterson
Stepps, 2014